Beyond the Screen

Written in an accessible style, this book explores the complex future of television across its different industries, providing professionals with key insights and pathways to adapt and prepare.

By exploring traditional media industries, and how they have come to make up today's streaming and broadcasting media world, this book provides a detailed discussion of the future of systems programming and television viewing. This includes a wide range of topics such as Internet Protocol television (IPTV), set-top boxes (STBs), ATSC 3.0, virtual reality (VR), holographic television and artificial intelligence (A.I.), as well as other cutting-edge technologies. Additionally, this book examines the future of content monetization by exploring the new and sometimes controversial methods of advertising, product placement, and search and promotion that will be required to be financially successful in this future television environment.

Beyond the Screen is an indispensable addition to the library of every television professional, academic, student, and television viewer who wants to know where this fascinating world of television is heading and what it will take to be successful within it.

Frank A. Aycock, Ph.D., is in his 39th year as a professor of communication at Appalachian State University. He received his doctorate in broadcasting from the University of Tennessee-Knoxville in 1989. A former local television and radio broadcaster and a futurist, Dr. Aycock is keenly interested in the development of the television industries in response to massive changes in technology and is a firm believer in the transformative power of new television technologies. He is the author of three books and has presented at numerous national and international conferences. Dr. Aycock presented a TED talk at the 2013 TEDx Conference in Nagoya, Japan; has been an invited speaker at numerous conferences including National Association of Broadcasters (NAB) and Consumer Electronic Show (CES) conventions and academic conferences including Broadcast Education Association (BEA) conventions for the last 35 years; and was a keynote speaker at the 2013 Cloud Computing Conference – West as well as the 2014 International Conference on Broadcasting Media & Film Industry.

Beyond the Screen
The Future of Television and Advertising

Frank A. Aycock, Ph.D.

Taylor & Francis Group

NEW YORK AND LONDON

Designed cover image: Shutterstock

First published 2026
by Routledge
605 Third Avenue, New York, NY 10158

and by Routledge
4 Park Square, Milton Park, Abingdon, Oxon, OX14 4RN

Routledge is an imprint of the Taylor & Francis Group, an informa business

© 2026 Frank A. Aycock

The right of Frank A. Aycock to be identified as author of this work has been asserted in accordance with sections 77 and 78 of the Copyright, Designs and Patents Act 1988.

All rights reserved. No part of this book may be reprinted or reproduced or utilised in any form or by any electronic, mechanical, or other means, now known or hereafter invented, including photocopying and recording, or in any information storage or retrieval system, without permission in writing from the publishers.

Trademark notice: Product or corporate names may be trademarks or registered trademarks, and are used only for identification and explanation without intent to infringe.

Library of Congress Cataloging-in-Publication Data
Names: Aycock, Frank A. author
Title: Beyond the screen : the future of television and advertising / Frank A. Aycock.
Description: New York, NY : Routledge, 2026. | Includes bibliographical references and index.
Identifiers: LCCN 2025026295 (print) | LCCN 2025026296 (ebook) | ISBN 9781041037873 paperback | ISBN 9781041037903 hardback | ISBN 9781003625384 ebook
Subjects: LCSH: Television broadcasting--Forecasting | Television advertising--Forecasting
Classification: LCC PN1992.55 .A94 2026 (print) | LCC PN1992.55 (ebook) | DDC 302.23/45--dc23/eng/20250709
LC record available at https://lccn.loc.gov/2025026295
LC ebook record available at https://lccn.loc.gov/2025026296

ISBN: 978-1-041-03790-3 (hbk)
ISBN: 978-1-041-03787-3 (pbk)
ISBN: 978-1-003-62538-4 (ebk)

DOI: 10.4324/9781003625384

Typeset in Times New Roman
by KnowledgeWorks Global Ltd.

To my beautiful wife, Gail,
my inspiration for all things,
my cheerleader, and the love of my life;
to my two sons and their wives,
who will enjoy all that the future of television
has to offer; and to my wonderful grandson, Elias,
for whom the future of television will be old hat,
and who will enjoy the dawning of
television in the 22nd century.

Contents

Acknowledgements ... ix

Introduction: Where Have We Been, Where Are We Now, Where Are We Going? ... 1

PART I
The Future of the Linear Media ... 11

1. The Future of the Broadcast Industry ... 13
2. The Future of the MVPD ... 28

PART II
The Future of the Streaming Media ... 43

3. The Future of Television Delivery Systems ... 45
4. The Future of Television Programming ... 69
5. The Future of Television Viewing ... 81
6. The Future of Cloud and Artificial Intelligence ... 103

PART III
The Future of Television Monetization ... 115

7. The Future of Television Advertising ... 117
8. The Future of Product Placement ... 143

9 The Future of Television Content Search and Promotion 153

10 The Future of U.S. Television in the Global Television Market 163

PART IV
The Future of Television in the Mid-21st Century and Beyond 177

11 Final Thoughts and Future Visions 179

Index *202*

Acknowledgements

Writing a book is a solitary endeavor and yet it is not. While the author writes the words, there are numerous others without whom the author might never finish the book. This book, especially, was a long time in the making. Trying to write about the coming television universe is not something I took lightly – it is too important, not only to the television industries, its professionals, and budding professionals now planning their careers in this ever-changing television universe, but to the consumers of television as well.

I want to extend a special note of thanks to Joe Mandese, the editor in chief of *MediaPost,* for his permission to use an extensive portion of the article "How Artificial Intelligence Ties Into Programmatic Media." The article provided key insight for the section on Programmatic Advertising in Chapter 7: The Future of Television Advertising, and I appreciate his willingness to permit me to use the article.

Likewise, I want to thank Patrick McKenna, CEO of Strikesocial.com, for his permission to use extensive portions of the article, "The Differences Between AI, Machine Learning, Programmatic Buying and Deep Learning." It, too, was a crucial part of the chapter on Programmatic Advertising, and I appreciate Patrick allowing me to use the article in depth.

Much of the thinking behind this book was inspired by my participation as a member of the press at National Association of Broadcasters (NAB) conventions over the last several years. The opportunity to attend numerous sessions and talk with leaders from the different industries was decisive to organizing the thoughts and words that have gone into this book. I want to express my deep appreciation for the NAB press coordination staff who provided press passes so I could do my research and say how grateful I am for them and their kindness.

I want to thank the publishing team from Taylor & Francis Group for believing in me and my idea for this book. I also want to thank them for their patience with me as a first-time author new to working with a book publisher. They have been covered over with my questions and their help has been immeasurable. So thank you, Danielle Zarfati, Daniel Kershaw, and Zoya Gayle; my copyeditor, Lauren MacGowan, who made me a much better writer; and everyone involved at Taylor & Francis – you are the best!

Finally, and most importantly, I want to thank my two sons and my daughter-in-laws for their encouragement and support; my amazing grandson who inspires me to continue to look ahead and try to understand the television world he will enjoy; and Gail, my beautiful wife of 45 years and the love of my life, without whom I know this book would be languishing in my mind. She has been my support and my cheerleader, she has been right beside me every step of the way, and she believes in my book and in me. I am truly a blessed man.

Introduction: Where Have We Been, Where Are We Now, Where Are We Going?

At the 2011 National Association of Broadcasters' (NAB) convention in Las Vegas, I had the opportunity to attend a number of panels. At one particular panel, during the question-and-answer period, an elderly gentleman approached the microphone and shared not a question but a series of comments on how television could deliver the Super Bowl to a nation, entertainment programs throughout television's history, and the major news stories of the day. His line of thinking concerned the importance of television to the viewing audience in the face of what he must have perceived as the growing threat from user-generated, online, and personal-choice video devices such as over-the-top (OTT) set-top boxes (STBs), the World Wide Web, etc. His point was that television was so important it was not going to be pushed out by those challengers. As you might imagine, this gentleman was working for a group owner, and it seemed to me that he had probably spent his whole career in broadcasting, and, likely, in local television. His comments were, predictably, well received by the audience.

However, what struck me about his comments was that the gentleman spoke of television as if it was a singular object, which made me think that, before anyone could take the comments of this gentleman seriously, the listener would have to know exactly what "television" the gentleman was talking about. More than likely, from his comments, his view of television was the traditional over-the-air (OTA) broadcast television delivered by the local affiliate to the local audience. His view was almost a pining for the halcyon days of the 1950s to the mid-1970s, when the only competition in the industry was between three networks and their affiliates; public television which, quite honestly, was no real threat to the networks' dominance; and a handful of independent stations in markets that could afford to support more than the three local affiliates.

Television in the future is not going to be as simple as it was during those past decades. Television is changing at light speed and trying to stay ahead of the technological curve is daunting at the very least. Each year, new television technologies are conceptualized, introduced, or brought to market. On the other side, every few years older television technologies begin to be phased out or disappear altogether. To bet on the future of television is to bet on continual change. To believe any current television technology will be around indefinitely is to be an ostrich with its head in the sand, anticipating the re-emergence of the manual typewriter.

DOI: 10.4324/9781003625384-1

So, how does one define television in light of the changes that have come about since the beginning of this century? In the past, defining television was much easier. For instance, in the 1950s the three major networks (and the occasional short-lived minor ones) along with early public television/educational television and (mostly) small independent local stations delivered black and white television over the airwaves to homes with television sets. Cable television was bare wires running from a master antenna directly to homes in primarily rural and mountainous portions of the country. That was it. The 1960s saw the introduction and ultimately the complete adoption of color television and the introduction of coaxial cable, a boon for the cable industry. Television added channels and improved the quality of its productions. Instant replay was introduced to television and in 1969, television was broadcast from the surface of the moon. The first half of the 1970s saw the continuing domination of the broadcast industry, but, beginning in 1975, the first satellite cable telecast heralded the start of major competition between the two industries. With the use of satellite, the cable industry was able to offer an "alphabet soup" of channels that began the fracturing of the broadcast dominance as viewers chose to watch the various alternative offerings that cable could provide. Additionally, viewers were introduced to a new form of "television" – the videocassette recorder (VCR). The VCR was introduced at about the same time as the first satellite-fed cable programming, so now viewers not only had choices other than the three networks and their affiliates, but also a way to "time-shift" their favorite programs and also record them to save for future viewings – the earliest beginnings of video-on-demand and binge-watching of programs, though those terms were not in the national lexicon at the time.

While the 1980s did not see the types of changes to television directly that the previous generations had, other technologies that would impact television in the coming decades began to be introduced – specifically the personal computer, the video game console, and the cell phone. All three technologies have altered the way television is defined today. Additionally, the Internet, which had started as a Defense Department project under the Defense Advanced Research Projects Agency (DARPA), became a technology for more than just defense contractors and researchers, although it and the web did not reach the average consumer until the next decade. However, while the VCR was introduced in the previous decade, it became an important household item during the 1980s. It was also during this decade that the "VCR rental store" became a major part of the video landscape, led by Blockbuster stores that proliferated around the country.

The 1990s is truly the decade that started the digital/streaming/OTT world, although that world has come to fruition in the last two decades. It was during the 1990s that the DVD player and, then, the digital video recorder (DVR) were introduced, Netflix began as a mail-order business to compete with Blockbuster and the other video rental stores, and the modern laptop/notebook computer in the form of the Apple Powerbook and the IBM Thinkpad became available to the public. Additionally, during the 1990s, the World Wide Web became available to the public, along with the first modern web browser, Mosaic. During the 1990s, Amazon started as an online book company; the Palm Pilot, the forerunner of the "smart" aspects of today's smartphone became available; Sony introduced the first Playstation; Google was founded; and the IBM Simon, the world's first smartphone, became available, which opened the door for the easily portable cell phones and smartphones of today.

Given the technological innovations that have been developed since the beginning of satellite cable in 1975, today the word "television" is not easy to define or to categorize. Before 1975, television was OTA, broadcast, and network-driven. Families watched television on their home sets, first in black and white and then in color. Television sets were often – especially in the early days of vacuum tube sets – pieces of furniture to go along with sofas, chairs, and coffee tables. Portable televisions were heavy and not especially portable despite the name.

Trying to define television today is another matter. No one will deny that the television the gentleman at the convention spoke so forcefully about is television. It has been since the beginning of television and remains so today. Consumers also consider programming coming into homes via a cable or a direct-to-home (DTH) satellite signal television as well, even though the local stations are but a small part of the television universe on any cable or DTH system. Even if the channel being watched through a local system is not ABC, CBS Television/Skydance, or NBC (and now Fox, the CW, and even the Spanish-language network Univision), but is ESPN, USA, A&E, TNT, or some other cable-only channel, it is still considered to be television. Longevity plays a role here, as does familiarity.

But what about programs viewed first using the VCR, then the DVD player, and now the DVR – are they television? In each case, the television is used to watch the programming. Does watching a movie telecast on NBC differ from watching the same movie telecast on HBO or rented from Red Box or even recorded on a DVR for later viewing? Do they qualify as watching television? Let us take it a step further – does watching a movie on pay-per-view (or the more modern term "video-on-demand") that will shortly be on HBO or some other premium channel and later on one of the networks and/or a cable movie channel qualify as watching television? Certainly, almost everyone would consider those scenarios to be television.

However, what about a movie downloaded from Netflix and viewed on the television through an OTT set-top box, a Blu-ray player, or a videogame console such as an Xbox Series X or a Playstation 5? Is that watching television, especially if the movie is of sufficient popularity that it is virtually certain to end up on video-on-demand, a cable premium channel, network television, and one of the basic cable channels? What about watching an episode of a television program on a television screen using an OTT set-top box such as Roku, Google Chromecast, Apple TV, or Amazon Fire TV – do any of these count as watching television? What if the program being watched on the television set is not a network program or a cable channel program, but original programming from HBO or Netflix? What if you are watching an entire season of a network program that you bought on DVD at a store, purchased from Amazon.com, or downloaded from iTunes – is that television? What about if the program that is watched on the television set is a network program being watched not at the time it is scheduled for telecast, but later through an Internet connection using Hulu, the network's own website, or YouTube – is that watching television? What if the program that is being delivered to the television screen is not a network program or a cable program, but a user-generated or professionally-produced program located on YouTube or one of YouTube's branded channels – could that also be television? You are watching it on a television set. What if you are watching any of the aforementioned on a connected (smart) television set through an operating system such as Roku or WebOS?

Now, let us change the location, but continue our ponderings. What if you are watching a network program at the time it is scheduled, but not on a television set? What if you are watching that program on a computer screen through a broadband or Wi-Fi connection, or on a tablet such as the iPad, Samsung Galaxy Tab, or Google Nexus using Wi-Fi or a 5G cellular connection? What if you are watching that program on a mobile phone through a 5G connection? Is any of those ways of viewing watching television? After all, the program you are watching on any of those alternative viewing devices is being telecast from ABC, CBS Television/Skydance, Fox, NBC, CW, or Univision. What if the program you are viewing on any of the alternative devices is a cable program such as ESPN or TNT? What if it is a program from a local television station? How about if the program is user-generated content from YouTube? How about if it is a downloaded or streamed movie or even an original program that is coming to you from Netflix? Remember, you are not at home watching your television set, but on the go somewhere, using one of the many (and growing) alternative devices to the television set.

The point of these ponderings and the view of this book is that all the aforementioned scenarios are "television" and should be considered and even embraced as such. That this monumental change is occurring seems obvious. According to YouTube's CEO, more U.S. viewers are watching the service over television sets than on mobile devices.[1] Four of the top ten linear TV providers in the U.S. are actually virtual Multichannel Video Programming Distributors (vMVPDs) and of those ten the only two that have grown in subscribers in each of the last three years are YouTube TV and Fubo TV.[2] Additionally, YouTube TV is the fourth largest MVPD/vMVPD provider in the U.S., surpassed only by Charter, Comcast, and DirecTV, and of the four, it is the only one that is continuing to see growth in subscribers – the other three are losing subscribers year over year.[3] Of all of Netflix's content, 70% is viewed over television sets rather than mobile devices.[4] In the first quarter of 2024, only 24% of streaming content viewed on smart TVs came from linear television and that percentage has continued to drop.[5] Even the most venerable of the broadcast networks, CBS, and its parent company, Paramount Global, recently merged with Skydance Media. The combined company is headed by David Ellison, the son of Oracle co-founder and billionaire Larry Ellison. The move is expected to allow the younger Ellison to leverage his tech knowledge with Paramount's intellectual property (IP) and CBS' audiences to produce a streaming competitor that combines traditional television with new tech to produce a streaming giant.[6,7]

Television is changing, much to the chagrin of that gentleman I mentioned at the beginning of this introduction, and will continue to change – most likely almost every day – for the foreseeable future. The television universe of the 21st century is and will be fundamentally different from that of the 20th century in ways that would be unimaginable to a television professional or viewer even at the turn of the millennium, to say nothing of those whose idea of television is the "golden age" of the 1950s and 1960s. By 2030, much of what is thought of as television today will seem antiquated and old-fashioned – certainly out-of-date. By 2040, the television of today will be relegated to museums of ancient technology, much as the early CPM-based portable computers of the 1980s had become pieces in museum exhibits by the early 1990s. (On a personal note, I experienced that specific scenario personally in Karvina, Czech Republic, in 1993. While in the city on business, I stopped by the local castle, which had become a museum. At that time, there was an exhibit on the development of electronic media from the phonograph to the television set to the computer. In the computer section, being exhibited as an example of an early portable computer was the Kaypro portable computer that I had written my master's thesis on just eight years earlier in 1985. It was an odd feeling to have gone from being "cutting edge" to a museum relic in eight short years!) The same will be true for today's most cutting-edge television technology in just a few short years. Television technology is moving so fast that looking forward is the only choice. Look back and you are history; look sideways and you are still history; do not look far enough ahead and shortly technology will have outpaced you and you will still be history.

In fact, while it is unlikely that the term "television" will disappear from use in the near future, given all the different possible ways of watching television so broadly defined in the previous paragraphs, perhaps the word television is itself just as antiquated and out-of-date as black and white television sets full of vacuum tubes. The one thing all these different iterations of "television" have in common is content – the delivery method differs, but there is always content. Perhaps to bring the entire television/video/gaming universe under one umbrella is simply to say "I am viewing (watching) content." Then, when the viewer is asked about the content, the answer can be more specific – the name of the program, the name of the platform or network, etc.

This book is an exploration of the future of television. While some of the points may seem controversial and so far in the distance as to seem unlikely to ever occur, it is important to remember that almost immediately before the iPad came out, the focus was on how the netbook was changing computing. After the iPad, the netbook market dried up almost overnight. Immediately after the first iPad was released, there were tablet computers produced by most of the major computer makers, and, later, even tablets from Amazon and Barnes and Noble – the Kindle Fire and the Nook Tablet, respectively. Additionally, since the introduction of that original iPad, the major players in the cable and satellite industries, and the OTT platforms have each developed applications (apps) not only for the iPad, but also for the other tablet computers running Android as well as other operating systems. Subscribers can now watch their favorite channels and their favorite programs while on the go wherever they may be, as long as they can get a Wi-Fi or cellular signal (for those tablets with both capabilities). So before discounting the more controversial portions of this book, remember how fast things are changing and keep an open mind.

This book is divided into four parts. The first two parts reflect the division of today's television industry into those industries that have been around quite a long time – called "linear (formerly legacy) television" – and those "new television" players (or streaming media), this book is similarly divided into two parts. Part I covers the linear (formerly legacy) industries. Chapter 1 looks at the broadcast industry, both the networks and the local stations. The chapter begins with a short history of broadcast television, then discusses the present and the future of the networks and the local stations separately. Broadcasters will likely disagree with the conclusions in this first chapter, as it suggests major changes in the network/affiliate relationship and in the networks' relationship to the cable, DTH satellite, and Internet industries. However, for the networks, which have seen their share of the prime-time audience sink lower and lower, especially among the lucrative 18–49-year-old age group, the changes stated in the chapter are inevitable. Additionally, the local stations will most likely disagree with the conclusions because the results suggest that there are major difficulties ahead for those stations, especially the affiliate stations who will be the most impacted by the changes in the networks. Local stations will struggle to survive, and many will not.

Chapter 2 looks at MVPDs, which consist of the cable industry, an industry currently undergoing and destined to see major changes, and the direct-to-home satellite industry, an industry with little to no future in its current form. After a short history of cable, this chapter, like Chapter 1, will focus on the future of the cable industry. However, unlike the broadcasters, the cable industry should fare very well as it seems to be embracing change. While the cable industry will have a period of shakeout, in the end, it should come back stronger than ever and be one of the leaders in the television universe of the future.

Chapter 2 also will discuss the DTH satellite industry. Only time will tell what will happen to the DTH satellite industry. Even as recently as 2010, the prospects for the industry were not promising, because it was at a disadvantage in its lack of ability to provide a "one-stop-shop" for the television viewer's needs. Despite changes in the industry, the jury is still out as will be described in the chapter.

Part II considers those industries that constitute the Internet-based streaming media industries. Chapter 3 explores the impact of the future of television delivery systems. The chapter first focuses on the impact that Internet protocol television, or IPTV, is having and will have on the future television universe. By 2035, most, if not all, television will be delivered by IPTV. As far back as the 2015 NAB convention much of the discussion on the convention floor and in panels throughout the week concerned the move to an all-IP infrastructure. Once IPTV is the delivery system for television, the whole industry changes, as the choices the viewer has will be limited only by his or her own imagination or desire to watch programming. Programs that might otherwise be canceled for lack of large enough audiences on the networks will find their niche in the universe that will be IPTV. New genres of programs will be developed and offered to viewers. Programs long since canceled or retired will find new life in a variety of ways, and not just on TVLand, Game Show Network, or other such channels that are currently available on cable and satellite systems. The impact of IPTV on the 21st century television universe will be profound.

The chapter also investigates the development of ATSC 3.0. At this time – at least publicly – the broadcasters are hoping ATSC 3.0 will slow or even reverse the continuing move away from traditional OTA television in favor of the new television forms of IPTV, both broadband and Wi-Fi. The chapter will discuss if ATSC 3.0 can be the savior of traditional broadcast television.

Finally, the chapter focuses on the OTT set-top box and its impact on television. Starting with the earliest forms of set-top boxes from the beginning of consumer television viewing, the chapter explores the role of the set-top box as both a way of assisting legacy television to bring programming to the viewers and a form of alternative television in today's transitional stage. The chapter also looks at the current impact of set-top boxes on the legacy industries and considers the future role of the set-top box in the 21st century television universe.

Chapter 4 looks at the future of television programming. The chapter first explores video-on-demand or VOD. If IPTV is the delivery mechanism of television in the future, VOD is the programming – or more correctly, lack of programming – scheme that will run on the IPTV system. Video-on-demand means exactly that – the program the viewer wants to watch is available for his or her viewing pleasure whenever and wherever (s)he wishes to watch it. Television of the future will take the viewing times and locations for viewing out of the hands of the channel's programming department and put the decision-making into the hands of the viewer. Appointment viewing will most likely be limited to live events, but even then only for those who wish to watch the event as it unfolds. Viewers will watch scripted programs when they so choose, not when a network or cable channel decides that they should. After discussing VOD overall, the chapter looks at the various types of VOD.

Next the chapter considers a new industry that is becoming increasingly popular and is an alternative to the various VOD offerings of today. Free ad-supported streaming television, or FAST, is a free alternative to subscription choices and provides viewers with both classic and new niche programming designed to appeal to very specific audiences. The only cost to the viewer is having to watch commercial breaks within the programming.

Finally, the chapter wraps up with a look at an Internet-driven alternative to cable and satellite television, the vMVPD. These offerings, led by YouTube TV and Hulu+LiveTV, provide viewers with a lower cost alternative (although the prices are rising) to cable and satellite television, with the added enhancement of no contract and the ability to view on computers, tablets, and smartphones in addition to television sets.

Chapter 5 explores the future of television viewing. The chapter begins with a look at the connected television (CTV) industry. Connected TVs are television sets that are designed to deliver not only linear television, but also the various forms of streaming television, and have pre-loaded software that allows the viewer to access the World Wide Web, social media, e-mail, etc., at the same time. The CTV market will continue to grow exponentially in the next few years, with the move from the current 4K television to 8K television taking place in the 2030–2035 timeframe. This will be determined in part by when the production houses choose to produce their programming in 4K and 8K.

On the horizon – for television, at least – is the use of virtual reality (VR) equipment to view and interact with television. While VR has been – and continues to be – a useful tool for science and an entertaining form of gaming, it has not moved into the television world in any meaningful way. That will change as more consumers prefer to interact with their favorite shows, and the production houses start to design those programs for interaction. Additionally, the use of VR will make it possible for advertisers to reach their consumers in ways not possible now. With the use of VR, consumers will be able to see in three dimensions (3D) what their purchases, especially fashion purchases, will look like on their bodies and in their homes. VR will be the transition device that will ultimately usher in the world of holographic television, around mid-century.

Finally, the chapter discusses the exploding iWorld of tablet computers, smartphones, and other devices as CTV devices. Apple has set the standard for both the truly television-capable smartphone, with its iPhone series, and tablet, with the iPad series, so it seemed natural to refer to this segment of the chapter as the iWorld. But the section looks at more than just Apple products and considers the other major players in tablets, smartphones, VR, augmented reality (AR), and other devices, and their operating systems.

Chapter 6 focuses on cutting edge cloud technologies for television as well as the development of artificial intelligence (AI) as a television tool. Already, cloud computing is making a real difference in almost all phases of television, from news to production to programming. AI, on the other hand, is just getting started. It is interesting to consider the roles AI will play and how it will impact the future of television.

Part III considers how the monetization of television will change, develop, and explode in the coming years. In some aspects, this portion of the book is the most direct reaction to NBC's former CEO Jeff Zucker's famous pronouncement of more than a decade ago of "trading analog dollars for digital pennies," and is a crucial focus of this book. The chapters in Part III are designed to show that, not only is it possible to develop ways of producing revenues and profits from the coming television universe, but there are opportunities for it to be even more profitable than television is today.

Chapter 7 focuses on the future of television advertising and looks at how addressable, personalized advertising will develop in the future to reach each viewer with advertising that appeals to her/him, for the products (s)he prefers. As such, the chapter discusses the interaction of today's cutting-edge programmatic advertising and dynamic advertisement insertion with a new step the author calls "aggregated targeted microadvertising" or ATMA. At this time, ATMA is still mostly a concept of the author, but it is just now beginning to appear in certain dynamic start-ups, one of which the book highlights in a case study. The author still chooses to use his term as no one has developed an alternative for this first step in the future of television advertising.

Following the chapter on advertising, Chapter 8 looks at another major type of revenue, product placement. Extensive product placement has been appearing prominently in certain reality television programs over the last decade, such as *American Idol* and especially *The Biggest Loser*, where everything from the foods the contestants eat, to the clothes they wear, to the water they drink has a product placement attached. The technology of the future has the capability to take product placement to a much higher level, one that allows every image on the screen to become a link to a website that will provide the viewer with more information about the image and, if the image is a product, ways to purchase it.

One of the most important aspects of television in the future is how to discover and how to promote television programs. To be successful, content providers and content distributors must be able to make it possible for viewers to easily and quickly find the programs they want to watch in a television world where there are no schedules and myriad choices of services and platforms from which to choose. Chapter 9 explores the future of television content search and promotion, discussing the ways in which content providers can make it easy for viewers to find their programs and to learn about new and different programs that would be of interest to them.

Part 3 wraps up with a discussion in Chapter 10 of the future of television: delivered over IPTV, as a global industry, distributing its programming and its various revenue streams worldwide. The chapter will look at how television, freed from its limitations of delivery structures, armed with new ways of reaching viewers successfully via advertising and product placement, and bolstered by its new promotional abilities, is poised to open the next chapter in its history. That next chapter will be one of global coverage where everyone can enjoy U.S. television programming anytime, anywhere, on any device, regardless of geographical location or nationality.

Part 4 – the final portion of the book – surveys the future of television through mid-century and beyond. Chapter 11, the final chapter, shares final thoughts and future visions. It opens with a report from the Cisco Corporation, which, in March 2011, introduced its vision of the future of television at a conference in San Jose, California. Its vision, based on interviews with a select group of industry leaders, paints a vivid picture of where Cisco sees television heading into the 2030s. The report is reproduced with permission in this chapter.

The chapter then discusses the author's personal vision of the future television universe. The author has let his mind run wild to the possibilities of what television could be like, and perhaps will be like, a half century or so from now – or even sooner. However, it is not idle speculation. Based on the fictional views of Ray Bradbury in his book *Fahrenheit 451*, the considerations of Cisco's panel of television experts, and the author's more than a decade of personal research, writings, and discussions with anyone who would listen, the vision put forth is plausible, feasible, technologically sound (given the current rate of development), and – if nothing else – hopefully entertaining and thought-provoking.

At the end of each of these chapters, the author provides likely future scenarios regarding the topics discussed and an expected timeline. These are my own expectations and timelines and are designed for you, the reader, to consider, ponder, and discuss with others if you have the mind to – I hope you will look forward to them. I provide a timeline or expected date for when each topic will occur or be occurring to provide concreteness to those scenarios as opposed to simply suggesting they may occur "sometime in the future." Some timelines and dates will be too aggressive with the scenarios occurring later than predicted; others will be too conservative, with those scenarios occurring sooner than anticipated. Some may be right on target or almost on target. Regardless, they are my expectations and mine alone.

Notes

1 Winslow, George, "YouTube CEO: More U.S. Viewers Are Watching on TV Than Mobile," *tvtech*, (February 11, 2025), https://www.tvtechnology.com/news/youtube-ceo-tv-overtakes-mobile-as-primary-device-for-viewing-in-the-u-s.
2 Dixon, Colin, "4 of the Top Ten Live, Linear US TV Providers are vMVPDs," *nScreenMedia*, (September 9, 2024), https://nscreenmedia.com/top-ten-live-linear-tv-providers-q2-2024/.
3 Dixon, "4 of the Top Ten Live, Linear US TV Providers are vMVPDs."
4 "TV vs. Smartphone: How Netflix Viewing Changes by Device," *digital i*, (April 1, 2022), https://www.digital-i.com/insight-articles/tv-vs-smartphone-how-netflix-viewing-changes-by-device.
5 Adgate, Brad, "Viewers Continue to Watch More Streaming Content on Smart TVs, Report Shows," (June 4, 2024), https://www.forbes.com/sites/bradadgate/2024/06/04/report-viewers-continue-to-watch-more-streaming-content-on-smart-tvs/.
6 Bauder, David, "Paramount Gets Green Light for $8 Billion Merger. But What Is the Psychic Cost for Company?" *AP,* (July 26, 2025), https://apnews.com/article/paramount-skydance-merger-cbs-news-trump-85560c3c7aaaa1fe894380683e66a89c.
7 Cunningham, Kevin, "4 of Golf's TV Partners are Quietly Undergoing a Major Shift. Here's What's Happening," *Golf,* (July 28, 2025), https://l.smartnews.com/p-5UdPf2y4/UD85A9.

Part I
The Future of the Linear Media

1 The Future of the Broadcast Industry

Today, the broadcast industry is going through unprecedented upheaval. Historically, the three networks (now four, five, or six, depending on how you define Fox Television, CW Television, and Univision) and their owned-and-operated and affiliated local stations across the country were, for those who grew up watching them, a stable presence in audiences' lives. Throughout the late 1940s, 1950s, 1960s, and the first half of the 1970s, the networks brought the viewer the day's national and international news and kept him or her entertained with a variety of scripted programs, while the local stations delivered the network programs to their audiences and provided the viewers with the day's local news, sports, and weather, along with special programming for kids during the weekday afternoons and on Saturday mornings. Before the mid-1970s, if viewers were going to watch television, they were going to watch one of the three networks on the local market affiliates or the networks' owned-and-operated stations. The networks and their local stations had to contend with public television stations and a smattering of local independent stations (if one or more was in the market) but neither of the two competitors was a threat, generally speaking. However, all that has now changed.

Today, broadcasters are facing a fight for their lives. Their entire relevance – especially among generations younger than the aging Baby-Boom population – is being brought into question. The audiences for the networks and their affiliates continue to erode as viewers choose to go elsewhere. Where elsewhere? Well, everywhere elsewhere, whether it is the myriad of narrowly-focused channel options on cable or direct-to-home satellite services, or, increasingly, through other alternative delivery systems (alternative to over-the-air [OTA] and mainly through the Internet). Almost nine out of ten viewers get their television by some means other than OTA television.[1] With cable, direct-to-home (DTH) satellite delivery, over-the-top (OTT) set-top boxes (STBs), Blu-ray and DVD players, digital video recorders, online options such as Hulu, YouTube TV, Philo TV, Crunchyroll, and hundreds other, and YouTube itself, viewers are going anywhere and everywhere to "watch TV."

In a recent weekly ratings report, the "Big Three" (ABC, CBS Television/Skydance, and NBC) combined for a total rating of 3.54 for the P2+ age group. To put it another way, the three networks combined have 3.54% of the total population of the U.S. – a far cry from when the share for primetime was upwards of 98% of the

DOI: 10.4324/9781003625384-3

viewing audience. Even combining all six of the networks – including Fox, CW, and Univision – the total rating of the U.S. P2+ audience was only 4.66 or 4.66% of television viewers. The networks and their local stations are struggling to stay on top with advertisers and viewers.[2]

The Networks

Network television is the most enduring of the legacy industries. For more than 70 years, the networks have been the largest source of information and entertainment programming for American audiences. For sheer numbers of viewers, the networks reign supreme in all dayparts. They have from the beginning of television and will likely continue to do so at least in the near future.

However, the networks have seen their audiences – especially the most coveted daypart of prime time – be continually eroded by other choices, whether it is the traditional cable and satellite only channels that have been available in ever-increasing numbers since the mid-1970s, or the new choices of today that will be discussed throughout this book.

History

Television, from its beginning until the mid-1970s, was delivered primarily over the air. This was done partly out of tradition – radio had been delivered over the airwaves – but mostly because of technological limitations. Over the air signals were the most efficient way of getting the networks to their local audiences. The Big Three networks – ABC, CBS Television/Skydance, and NBC – had virtually all of the primetime television audience, with whatever miniscule audience was left going to the public television stations and the occasional independent station in markets that could support them.[3] Local stations battled among themselves for market supremacy in the local news and syndicated programming time slots during the week. The networks ran lavish productions during the four sweeps months to bolster their ratings numbers, while the local stations provided numerous promotional announcements for their networks and enticed viewers with their most exciting news reports to keep their local ratings numbers as high as possible. Ratings were the name of the game, deciding the price for advertising time and determining which programs remained on the air and which ones did not. One advantage during the days before 1975 was that critically acclaimed programs often had the time to grow their audiences, so programs such as *Hill Street Blues*, which started out with modest viewership, had the chance to become ratings winners over time.

Cable television was originally a retransmission device for the local network affiliates' programs. The cable systems provided their mostly rural audiences with the ability to watch one or more of the network affiliate stations when distance or topography denied households the ability to receive the stations and their programs through the television-top antennas – the ubiquitous "rabbit ears" – or through an individual home tower antenna connected to the television set. For the broadcasters during this time, all was right with the world. Cable systems were small but growing, and of little worry to the networks themselves, although some local stations had cause to be concerned when their local market area was intruded upon by the cable company's ability to deliver a different market's local affiliate of the same network.[4] Nevertheless, in cities and towns of any size across the United States, television viewers saw little to no need to spend money on cable when they could see all that cable could offer free of charge on their local network affiliates.

In 1975, HBO's decision to deliver its programming via satellite and Ted Turner's 1976 decision to give the viewing audience the world's first superstation by putting his local Atlanta-based UHF television station onto the satellite began a movement that has turned the nice, neat little world of network television and its local affiliates upside down. Thanks to the decisions of HBO, Turner, and others, the cable industry had something to offer potential subscribers that they could not receive over the air.[5]

Today Americans enjoy hundreds of programming choices on cable and direct-to-home satellite systems, and a myriad of additional choices over the Internet. As such, the networks' combined primetime audience is now a mere shadow of its former glory.

Additionally, this multichannel universe is experiencing an explosion of specialized cable channels that started in the mid-to-late 1970s and has continued on for a number of years. These specialized channels fragment the audiences further and erode the ratings numbers of the networks. Further, with the current surge of Internet offerings providing everything that cable and satellite services can, plus numerous other offerings through subscription and advertising-driven choices, the opportunities available for viewers grow and the size of the broadcast audience continues to diminish. Finally, according to the February 2024 *Statista* report, the percentage of homes that watch television by some means other than over the air is right at 90%, although, interestingly, the percentage of viewers who watch some TV using an antenna, but still have cable or satellite is 33%.[6] That discrepancy can be attributed to the rising cost of cable subscriptions and the desire of viewers to pick and choose their cable offerings. That will continue to change in the future as the number of viewers using an antenna and an MVPD (multichannel video programming distributor – a catch all for cable and DTH satellite) will fall as viewers move to Internet-driven virtual MVPDs (vMVPDs) such as YouTube TV and Hulu+ Live TV. Regardless of the argument made, the number of people watching television over the air only is, at best, small. This fracturing of the television viewing public has left the networks and their local affiliate stations in a dire situation.

The Networks Today

Today, the networks are fighting for their existence. Every year, the networks – whether it's the traditional Big Three, or the Big Three plus Fox, CW, and Univision – continue to lose market share as more and more viewing alternatives become available to the television consumer. Today the networks have to contend with numerous cable or direct-to-home satellite channels, many telecasting reruns of network programming, while others provide original programming that are of special interest to niche, but important, audiences. Additionally, the networks must contend with streaming media that deliver their programming through the Internet to audiences – not only to their computers, but on the go to their notebook computers, tablets, and mobile phones – and their homes via big-screen home smart television sets that connect directly to the Internet, or that can connect through one of the various types of OTT set-top boxes.

Whether it is Netflix or Amazon Instant Video offering movies, television programs, and original programming streamed to the television on-demand through a variety of devices, iTunes providing downloads of movies and television programs, user-generated programming through YouTube being delivered, or even their own programs being streamed through Hulu/Hulu+, YouTube TV, or any of the other virtual multichannel video programming distributors, the networks and their local affiliates are having to battle competitors, many of which were not around as recently as the beginning of this century. Further, the cable and DTH satellite companies themselves have begun to offer movies and programs as video-on-demand (VOD) for a fee, uncut and uninterrupted, even sooner than HBO and the other premium pay-television channels. Finally, the networks and their local affiliates must compete with original programming from not only HBO, Showtime, and the other premium pay-television cable offerings, but also from Internet sites such as Yahoo and YouTube, which have begun specialized channels in their Internet space for long-format, professionally produced programming.[7,8]

At this time, the networks' local OTA affiliates are embroiled in a battle with the mobile telephone industry and the Federal Communications Commission over bandwidth usage by the affiliates.[9] Traditionally, every OTA television channel was provided six megahertz of bandwidth on which to deliver its signal to the home. Today, with the various means of compressing that same television signal without loss or degradation of signal quality, television stations need only a portion of the original six megahertz of bandwidth to broadcast their signals. With digital television – as almost all television is today – the programmer can adjust the amount of space needed for a program, making it possible for several compressed channels to be located within one analog channel and still look high quality to the viewing public.[10]

Because of the proliferation of smartphones and tablets capable of surfing the World Wide Web, sending and receiving e-mails, texts, and multimedia messages, and downloading and playing music, movies, and even television programs in their entirety, the amount of bandwidth set aside for the mobile telephone industry is dwindling rapidly. The largest amount of additional bandwidth is the extra bandwidth the television stations have as part of their original six megahertz. However, because the broadcasters are in a furious battle for survival against *all* their competitors – including the mobile phone and tablet industries – the broadcasters' willingness to give up that extra bandwidth, even if they are paid for it, is extremely mixed. Regardless of whether or not individual stations are willing to give up part or all of their bandwidth, overall the broadcast industry simply does not appear ready to give in to the inevitable – the day of OTA broadcasting is dying and will not return.

Future of the Networks

The seeds of the future of television broadcasting have already been sown. With the introduction of the original CBS All Access streaming service by former CBS head Les Moonves and the former joint venture that is Hulu, what will be the ultimate move to streaming by the networks has already been set in motion. It is reasonable to assume that, sooner rather than later, the networks will determine that the traditional model is no longer cost effective or even necessary. Nevertheless, as long as the networks continue to dominate the telecasting of both major and minor sporting events, the networks will hang on to their affiliates. However, by the end of the 2020s, it is likely that most if not all live sports will have moved to the major tech companies such as Amazon, Apple, Google (YouTube), Netflix, etc. These companies have deeper pockets than the networks and have already begun to experiment with streaming live football and other sports. Without their major sporting events, the networks will be reduced to airing scripted programs, for which no time frame for airing is needed – nor are affiliates needed.

When that happens, one by one the networks will do what has long been coming: they will jettison their local affiliates for the new possibilities of direct delivery of their programming to audiences through the ever-growing variety of screens and devices. This is already in the early stages with the parent company of CBS Television/Skydance, Paramount Global, establishing Paramount+ and Comcast, the parent company of NBC, establishing Peacock. Disney, of course, today owns Hulu and Disney+. Fox, while not having a streaming service similar to Peacock or Paramount+ does offer Fox Nation, a news-oriented streaming service. While all of the aforementioned services charge a monthly fee, the CW Network's streaming service, CW TV is free for viewers and is somewhat similar to Peacock or Paramount+. It also makes good use of its website to provide programs to its audience.

Opportunities for the networks to reach their audiences using these services directly are too profitable for them to ignore. In addition to delivering their programming through the traditional cable and DTH satellite companies – at least in the near term, but unlikely in the longer term – the networks will reach their viewers through connected "smart" television sets that will rival the IMAX screens of today[11] with the possibility of full television rooms, as Ray Bradbury imagined in his novel *Fahrenheit 451*, and will provide connections to a multitude of (VOD) choices and aggregator streaming sites. They will reach their audiences on-the-go through smartphones and tablets, capable of delivering HDTV, UHD, and even newer television delivery technologies.[12] The networks will reach audiences directly through high-speed broadband, Wi-Fi, and cellular services. Most importantly, they will reach viewers anywhere in the world that the viewer can connect to the Internet.[13]

It is inevitable that the networks will deliver their programming to their audiences directly for the following reasons.

1 Continuing the affiliate/network relationship is no longer cost-effective.
2 Technology makes the affiliate/network relationship obsolete.

3 Providing direct delivery of programming to the consumer is more profitable and opens more avenues for revenues.
4 The up-and-coming generation does not watch OTA television. Increasingly, it does not even watch cable, DTH satellite, or current Internet Protocol television (IPTV) in the form of AT&T's U-verse and Verizon's FiOS, choosing instead to watch true 21st century television platforms.

First, continuing the affiliate/network relationship is no longer cost effective. Traditionally, the affiliate relationship has been a cost to the networks, either through direct payments of cash, more recently, the providing of additional time in network programs for local advertisements, or a combination of the two. When OTA delivery was the way most or virtually all of the audience received their television, the return received by the network more than compensated for the cost of the affiliate relationship. Further, at that time there was no other way for the networks' programming to reach their audiences. The networks and the local stations had a symbiotic relationship that provided mutual benefit to each industry.

Today, the affiliate/network relationship has changed dramatically. While the cost for a single advertisement in high-profile sports events such as the Super Bowl continues to escalate, overall the revenues for network programming continue to dwindle. Jeffrey Cole, the founder and director of The Center for the Digital Future at USC Annenberg, reported in his May 10, 2023 article that *The Late, Late Show with James Corden* was costing CBS $65 million a year to produce while only bringing in $45 million a year in advertising.[14] Another example from that same article comes from the program *Bob Hearts Abishola*, one of the stronger programs on the network. The show has two major characters and a dozen recurring characters who appear on a regular basis throughout each 22-episode season. Going into the 2023 season, to save money, CBS cut all 12 of those recurring characters from the 22-show commitment down to only a 5-show commitment, with the possibility of occasionally appearing in additional episodes should the programming arc warrant it.[15]

One way that the affiliate/network relationship can remain cost-effective enough to delay its death is through the continued sharing of the retransmission consent fees that the local stations charge cable systems to carry their programming.[16] Charging retransmission consent fees is a significant battle between the cable, DTH satellite, and vMVPD industries and the broadcasters that continues to this day. Retransmission consent fees are paid by the cable, DTH satellite, and streaming aggregator industries to the local broadcast affiliates and the cable-only channels, while the networks are left out, except for the fees they collect from their owned-and-operated local stations and the cable-only channels which they own. The amount paid to the local stations (and their group owners) for 2023 was $15.09 billion.[17,18] With the continuing costs of programming, including the ever-increasing costs of sporting events and the continued dwindling of their advertising revenue, the networks are demanding an ever-increasing share of those retrans dollars. The local stations, naturally, do not want to give up any more of their retrans dollars than absolutely necessary, and would prefer to keep all the fees for themselves.

Therein lies the battle. As early as 2009, then-CBS Chief Executive Officer Les Moonves stated, "As each new affiliation agreement comes up, there will a sharing of the retrans fees."[19] The affiliates did not agree. Nexstar CEO Perry Shook responded, "With all due respect to my friends at the networks, I contend that the network programming is not the main reason that we are receiving compensation. It's our local programming."[20]

However, from the networks' point of view, why should they give up even a portion of the retransmission consent fee bonanza when it is the networks that provide the programming for the largest portion of the day, as well as that portion of the broadcast day that is by far the most lucrative to the networks and the local affiliates? As the amount of total revenue continues to grow, the networks will realize that the whole amount could be – and should be – theirs. By going straight to the audience instead of through their local affiliates, the networks will receive the revenue from the retransmission consent fees that they desperately need and deserve. The odds are the network/affiliate revenue-sharing of retransmission consent fees will be short-lived.

The second reason is that technology makes the affiliate/network relationship obsolete. Already the viewing audience is moving and will continue to move from the legacy industries to the streaming offerings available today, and the continuing development of additional future television technologies will make delivery of all network television directly to the consumer virtually guaranteed in the next five to ten years, possibly sooner. Without the need for the strict scheduling of programs that is required of today's network television, the networks will simply provide starting dates for programs and/or episodes and viewers will be able to watch episode by episode, catch up on past episodes when they want, or binge-watch an entire season, directly competing with the subscription video-on-demand (SVOD) and advertising-driven video-on-demand (AVOD) offerings currently available or in the future.

Additionally, in the future the networks will have the ability to deliver complete interactivity to the television viewing experience, which will be a boon for network television. This will open opportunities for personalized advertising targeting the individual viewer with products that (s)he likes, enjoys, and desires via the types of advertisements that s(he) prefers.[21]

Further, as current technology continues to improve and adapt, on the near horizon is the use of immersive technologies such as virtual reality (VR) headsets that are being adapted for use in more than just video games. VR headsets are currently being improved to allow viewers to interact more closely with television programs, especially sports events, where the viewer can become a part of the excitement of being at the event and enjoying it live virtually. VR headsets could also be used by viewers to feel more involved with scripted programs in many of the same ways that they do now when gaming. Full VR immersion into television programming (and advertisements as well) could speed up the introduction of holographic television – the logical extension of television in the future after VR.

Finally, television of the future will be global in nature, with every content provider becoming a global provider. Networks will become direct-to-consumer global providers of programming, with audiences in countries around the world watching the same programs, in the same manner, on the same or similar screens, at the same or similar times of their choosing, as those in the U.S.[22] To think of television as country specific or region specific is to shortchange the power and interest in television of the future. Already audiences across the world can watch programming on streaming services such as Netflix and Amazon Instant Video, and U.S. audiences now have the ability to watch British programming through BritBox and other such streaming services. Network television of the future will offer the same abilities to audiences around the world through streaming services such as Paramount+, Peacock, and Hulu.

Third, providing direct-to-consumer delivery of programming is more profitable and opens more avenues for revenues. Much of what has already been written supports this position. Direct delivery of programming through cable, DTH satellite, and streaming aggregators provides the networks with a continuing stream of revenue from retransmission consent fees. Additionally, without the need to provide local television stations with any compensation, opportunities for additional advertising revenue would exist during those advertising slots that would normally go to the local affiliates. Further, the networks would not have to worry about those local stations that, for technical or other reasons, perform poorly in their respective markets even when the network may be doing well overall nationally.

The ability to deliver television in the future using the various Internet-driven technologies will provide the networks with the opportunity to reach audiences with highly targeted advertisements. These addressable, personalized advertisements will be designed with the individual viewer in mind, rather than an undifferentiated mass audience. Advertising availabilities will be sold numerous times, with specifically developed advertisements being viewed by the targeted individuals. Such advertising strategies will make it possible for the advertisements to produce success rates as high as 80% or greater.[23]

In addition to advertising, television in the future makes it possible for the networks to take advantage of extensive product placement opportunities. With television delivered over the Internet, every aspect of every scene in a program can become a clickable link, allowing the viewer the opportunity to make purchases of anything (s)he might see in a television program. Such product placement opportunities will provide the networks with numerous new opportunities to attract advertising dollars and sales through planned and impulse buying.[24]

Fourth, the younger generations and the up-and-coming generation do not watch OTA television. In fact, they most often do not even watch cable, preferring instead to watch movies and original programming on Netflix, Amazon Prime, and Hulu/Hulu+; user-generated videos on YouTube and other such sites; and traditional television programming on streaming aggregator sites or even the networks' own websites. The younger generations enjoy all the alternative forms of television delivery that have been mentioned earlier.[25] Both the Deloitte Corporation and the Pew Research Center have continuously documented in detail the changing television viewer over the last decade and beyond. The results of those surveys show that the media use landscape is changing in a significant way, especially for generations younger than the baby-boomers.

Network television is in a major transitional period – one that will make or break the networks. Either they will hold onto the traditional ways of delivering programming to their continually shrinking audiences – such an unlikely scenario as to be discounted (these are intelligent people who run the networks) – or they will move to a more competitive alternative, becoming the major general-programming channels on cable, DTH satellite, the aggregate streaming alternatives such as YouTube TV and Hulu+Live TV, and possibly, the free ad-supported streaming television (FAST) channels as they move away from traditional television delivery. Finally, the networks may also choose to go directly to consumers using their own apps such as Paramount+ or Peacock. Regardless, the networks will deliver their programming in a variety of ways, but not over the air using local television affiliates. That much is virtually certain.

The Local Network Affiliates

The local network affiliate television station industry is dying. It is the dirty little secret that the television networks do not want to say out loud and the local stations do not want to think about. But the local network affiliate is dying. The network affiliate arrangement with local stations around the country is an antiquated artifact of a bygone era. As mentioned in the previous section, the networks simply do not need their affiliates any longer, given the current television universe, and will soon be jettisoning them, leaving any local station that has not already developed plans for going it alone either scrambling for survival, or, most likely, simply shutting its doors.

History of the Local Television Industry

The local television station affiliate relationship grew out of the relationships developed in the 1930s between local radio stations and the radio networks. When the Federal Communications Commission (FCC) froze television growth between 1948 and 1952, in an effort to ward off a situation similar to the chaos of 1920s radio, the FCC developed non-overlapping geographical areas designated for certain channels. These non-overlapping areas are today's television markets.[26]

In each market, the FCC designated a set number of stations and assigned channel locations to each station, making sure that stations would not interfere with others in the market or in adjacent markets. Depending on the markets, some would have only very high frequency (VHF) stations (channels 2–13 for OTA signals), some would have only ultra high frequency (UHF) stations (channels 14–83 for OTA signals), and many markets would be "intermixed" – having both VHF and UHF stations in the same market. The intermixing of the markets caused immediate problems as the UHF signal was neither technically as good, nor as strong, as the VHF signal, putting any network having to affiliate with a UHF station in an intermixed market at a decided disadvantage.[27] Further, until Congress passed the All-Channel Receiver Bill, which took effect in 1964 and required all television sets to have both VHF and UHF tuners built in, television sets had only one tuner built in, and that was for the VHF channels.[28] UHF channels could only be seen on television sets if a household purchased a UHF converter box.[29] In most intermixed markets, though not all, NBC and CBS networks were affiliated with the VHF stations, leaving ABC at a disadvantage that it would not overcome until the 1970s. Throughout the early decades of television, the network-affiliate relationship was necessary as the local stations were the only way the networks could reach a nationwide audience.

Programming for the networks' affiliates in the early days of television was similar to that of 1930s and 1940s radio. The programming was broad-based and attempted to capture the largest portion of the market share possible. Competition in local markets was often fierce, not only in the area of network programming, but also in local news, information, and entertainment programming where local stations went head-to-head for viewers. The local network affiliates had only each other to worry about and to compete against in each market, even though there were early public television stations and the occasional independent station, but their total share of virtually any market was negligible.

The Local Television Industry Today

The local television industry today is in dire straits. As television in the 21st century continues to evolve and change, so too must the local television station. No longer will the local station be able to depend on the network for programming, as there will be no network/affiliate relationships for the reasons discussed in the previous section on networks. Each local station will be on its own, scrambling for programming to fill its day. Those that are able to transition successfully will flourish; those that cannot, or do not, will cease to exist.

Today, while putting forth a brave face and battling both the streaming technologies in the courts and the FCC to keep broadcasting the way it has always been, in reality, many – if not most – of the local stations in the country are making plans for the major changes that will affect them sooner rather than later. Virtually all have websites where they deliver both written and video pieces from their news, sports, and weather departments. Most of the stations put portions or even entire newscasts on their websites for viewers to watch. Most, if not virtually all, local stations have apps for both the iPhone and Android operating systems, which allow viewers to go directly to their websites, often optimized for mobile phone use.[30]

Additionally, almost all local television stations are making good use of social media, such as Facebook, Instagram, and X (formerly Twitter), and they are beginning to use the video power of Tik Tok and Reels to stay in touch with their audiences and keep them informed throughout the day.[31] Further, their air personalities are encouraged to maintain and actively participate in Facebook fan pages, and those same air personalities often tweet throughout the day.[32]

For the local broadcast stations, the future of the survival of the industry as a major force may depend on the ability to successfully roll out their new delivery system, called ATSC 3.0, nationwide. When/if the local stations are able to put

ATSC 3.0 into place fully, the technology is expected to be a breakout system that will allow the broadcasters to compete with the streaming platforms.[33]

Local stations' creation of an online presence during the past few years has begun to pay off in terms of revenues. "The growth of local broadcast stations' online and mobile offerings is driving rapid advertiser adoption and is proof positive that digital media is a perfect complement to local television stations' proven reach and targeting," said TVB President-CEO Steve Lanzano. "As a result, broadcast-plus-digital packages have become tremendously more powerful than just stand-alone digital media buys."[34] Borrell Associates' CEO, Gordon Burrell, further highlights the point:

> When it comes to local media companies transforming to this new 'digital' marketplace, local TV broadcasters are in a very envious position. [...] Broadcasters have an exclusive on the mass reach and targeting that advertisers want, through a unique combination of the traditional television and digital media platforms. It's a very powerful package, which is why we're seeing this growth.[35]

Further, CPMs for video advertising rates are twice as high as banner ad rates for local television stations.[36]

While the percentage of online and even mobile advertising revenues is not that large compared with the overall revenues of the local television station industry in the U.S. today, in the future they will be a much larger source of revenue for the stations. As local stations lose their network affiliations, and with that loss, their retransmission consent fees and their strong revenue-generating network programming, local stations will have no other choice but to find new avenues to profitability or they will go out of business.

The Future of Local Television

Where does all this leave the local television station? There is a monumental change occurring in the relationship between the local stations and the networks with which they are affiliated. No longer can local television stations depend on the millions upon millions of dollars they receive from retransmission consent fees – those fees paid by the cable, satellite, and IPTV companies to re-telecast the local stations' programming; the networks are demanding at least half, if not more, of those dollars to help offset their declining advertising revenues. In addition to demanding a large portion or even the majority of the local stations' retransmit, it is the networks that negotiate those same fees with the vMVPDs, such as YouTube TV and Hulu+LiveTV, not the local station or station groups.[37] Additionally, with the networks all establishing their own streaming services designed to deliver network programming in real time, can the day be far away when the networks decide they no longer need their affiliates and can go directly to their viewers anywhere, anytime, and on any platform?

What does the local television station do once it has lost its network affiliation? There is really only one long-term alternative. That alternative, the one most likely to occur, at least initially, when the local affiliates lose their network contracts, is to become hyperlocal independent stations. Regardless of whether the local stations become hyperlocal ones or choose some other – likely digital-only – option, the road to continuing profitability will be difficult. Most likely, many stations will cease to exist because the average television market will not be able to support more than three stations and could support only one, depending on the size of the market.

Ultimately, those that do survive will do so by becoming hyperlocal stations. Hyperlocal stations are stations that focus their resources primarily on the local community, although they will supplement their local programming with syndicated programs that they can afford to purchase as well as programs from independent producers, both local and non-local. Those stations that can take advantage of ATSC 3.0, should it become fully realized, will have the additional option of being the backbone for delivering OTA broadband signals to homes. The ability to deliver ATSC 3.0 will give those stations opportunities for additional revenue streams, both from the cost to the consumers for the service and the ability to include targeted advertising on streaming channels.

Today's hyperlocal stations are often the low-power stations in a given market, serving either a rural community or an area or neighborhood within a larger market. Hyperlocal stations firmly belong to their communities, rather than being local stations delivering network programming for most of the day, and syndicated programming for the rest of the day (except for the local newscasts and any public affairs programs that might run either late at night or on the weekend). In one sense, the transition of the current local stations to hyperlocal stations takes them back to their original purpose – that of being local television voices in the community, like radio stations are local radio voices in the community.

Already there are examples of the possibilities that could be on the horizon for the new hyperlocal stations of the near future. According to Jaime Spencer of Frank N. Magid Associates, with the addition of large and medium markets joining small markets around the country during the past five years or so, more than half of all the television stations in the country that produce newscasts are including coverage of high school and prep sports. Not only does that coverage include football, as might be expected, but it also includes everything from basketball to the spring sports, and even high school bowling matches. Additionally, many of the stations supplement their on-air coverage of high school sports with websites encouraging their viewers to interact with the station by voting for games of the week or uploading their own videos of the contests. Spencer claims that the online component for the local television stations' prep sports coverage is "huge." Spencer goes on to say, "…when we look at what the newsroom of the future [will be], it certainly is going to have more room for creating compelling local content."[38] Other examples include Houston's Fox O&O station KRIV-TV's inclusion of a 30 minute daily Web program that airs immediately before the evening news,[39] and Tribune SVP of news, Bart Feder's statement:

> … that at a time when consumers are juggling multiple devices at once, even while watching local newscasts, TV can no longer be considered the

primary medium at play. In turn, digital editors need to have a larger role in newsrooms, as they, more than any other staffer, have their pulse on the community they are serving, and the hot button topics they are interested in. We talk about the second screen, but we are the second screen a lot. We are the companion. [...] That puts the onus on us to continually call the audience back.[40]

Any of the possibilities listed above would provide the local audience with local programming and advertising and would be ways of alleviating any worries the FCC might have concerning a lack of localism in television.

Summary

The OTA broadcasters face a very turbulent future in the short-term. Challenges from IPTV, VOD, mobile phones, tablets, as well as enhanced services from their traditional rivals in the cable and DTH satellite industries, will make it difficult for the broadcasters to continue to compete in the coming television universe. The longer the broadcasters continue to resist the obvious need to move away from OTA delivery to total anywhere, anytime, on any platform delivery, the harder it will be for them to remain profitable. Ultimately, the networks will be forced to cease relationships with their local affiliate stations and deliver programming directly to their audiences using all current and future television technologies. Additionally, broadcasters will need to adopt new advertising models that will deliver specific advertisements to the audiences that make up the advertisers' particular target markets. without wasting advertising dollars on audiences that have no interest in their products or services.[41]

Next, the networks will retake complete control of their entire inventory of current and classic television programming, delivering those programs to audiences through VOD, allowing audiences to watch their programs anytime, anywhere, on whatever screen they choose. For the networks, VOD is and will be an exciting revenue maker as they will be able to sell advertising for their entire inventory again and again as audiences continue to watch and to discover programs they find interesting. While advertisements may not reach the same size of audiences as the current method of advertising does, the fact that the advertising will reach only those who are interested and most likely to buy the product will make each advertisement significantly more valuable.[42]

For the local stations, the picture is not good. Many stations will close as they are not able to compete without their network affiliations. Those that survive will become, in some form, hyperlocal stations, providing the programming of local importance that their communities both need and want to watch. The newfound relationship between the local broadcaster and the community will be the key to the growth and profitability of those stations. Like the networks, the hyperlocal broadcasters will take advantage of future television technologies available to them to reach audiences that are both local as well as, potentially, global.

Notes

1. A. C. Nielsen, Co., "The Total Audience Report – Q1 2015," *The Total Audience Series*, (2015), http://www.nielsen.com/content/dam/corporate/us/en/reports-downloads/2015-reports/total-audience-report-q1-2015.pdf.
2. "US Cable & Broadcast TV Network Rankings," *National Media Spots*, (April 2024), https://www.nationalmediaspots.com/stats-us-cable-broadcast-tv-network-rankings.php.
3. Aycock, Frank A. (1989), *A Comparison of Blunting, Hybrid, and Counterprogramming Television Strategies and Their Effects on Total Network Television Viewing*. Doctoral Dissertation.
4. See Chapter 2: The Future of the MVPD.
5. See Chapter 2: The Future of the MVPD.
6. Stoll, Julia, "Share of Adults Using Over-the-Air Antenna (OTA) to Watch TV in the United States from 2020-2023, *Statista*, (February 15, 2024), https://www.statista.com/statistics/1440344/television-access-over-the-air-antenna-usage-united-states/.
7. See Chapter 2: The Future of the MVPD.
8. See Chapter 3: The Future of Television Delivery Systems.
9. See, for example, http://broadbandandsocialjustice.org/2012/04/spectrum-reallocation-how-will-the-national-broadband-plan%E2%80%99s-goals-be-realized/ and http://www.broadcastingcable.com/article/482409-NTIA_Spectrum_Plan_Could_Force_Second_ENG_Exodus.php.
10. Brain, Marshall, "How Digital Television Works," *howstuffworks*, http://electronics.howstuffworks.com/dtv.htm.
11. During the 2025 NABShow, on the floor of the convention hall, I had the opportunity to see a literal television room, where the walls were screens and the floor was interactive. See the section on Connected TVs in Chapter 5: The Future of Television Viewing for more discussion of this setup.
12. See the section on the iWorld in Chapter 5: The Future of Television Viewing.
13. See Chapter 10: The Future of U.S. Television in the Global Television Market.
14. Cole, Jeffrey, "The End of Broadcast TV," *Center for the Digital Future*, (May 10, 2023), https://www.digitalcenter.org/columns/cole-broadcast-tv/.
15. Cole, Jeffrey, "The End of Broadcast TV."
16. See Chapter 11: Final Thoughts and Visions.
17. Lieberman, David, "Retransmission Consent Payments to Hit $9.3 Billion In 2020: SNL Kagan," *Deadline Hollywood*, (October 27, 2014), http://deadline.com/2014/10/tv-station-retransmission-consent-payments-862748/.
18. "Broadcast Outlook 2024: Challenges, Opportunities Facing US TV, Radio Stations," *S&P Global*, (February 23, 2024), https://www.spglobal.com/marketintelligence/en/news-insights/research/broadcast-outlook-2024-challenges-opportunities-facing-us-tv-radio-stations.
19. Ware, Holly Sanders, "Poor Reception," *New York Post*, (November 12, 2009), http://www.nypost.com/p/news/business/item_rd7p88ycaZIfEZfHtfiX4M.
20. Ware, Holly Sanders, "Poor Reception."
21. See Chapter 7: The Future of Television Advertising.
22. See Chapter 10: The Future of U.S. Television in the Global Television Market.
23. See Chapter 7: The Future of Television Advertising.
24. See Chapter 8: The Future of Product Placement.
25. See the various chapters in Part I: The Future of the Streaming Media.
26. Sukhanova, Kate, "TV Viewership Statistics Explored: The Changing Landscape in 2023," *TechReport*, (May 27, 2024), https://techreport.com/statistics/entertainment/tv-viewership-statistics/.
27. Head, Sydney W. and Christopher H. Sterling (1990), *Broadcasting in America*, (Boston: Houghton Mifflin), 65–68.
28. Head and Sterling, *Broadcasting In America*.

29 Head and Sterling, *Broadcasting In America.*
30 See Chapter 3: The Future of Television Delivery Systems.
31 See the section on the iWorld in Chapter 5: The Future of Television Viewing.
32 Miller, Mark, "Local TV Stations Evolving Social Media Use as Platforms Change," *TVNewsCheck*, (August 14, 2023), https://marketshare.tvnewscheck.com/2023/08/14/local-tv-stations-evolving-social-media-use-as-platforms-change/.
33 See Chapter 9: The Future of Television Content Search & Promotion.
34 See the section on ATSC 3.0 in Chapter 3: The Future of Television Delivery Systems.
35 "TV Stations To Generate $3B in Digital Ad Rev," *TV NewsCheck* (August 5, 2014), http://www.tvnewscheck.com/article/78215/tv-stations-to-generate-3b-in-digital-ad-rev?ref=search.
36 Borrell Associates (July 2014), "Benchmarking Local TV Stations' Online Revenues," *Special Report for TVB*, pg. 7.
37 Borrell Associates, "Benchmarking Local TV Stations' Online Revenues."
38 Adgate, Brad, "TV Stations & Broadcast Networks at Odds Over Streaming Content Fees," *Forbes*, (May 3, 2024), https://www.forbes.com/sites/bradadgate/2024/05/03/tv-stations-broadcast-networks-at-odds-over-streaming-content-fees/.
39 Marszalek, Diana, "High School Sports News Scores For Stations," *TVNewsCheck*, (March 13, 2012), http://www.tvnewscheck.com/article/2012/03/13/58037/high-school-sports-news-scores-for-stations?utm_source=Listrak&utm_medium=Email&utm_term=High+School+Sports+News+Scores+For+Stations&utm_campaign=Stations+2012+Online+Rev+To+Soar+35%25+To+%242.7B.
40 Marszalek, Diana, "Houston's KRIV Launches Web-Only Personal Take on News," *NetNewsCheck*, (April 24, 2015), http://www.netnewscheck.com/article/40525/houstons-kriv-launches-webonly-personal-take-on-news.
41 Marszalek, Diana, "How to Insure TV Stays No. 1 in Local News," *TVNewsCheck*, (April 16, 2015), http://www.tvnewscheck.com/article/84608/how-to-insure-tv-stays-no-1-in-local-news?ref=search.
42 See Chapter 7: The Future of Television Advertising.

2 The Future of the MVPD

The multichannel video programming distributors, or MVPDs, consist of the cable television and the direct-to-home (DTH) satellite industries and are the traditional "alternative television" industries (alternative to broadcast). Both MVPD industries have seen growth periods, and both are currently facing an ultimatum: "change or die." This chapter will look first at the cable television industry, then the DTH satellite industry. Both are facing massive changes in the coming years, and there are serious questions facing both industries if they are to survive.

The Cable Television Industry

From open wires over tree limbs to today's fiber optic connections to TV Everywhere, cable television has been the major alternative way of delivering television to audiences across the country. In the coming years, cable companies will continue to see a host of industry-shifting changes. Competitors will continue to challenge and dramatically impact the domination of cable in the U.S. By 2035, the cable industry will look nothing like it does today.

History

The forerunner of today's cable industry began during the television freeze of the late 1940s and early 1950s as community antenna television, or CATV. During that time there were communities where television reception was sporadic or nonexistent even when citizens used their home television "rabbit-ears" antennas or even their home tower antennas. Communities in those regions would get together and erect a community "tall-tower" antenna on the highest surrounding location to get a direct line-of-sight view of whatever television signals might be available. Households in the community would then be connected to that tall tower for a fee. The antenna would deliver to each connected CATV household whatever television signals the antenna could receive.[1] If there were enough operational television stations within the antenna's range, then the households connected to the community antenna might be able to watch all three networks – provided, of course, that none of them was on an ultra high frequency channel (UHF) station. Watching a UHF station would only have been possible if the household had a UHF converter box

DOI: 10.4324/9781003625384-4

attached to the television set and the antenna connection.[2] Unless there was an independent television station in the market (one without a network affiliation) or a public television station close by, the only programming CATV households could watch was the networks and local programming – which, of course, was all that was available to anyone else in the U.S. at that time.

For those communities that were on the fringe of two or more markets, households would often have the additional ability to receive duplicate network broadcasts from the television stations located in those markets. In those communities the households would be able to choose between or among the various network and local broadcasts for the best or their favorites. The ability of cable to deliver signals from further than just the immediate market area led to the early battles between the cable and broadcast industries, battles which continued until the late 1970s and 1980s, and in some areas, even until today. Throughout the 1960s and early 1970s, cable continued to be primarily for rural communities, communities on the fringe of markets, and communities where natural formations such as mountains interfered with the ability of households to receive all three network signals.

That all changed in 1975 with the Home Box Office (HBO) broadcast of the Muhammad Ali/Joe Frazier heavyweight championship boxing match from Manila in the Philippines (known as the "Thrilla in Manila"). HBO, at the time was a microwave-delivered, pay-television programming service only for the northeastern U.S., where there were large population centers in a very small geographical distance. Because the Thrilla in Manila took place halfway around the world from the Wilkes-Barre, Pennsylvania, headquarters of HBO, the cable network chose to distribute the telecast of the fight using satellite distribution. The decision was a tremendous viewing success, as fight enthusiasts around the country were able to watch the boxing match between the two heavyweight giants of the time. In the wake of the success of this initial attempt at satellite delivery, HBO used the fight to launch their full satellite-fed programming schedule nationwide.[3]

Additionally, in 1976, Ted Turner decided to go nationwide, putting his local Atlanta-based UHF station, WTCG-TV, onto the satellite as well, and christening it the "Superstation."[4] Turner's use of satellite distribution for his television station helped popularize the idea of satellite distribution of programming for nationwide delivery as an alternative to the network delivery system of the "Big 3." Further, satellite delivery of Turner's Superstation and HBO's movie channel for the first time provided cable operators with additional programming that viewers could only get by subscribing to the local cable system. HBO and Turner showed to others the possibilities of satellite distribution of cable-only channels and led to the "cable gold-rush era" of the late 1970s and 1980s, where enterprising organizations developed the numerous specialized programming channels that comprise today's multichannel cable universe.

HBO's demonstration of its ability to deliver programming profitably to a nationwide audience opened the way for a host of entrepreneurs to develop and offer to audiences across the country (and now throughout the Western hemisphere) programming of all types. From all sports networks (ESPN, Versus, and many others) to all news and/or business networks (CNN, MSNBC, CNBC, Fox Business

Channel, and others) to do-it-yourself networks (HGTV, DIY), the cable industry has gone from a minor industry to a multichannel universe of niche programming designed to fracture a once more-or-less monolithic, prime time, three-network television program schedule into hundreds of audience shards.

Cable Today

The cable industry today is undergoing tremendous, dynamic change. Cable in 2035 will not resemble the way it looks today. In fact, the cable industry is one of the more forward-looking of all the linear industries, because the industry realizes that it must change to meet the new and developing technologies delivering television to the consumer.

Cable use has dropped significantly and rapidly over the past years. As of May 2024, cable penetration hit a low of 40% of the television population, down from 47% in January 2019,[5] and from a high in 2005 of just under 71%,[6] while DTH satellite penetration had also dropped dramatically, with both DirecTV and Dish Network losing between half (DirecTV)[7] and more than half (Dish)[8] of their subscribers. Not surprisingly, the percentage of adults who subscribe to a cable TV service goes down according to the age of the subscriber: for those aged 65 and older, 50% subscribe; for 45–64s, the percentage drops to 41%; for 35–44s, the percentage drops again to 35%; and for 18–34s, the percentage drops slightly to 34%.[9] With only about one third of adults aged 44 or younger subscribing to a cable TV service as of January 2023, and with the number of subscribers continuing to drop each quarter, the outlook for traditional cable is extremely bleak.

Additionally, television delivery by the telephone companies – predominantly AT&T and Verizon – was at 12% as of October 2022.[10] Further, the percentage of those who watch television using an over-the-air (OTA) antenna only is 4.1%, but an additional almost 12.5% use an OTA antenna along with a subscription streaming service such as Netflix or Amazon Prime Video.[11]

The cable industry is looking at significant competition not only from the competing alternative delivery systems, but also from those who choose to watch their television through some means other than the linear systems. For virtually the entire life of cable, the industry has had a monopoly on supplying alternative delivery of television to the country. Even when the DTH satellite industry began, cable was the dominant alternative delivery system in the U.S. While the numbers have been dropping significantly since 2005, cable is still the dominant alternative delivery system today. What cable did not, would not, or could not cover, DTH satellite systems did. It was a good partnership, especially for the cable industry.

Now, however, the cable industry is facing life-changing competition from a variety of sources, in addition to the DTH satellite services with whom they have been battling for many years.

In no specific order, the first of the competitors are various virtual MVPDs (vMVPDs) such as YouTube TV, Hulu/Hulu+LiveTV, Sling, and other such services delivered over the top (OTT) to connected TVs and connected devices, allowing viewers to watch television online. These vMVPDs have become direct competitors to critical portions of the traditional cable industry, and the largest, YouTubeTV, has now become the fourth largest alternative television provider in the U.S.[12] Additionally, for the younger age groups, and especially those who are 25 years old and younger, the traditional way of watching television through appointment viewing is no longer their first choice. Instead, more and more, they are choosing to watch television in a video-on-demand (VOD) style, rather than according to a schedule. The choice by these younger generations to watch television on-demand rather than the traditional scheduled, appointment-viewing manner will have a major impact on television in the coming years.[13]

The second form of competition, related to the first, is the myriad of online video streaming options available to the viewer today. The online video streaming industry takes in not only the online television viewing discussed above, but also subscription video-on-demand (SVOD), advertising-driven video-on-demand (AVOD), and free ad-supported streaming television (FAST) channels such as Netflix, Amazon Prime Video, Roku Channel, and Disney+ that use the Internet to stream programs to a variety of devices. Once again, for the younger generations, online video streaming is simply another form of television, one that is as equally acceptable to them as traditional television. With the ability to access the Internet not only from computers, but also smartphones and tablets, online video streaming is a powerful alternative to the cable industry, especially for the younger generations who are the future consumers of television.

A third competitor to traditional cable is the OTT set-top box (STB). OTT STBs were one of the first alternative delivery methods to traditional cable before the advent of the connected/smart TV. The most popular of those boxes, Roku, has now become the internal software for a number of those connected TVs, although viewers still get their favorite programming from Roku boxes, and others, especially when they are travelling as most TVs today have "plug and play" abilities. The term "over-the-top set-top box" is a general term encompassing not only stand-alone boxes like the Roku, Apple TV, Chromecast, and Amazon Fire TV delivery systems, but also videogame consoles, DVRs, and Blu-ray DVD players that have Internet capability built in.[14] OTT STBs were the original favored delivery system of "cord-cutters" – those consumers who are fed up with the "same-old, same-old" of linear television fare.

A fourth alternative to cable is the connected or "smart" TV. A CTV set is one where the television set itself receives streaming signals from the Internet. While the original connected TV operated with an STB, connected TVs operate with software built in, making it a fully-integrated television set. According to Hub Entertainment Research, in April 2024, 79% of U.S. homes have CTV sets, up from 66% just four years earlier, in 2020.[15]

Cable's Future Is Now

With all the alternatives to cable, one would think that cable's days might be numbered. However, that is not the case – for the industry, at least. Of all the linear TV industries, the cable industry has been the most forward-thinking and most willing to embrace the changes it needs to make to stay at the forefront of the competition. The cable industry has made it a point to adapt to developments in the industry that will ensure its survival.

Cable's first major change was to move from its traditional method of delivering television programming through a wire to its subscribers to providing what was called a "triple-play" of services. This triple-play service was a combination of traditional cable, broadband Internet, and landline telephone service. Triple-play service was introduced by Time Warner Cable and Comcast in 2004 and 2005 respectively.[16] In May 2015, Charlie Ergen, CEO of Dish Network, also began a push toward directly competing in the triple-play arena by rolling out a wireless video and data bundle to go with the "skinny-bundle" Sling TV[17] that Dish introduced at the 2015 CES convention.

The cable companies' offerings of triple-play – and now, quad-play – services move cable from simply a television transmission/retransmission service to a multifaceted industry capable of challenging Internet service providers and telephone companies in delivering the best and fastest Internet connectivity. Cable companies have the potential to become the primary wired broadband service in the U.S., challenging the major broadband deliverers of today for dominance and influence until power companies implement broadband over power lines technology, if that ever becomes a reality (which at this time appears highly unlikely in the U.S.).[18]

Furthermore, cable's ability to deliver high-speed broadband to its subscribers makes it possible for cable to continue to be the delivery mechanism for the CTV sets of the future. As mentioned earlier, connected TVs dominate the television set landscape. Given that CTVs receive their programming through an Internet connection, cable companies are a natural partner, delivering the programming to the television sets. Further, because cable's broadband service also delivers the Internet to a home's wireless router, CTV sets that have Wi-Fi capability can receive programming wirelessly in every room of the home.

Today, due to the proliferation of technologies capable of showing video signals in real time, the cable industry has introduced what is described generically as "TV Everywhere." TV Everywhere is generally thought of as the cable company offering its subscribers the ability to watch television anytime, anywhere, and on any platform. Using apps[19] that deliver the cable signal over broadband, wireless, or even cellular connections, cable companies have been one of the more progressive of the linear television industries when it comes to embracing the TV Everywhere system.

TV Everywhere makes it possible for viewers to enjoy their favorite programs while on the go. Subscribers to the cable companies offering their versions of TV Everywhere can watch their favorite programs anywhere they can get an Internet signal, either Wi-Fi or, increasingly, cellular. With TV Everywhere, the viewer no longer needs to remember to set his or her DVR to record a program while (s)he is out. TV Everywhere gives the viewer the ability to watch that program immediately on his or her smartphone, tablet, or notebook/laptop computer, as long as the device has wireless capability. The problem, though, is that the service is open only to each cable company's subscribers.

As is so often the case with the linear television industries, cable views TV Everywhere merely as an add-on benefit for its subscribers instead of an entirely new revenue stream of additional subscribers to its cable systems. Subscribe to the cable service and get TV Everywhere as an add-on. If you do not subscribe to the cable service or live within the coverage area, you are out of luck. Cable companies will even refer the potential TV Everywhere service subscriber to the competitor cable company that has the coverage for the area where they are located, even though it means losing that subscriber.[20]

It is likely that, in the future, TV Everywhere will eclipse traditional cable in terms of revenue generation because it will not be limited by area or even national or international boundaries. With the future of TV Everywhere, viewers will be able to watch favorite programs on the go whether they are in the U.S. or around the world. Additionally, because TV Everywhere will not necessarily have to be limited to national borders, U.S. cable companies will have the opportunity to deliver their programming to audiences in other countries, not just U.S. audiences or U.S. citizens living, working, or visiting international locations. TV Everywhere would make it possible for cable companies to have substantial numbers of subscribers in international locations. For example, Comcast could have subscribers in every European country; Charter could have audiences throughout South America; and Cablevision could be receiving revenues from subscribers across India – all through the use of TV Everywhere's ability to connect with the subscriber anywhere with an Internet connection. Considering the enormous revenue potential of TV Everywhere, expect the service to explode in the coming years. Already, Comcast's mobile phone service provides its users with the ability to make calls, text, and use their data services in more than 200 countries throughout the world.[21] Charter, through its Spectrum brand offers free calling throughout the U.S. (as expected), but also to Puerto Rico and to the U.S.'s overseas territories of Guam, U.S. Virgin Islands, Northern Mariana Islands, and American Samoa through its international calling plan.[22] Additionally, using Spectrum's mobile service through its flexible travel options, customers have free international texting around the world and international data in 180 countries.[23] Further, Comcast owns Sky Television, a major European entertainment company. It includes not only entertainments networks, but also Sky News and Sky Sports networks, along with high-speed internet, voice, and wireless networks, giving Comcast a major international reach.[24] While Charter, at this time, has no reach outside the U.S. except for mobile phone services, Comcast's ownership of Sky and the international reach of Netflix, Amazon Prime Video, and YouTube may force Charter to fully expand internationally to remain competitive.

TV Everywhere, though, is not the only major change for the cable industry before the end of the decade. Cable is not the future of the cable television industry – broadband is.[25] The best demonstration of this change to a broadband-first industry is the fact that the small cable companies around the U.S. are dropping the cable portion of their businesses and delivering only broadband and telephone services.[26] Other companies, including Suddenlink Communications, are finding customers do remain loyal as the cable companies pare back their cable channel offerings to keep prices lower.²⁷ In fact, as of September 2022 (the latest figures available), one third of U.S. homes access their television shows through broadband only, up from 5.9% just five years earlier (Sept. 2017).²⁸

Summary

The next five to ten years will be crucial for the cable television industry, as they will be for all the television industries. Cable is at a crossroads – either the industry will continue to innovate, or it will slowly lose out to newer television technologies.

The cable industry must envision itself as a broadband service to homes rather than as a traditional cable service. With networks and all other future television content providers deciding to retain their entire inventories and to deliver their programming directly to audiences using their websites or apps on connected TVs, smartphones, and tablets, the need for traditional cable services will evaporate. vMVPDs such as YouTube TV and Hulu+Live TV, FAST channels, and VOD services will further drive traditional cable services into extinction. Internet Protocol (IP) infrastructure has been on the minds of the participants, and a discussion point during most of the panels, since the 2015 National Association of Broadcasters (NAB) convention, so the parts of the industry have already acknowledged the need to move to IP.²⁹ Cable companies that do not innovate will be forced to close, or more likely be bought out by more successful, innovative companies.

The next ten years will be crucial for the cable industry. With the constant development of new and innovative technology, cable companies will need to be at the forefront of any technological revolution that will impact the industry. Already the industry is seeing mergers and attempts at mergers. The move toward consolidation is continuing and will rapidly expand in the coming years.³⁰ By 2035 there will probably be only a few cable mega-companies providing services. While the next few years may be rough, overall, the future for the cable industry can be very bright. Constant innovation and the embracing of the future of television with all its cutting-edge technologies will be the key.

The Direct-to-Home Satellite Industry

Of the linear media industries, the youngest is the DTH satellite industry. Through the delivery of DirecTV and Dish Network, the DTH satellite industry was, throughout the decade of the 2000s, the fastest growing of the media industries, taking audiences away from the cable industry, and delivering programming to 30% of the total television audience.

However, the DTH satellite industry potentially has the most to lose in the technological explosion that is the television landscape today and, in the future, because the industry has no way to compete fully with the different offerings that cable and other new technology industries can provide. If the DTH satellite industry is to survive, it will have to change dramatically. Those changes will mean the end of the DTH portion of the industry, but will allow the industry in its new form to continue and, potentially, to become even stronger.

History of the Direct-to-Home Satellite Industry

The notion of a DTH satellite delivery system was first described by the famous science-fiction writer, Arthur C. Clarke in an article he wrote entitled "Extraterrestrial Relays" that was published in *Wireless World Magazine* in 1945. In his article, Clarke shared an initial description of what satellite television would become in the future – continuous communication around the world could be achieved, he argued, by placing three space platforms into specific orbits 22,300 miles above the equator. Today, the equator is where not only the DTH satellites are located, but virtually all communication satellites as well.[31]

The first communications satellite (but not DTH satellite) was launched in 1962. It had an elliptical orbit, which meant that it was not able to transmit a continuous signal. The first commercial communication satellite to be geosynchronous – that is, to have the ability to revolve around the earth at the same rate that the earth rotates on its axis, making its footprint stationary – was the Intelsat I satellite, more commonly known as Early Bird I.[32]

Following in the footsteps of HBO (and their nationwide launch after the success of the previously mentioned Thrilla in Manila boxing match), entrepreneurs such as Ted Turner (WTCG-TV, Channel 17 in Atlanta, later TBS) and Pat Robertson (CBN, Christian Broadcasting Network, later The Family Channel) turned their attention to satellite delivery for their programs. The combination of HBO, Turner, and Robertson showed others what was possible with satellite delivery and thus began the direct broadcast satellite industry.[33]

The early days of satellite delivery to the home saw all programming made available free to the viewer. For the first ten years of direct broadcast satellite delivery around the country, television viewers who were not able to receive cable could buy a very large (about 10 feet in diameter) C-Band television receive-only (TVRO) dish and system that allowed the viewer to watch more than 100 channels of programming free of charge. The programming they could receive included the "raw take" from the networks without any local commercials (network commercials were still delivered). This ability to view the raw programming allowed the viewer to see newscasters "primping" between news segments and during commercial breaks or blowing their noses, etc.

These C-Band satellite systems were initially extremely expensive, with the system costing about $10,000 in 1980. As more and more people invested in the systems, however, the prices fell quickly – by 1985, the price of a C-Band home satellite system had dropped to less than $3000. Furthermore, because the signal came directly from the source to the consumer, the programming was of the highest quality, the same quality that the cable systems were receiving at the headend before sending the signals to the homes.[34] The advantage to the purchase of the C-Band satellite system was that, once the system was purchased, the programming was free, making the long-term cost less than having to pay monthly cable rates. However, as mentioned earlier, most systems were purchased by people in locations that could not receive cable. Further, a person purchasing the system had to have enough open space to put a satellite dish that was 10 feet in diameter. The size and the weight of the system precluded its use in small spaces as well as in apartments and townhomes.

The ability of home TVRO satellite owners to watch programming free of charge came to an end through the lobbying efforts of the cable industry. Because of those efforts, in 1984, Congress passed the Cable Act which allowed programmers to encrypt (or scramble) their signals, making it impossible for the home satellite owners to receive a picture without some form of decoding system. Almost overnight, the C-Band home satellite system industry dried up, with half of the satellite retailers nationwide having to close their businesses.[35] In place of the TVRO home system, a new industry developed – the modern-day DTH satellite industry, best known to viewers as DirecTV and Dish Network.

The first modern direct broadcast satellite (DBS) company was Primestar. Primestar was launched in July 1991 by a group of cable owners as the first-generation DBS service. It used transponders on GE American's Satcom K1 satellite to provide 67 channels to its subscribers. Primestar subscribers were charged between $25 and $35 a month for the service, along with a $100–$200 fee for having the satellite dish installed in their home.[36] While the subscriber did not have to buy the equipment (a major selling point in the Primestar advertising), the company continued to own the subscriber's home system. By 1997, Primestar was advertising that it had 160 channels available for subscribers.[37] Primestar was eventually bought by its major competitor, DirecTV, in 1999. Its assets and subscriber base were absorbed into DirecTV and Primestar ceased to exist.[38]

The U.S.'s largest and most powerful DTH satellite corporation today is DirecTV, with 11.3 million subscribers (in the U.S.), down significantly from a high of slightly more than 21 million subscribers.[39] DirecTV was originally a division of Hughes Electronics, a subsidiary of General Motors. At the same time, Stanley S. Hubbard, a visionary and the leading proponent of direct broadcast satellite in the U.S., had founded United States Satellite Broadcasting (USSB) in 1981 with the idea of developing his own DBS satellite system. In 1994, Hughes Electronics was awarded a contract to build and launch new high-powered satellites. USSB and DirecTV agreed that the new satellites would carry both USSB and DirecTV programming services. On June 17, 1994, both services were launched. The two services continued to compete until 1998, when DirecTV bought USSB for $1.3 billion.[40] As stated above, the next year DirecTV also bought its competitor, Primestar. In 2003, News Corporation bought controlling interest in DirecTV[41] which it ultimately sold to Liberty Media in 2008.[42]

Two years after the launch of DirecTV, in 1996, the company destined to be DirecTV's only DTH satellite competitor was founded. Dish Network was originally a wholly owned subsidiary of Echostar Communications Corporation. Echostar was founded in 1981 by Colorado entrepreneur Charles Ergen, his wife Cantey, and a family friend by the name of James DeFranco. Echostar started out as a C-band satellite TV retailer, but became a manufacturer of satellite receiving equipment.[43]

Dish Network began operations in March 1996 and has become DirecTV's biggest rival. In 1997, six years before News Corp purchased controlling interest in DirecTV, Dish Network entered into negotiations with News Corporation to merge the two companies for $1 billion. Had the merger occurred, Echostar, through Dish Network, would have been able to offer more than 500 channels to its customers. However, the merger negotiations fell apart.[44]

Five years later, Echostar and Dish Network attempted to purchase Hughes Electronics and its rival, DirecTV. Once again, however, it was not to be. Had the takeover occurred, it would have given Echostar a virtual monopoly of the DTH satellite market. After more than a year of speculation, the bid was officially blocked by the Federal Communications Commission (FCC) and the U.S. Department of Justice for fear of monopolistic abuse.[45]

Finally, in 2008, Dish Network became its own corporation. That year, Echostar officially split into two separate companies, with EchoStar providing the technology Dish Network uses to offer TV services. Charlie Ergen, the founder of both companies, is still the chairman of both Echostar and Dish Network.[46]

Direct-to-Home Satellite Industry Today

Today the DTH satellite industry is in decline, with little to no future as a DTH delivery system. In reality, the industry is comprised of only two DTH satellite companies, DirecTV and Dish Network. Both are nationwide organizations, both provide an alternative to cable television, and both are losing subscribers at alarming rates.

As mentioned earlier, DirecTV is down to 11.3 million subscribers from a high of slightly more than 21 million just seven years earlier. Dish Network is also down by more than half, at slightly less than 6.5 million subscribers as of Q4, 2023, down from a high of 14.1 million subscribers in Q1, 2014.[47] In 2023 alone, DirecTV lost 1.8 million subscribers and Dish lost 945,000 subscribers,[48] and those losses will not be recouped as more and more households continue to cut the "space cord" just as they have been cutting the cord on cable. (To be fair, during 2023, the two largest cable companies, Charter and Comcast, lost 1.025 million and 2.036 million subscribers respectively, and the cable industry as a whole lost 11.2% of their subscriber base.[49])

However, both companies are trying – albeit late to the party – to offer streaming options as part of their DTH services. DirecTV offers a streaming alternative called DIRECTV STREAM (formerly known as AT&T Now[50]) through its parent company AT&T, which owned a 70% share of DirecTV – at least until July 31, 2024, when it sold its stake to private equity firm TPG for $7.6 billion.[51] As mentioned earlier, Dish Network was the first to offer a streaming alternative to its DTH service through its Sling TV service. Sling is still viable, being the third largest vMVPD behind YouTube TV and Hulu+Live TV, with 2.055 million subscribers; however, it is the only one of the major vMVPDs to lose subscribers in 2023, losing 279,000 subscribers.[52]

Possibly the most ambitious move Dish Network has made is the purchase of two bankrupt companies with wireless spectrum inventories. Early in 2011, Dish Network purchased Terrestar and DBSD, which gave the company 40 Mhz of wireless spectrum. On August 22, 2011, Dish Network entered a filing with the

FCC requesting the right to build out a wireless broadband network, using 4G LTE (long term evolution) advanced technology – which was not available at that time. The move, if it had been approved, would have allowed Dish Network to enter the wireless broadband business and provided it an additional way of courting new subscribers while retaining current ones by using a hybrid satellite-terrestrial broadband capability.[53,54]

Dish Network's plan was to build out a cellular broadband network to compete directly with Verizon and AT&T, to provide a triple-play of its own, combining video, Internet, and mobile phone services. The Dish Network triple-play would have differed from the cable companies' in that – at the time – the cable companies offered only landline telephone service. Ergen said that to ensure the cellular service was backed by the right expertise, Dish Network would be open to partnering with one of the mobile phone companies, most likely either T-Mobile or Sprint Nextel (which was still a separate company at the time). While T-Mobile did not comment, Sprint Nextel said that it was "open to opportunities with spectrum holders who can't or don't want to build a network for their spectrum."[55] In April 2013, Dish made good on that possibility, offering to buy Sprint for $25.5 billion in an effort to stop an intended takeover of Sprint by Softbank, a Japanese phone and Internet company, and its boss, Masayoshi Son.[56] Dish was unsuccessful in its attempt, and three months later, in July 2013, the Sprint/Softbank merger was finalized.[57]

Dish's Ergen has not shown himself as one to stand still. In the FCC's "Block H" round of spectrum auctions, Dish purchased the entire block for $1.5 billion. The purchase added to Dish's spectrum inventory an additional 10 MHz.[58] With the addition of the Block H spectrum, Dish is continuing work on the 4G LTE advanced wireless broadband plan it initially filed for in 2011.[59] Ergen and Dish were also winners in a second round of auctions in November 2014, and Ergen said he would contend for additional spectrum in upcoming spectrum auctions.[60] In May 2015, Ergen announced that Dish Network would develop and implement a wireless video and data bundle combining Dish's Sling technology with a cloud-based data service using a portion of the wireless spectrum Dish won in the FCC spectrum auctions.[61]

Today, Dish Network is a player in the cellular phone business, even as its DTH satellite business is declining. Dish has been able to provide both domestic and worldwide coverage through its purchase of Boost Mobile and its development of Genmobile cellular companies.[62] Ergen's dream of competing has become a reality, although now, the cellular landscape is crowded not only with the major telephone companies (AT&T, Verizon, and T-Mobile), but with additional newcomers like Comcast and Charter. What the future will hold for Dish Network's offering – whether it will survive and thrive or not – is yet to be seen.

Future of the Direct-to-Home Satellite Industry

Today, the DTH satellite industry is in decline – precipitous decline, many would say. Both players in the industry – DirecTV and Dish Network – are shadows of what they were just a few years ago. Both are losing substantial numbers of subscribers each quarter.

For DirecTV, the question of what is next is still up in the air. Private equity firm TPG owns both DirecTV and its streaming service, along with Internet Protocol television (IPTV) service U-verse, all purchased from AT&T.

For Dish Network, the view is equally bleak. Its wireless service is struggling to find an identity and is hemorrhaging customers, as is its satellite service. Dish merged with EchoStar in 2023, but that has not helped the situation. While Dish executives expected 2024 to be a transition year, as they finished the build out of their nationwide 5G wireless network, the full picture for Dish has the shadow of a possible bankruptcy looming. The company is facing debts that they are struggling to meet.[63]

One possible short-term option would be for DirecTV and Dish Network to merge. This is not an unprecedented scenario – one only has to look at the merger in 2008 of Sirius and XM, which likely saved the satellite radio industry.[64] A merger between Dish and DirecTV could have the same effect. While there has been talk surrounding the possibility, it is still far from occurring. Shortly after purchasing DirecTV, TPG attempted to merge with Dish Network/EchoStar, but the merger quickly fell through.[65] However, a merger of the two would provide the new company with two streaming services in DirecTV Stream and Sling TV and a budding 5G cellular service (that could become a serious competitor in addition to DirecTV and Dish DTH services, which would most likely either be spun off or shut down). However, all this must be done quickly as the majority of subscribers to both companies tend to fall into the oldest generations, so the time frame for survival is growing shorter and shorter.

Ultimately, however, the DTH portion of the DTH satellite industry will disappear, replaced by the myriad streaming services that are available, the number and variety of which will continue to increase. The time frame for this is the next 5–10 years. However, it is possible that both DirecTV and Dish Network could continue to exist even after their satellite services have disappeared through their streaming and 5G offerings. Still, a merger of the two companies may be the best chance, however slight, not only for survival, but for continued competitiveness in the coming years.

Notes

1 Sterling, Christopher H. and John M. Kittross (1978), *Stay Tuned: A Concise History of American Broadcasting*, (Belmont, California: Wadsworth), 303.
2 See Chapter 3: The Future of Television Delivery Systems.
3 See Chapter 3: The Future of Television Delivery Systems.
4 Head, Sydney W. and Christopher H. Sterling (1990), *Broadcasting in America*, (Boston: Houghton Mifflin), 81.
5 Reese, Thomas, "Cable TV Statistics 2024 (Key Trends & Data)," *evoca.tv*, (May 21, 2024), https://evoca.tv/cable-tv-statistics/.
6 A. C. Nielsen, Co., *State of the Media: The Cross-Platform Report*, Q4 2011, http://www.nielsen.com/content/dam/corporate/us/en/reports-downloads/2012-Reports/nielsen-cross-platform-q4-2011.pdf.
7 Stoll, Julia, "Number of DirecTV Video Subscribers in the United States From 2nd Quarter 2014 to 4th Quarter 2023," *Statista*, (March 11, 2024), https://www.statista.com/statistics/497288/directv-number-video-subscribers-usa/.

8. Stoll, Julia, "Number of Dish Traditional Pay Subscribers in the United States From 1st Quarter 2014 to 4th Quarter 2023," *Statista*, (March 14, 2024), https://www.statista.com/statistics/497299/dish-network-number-subscribers-usa/.
9. Stoll, Julia, "Share of Adults Who Subscribe to a Cable TV Service in the United States as of January 2023, By Age Group," *Statista*, (March 18, 2024), https://www.statista.com/statistics/322958/pay-tv-penetration-rate-usa/.
10. "Pay TV in the United States" (report), *Statista*, https://www.statista.com/study/13111/pay-tv-in-the-us-statista-dossier/, p. 25.
11. A. C. Nielsen, Co., *Beyond Big Data: The Audience Watching Over the Air*, (January 2024), https://www.nielsen.com/insights/2024/beyond-big-data-the-audience-watching-over-the-air/.
12. Adgate, Brad, "YouTube TV Is Forecasted to Be the Largest Pay-TV Distributor In 2026," *Forbes*, (April 7, 2024, updated April 9, 2024), https://www.forbes.com/sites/bradadgate/2024/04/07/youtube-tv-is-forecast-to-be-the-largest-pay-tv-distributor-in-2026/.
13. See Chapter 4: The Future of Television Programming.
14. See Chapter 3: The Future of Television Delivery Systems.
15. Hardimon, Zharmer, 79% of U.S. Households Now Own a Smart TV," *The Current*, (May 22, 2024), https://www.thecurrent.com/americans-smart-tv-data-streaming-marketing.
16. See http://www.timewarnercable.com/ and http://www.comcast.com/ for more information.
17. Atkinson, Claire, "Dish's Ergen Set to Launch a Wireless Triple Play," *New York Post*, (May 14, 2015), http://nypost.com/2015/05/14/dishs-ergen-set-to-launch-a-wireless-triple-play/.
18. Buckley, Sean, "Broadband Over Powerline Last Mile Networks: More Hype Than Hope," *Fierce Telecom*, (January 10, 2012), http://www.fiercetelecom.com/story/broadband-over-powerline-more-hype-hope/2012-01-10.
19. See the section on the iWorld in Chapter 5: The Future of Television Viewing.
20. This is a personal example. In June 2012, I attempted to establish an Xfinity account with Comcast and a TV Everywhere account with Time Warner. In each case, I was directed to Charter Communications, which is the local service in my town. Further, I could download the apps for each company to my mobile phone, but could not access either one without an account number.
21. "Go Global," *Xfinity Mobile*, https://www.xfinity.com/mobile/my-account/international#:~:text=Go%20global,data%20in%20over%20200%20countries.
22. "Spectrum Voice International Calling Plan," *Spectrum*, https://www.spectrum.net/support/voice/countries-included-spectrum-voice-international-calling-plan.
23. "Mobile Plans with Flexible Travel Options," *Spectrum Mobile*, https://www.spectrum.com/mobile/plans/international.
24. Reiff, Nathan, "5 Companies Owned by Comcast," *Investopedia*, (updated May 3, 2025), https://www.investopedia.com/articles/markets/101215/top-4-companies-owned-comcast.asp#toc-3-sky.
25. http://money.cnn.com/news/newsfeeds/gigaom/media/2010_08_23_the_future_of_tv_is_not_on_cable.html.
26. Ramachandran, Shalini, "More Cable Companies Take TV Off Menu," *The Wall Street Journal*, (October 3, 2014), http://www.wsj.com/articles/more-cable-companies-take-tv-off-menu-1412120310?cb=logged0.8388166635099805.
27. Ramachandran, Shalini, "More Cable Companies Take TV Off Menu," *The Wall Street Journal*, (October 3, 2014), http://www.wsj.com/articles/more-cable-companies-take-tv-off-menu-1412120310?cb=logged0.8388166635099805.
28. "Tracking the Growth of Broadband-Only TV Homes," *Marketing Charts*, (November 9, 2022), https://www.marketingcharts.com/television/tv-audiences-and-consumption-227695.
29. I was able to observe this first-hand at the 2015 NAB convention, April 11–16, in Las Vegas. Time and again, in panel after panel, regardless of convention track (engineering,

management, etc.), discussion of the need to move to an all-IP structure was front-and-center on everyone's mind.
30 See, especially, Charter's and Comcast's attempts to acquire/merge with Time Warner Cable.
31 Marples, Gareth, "The History of Satellite TV – A Vision for the Future" http://thehistoryof.net/history-of-satellite-tv.html.
32 Sterling & Kitross, *Stay Tuned: A Concise History of American Broadcasting.*
33 "Industry History," *Satellite Broadcasting & Communications Association.* http://sbca.com/receiver-network/history-satellite-providers.htm.
34 Marples, Gareth, "The History of Satellite TV – A Vision for the Future."
35 "Industry History," *Satellite Broadcasting & Communications Association.*
36 "Direct Broadcast Satellite," Museum of Broadcast Communications, http://www.museum.tv/eotvsection.php?entrycode=directbroadc.
37 http://web.archive.org/web/19970512011951/http://www.primestar.com/.
38 Glasner, Joanna, "DirecTV Buys PrimeStar," *Wired*, (January 22, 1999), http://www.wired.com/techbiz/media/news/1999/01/17479.
39 Stoll, Julia, "Number of DirecTV Video Subscribers in the United States From 2nd Quarter 2014 to 4th Quarter 2023," *Statista*, https://www.statista.com/statistics/497288/directv-number-video-subscribers-usa/.
40 Grice, Corey, "Hughes Buys Satellite Firm for $1.3 billion," *c/net*, (December 14, 1998), http://news.cnet.com/Hughes-buys-satellite-firm-for-1.3-billion/2100-1033_3-219066.html.
41 http://www.msnbc.msn.com/id/3763546/ns/business-us_business/#.TwYaGXqZauI.
42 http://www.bloomberg.com/apps/news?pid=newsarchive&sid=a4JFvml25M_8.
43 http://www.satellitetv.digitalinsurrection.com/dishnetwork/dishnetwork.php.
44 http://www.satellitetv.digitalinsurrection.com/dishnetwork/dishnetwork.php.
45 http://www.satellitetv.digitalinsurrection.com/dishnetwork/dishnetwork.php.
46 http://press.dishnetwork.com/Corporate-Info/Company-Overview.
47 Stoll, Julia, "Number of Dish Traditional Pay TV Subscribers in the United States from 1st Quarter 2014 to 4th Quarter 2023," *Statista*, (May 14, 2024), https://www.statista.com/statistics/497299/dish-network-number-subscribers-usa/.
48 Frankel, Daniel, "DirecTV Lost 1.8 Million Subscribers in 2023, Analyst Estimates," *Next/TV*, (March 8, 2024), https://www.nexttv.com/news/directv-lost-18-million-subscribers-in-2023-analyst-estimates.
49 Frankel, Daniel, "DirecTV Lost 1.8 Million Subscribers in 2023, Analyst Estimates," *Next/TV*, (March 8, 2024), https://www.nexttv.com/news/directv-lost-18-million-subscribers-in-2023-analyst-estimates.
50 See DirecTV, https://www.directv.com/att-tv/.
51 "AT&T Sells Stake in DirecTV to TPG for $7.6 bln," *Reuters*, (Sept. 30, 2024), https://www.reuters.com/business/media-telecom/att-sells-70-stake-directv-tpg-76-bln-2024-09-30/.
52 Frankel, Daniel, "DirecTV Lost 1.8 Million Subscribers in 2023, Analyst Estimates," *Next/TV*, (March 8, 2024), https://www.nexttv.com/news/directv-lost-18-million-subscribers-in-2023-analyst-estimates.
53 Cheng, Roger, "Dish Unveils Plan for 4G LTE Network," *c/net*, (August 23, 2011), http://news.cnet.com/8301-1035_3-20095916-94/dish-unveils-plans-for-4g-lte-network/?tag=mncol;5n.
54 Goldstein, Phil, "Dish's Wireless Plan Unveiled: Satellite-terestrial LTE-Advanced Network," *FierceWireless*, (August 23, 2011), http://www.fiercewireless.com/story/dishs-wireless-plan-unveiled-satellite-terrestrial-lte-advanced-network/2011-08-23.
55 Ramachandran, Shalini, "Ergen Spies an Opening for New Wireless Network," *The Wall Street Journal*, (June 8, 2012), B4.
56 Chen, Brian X. and Scott, Mark, "Dish Offers to Buy Sprint, Joining Phone to TV Service," *The New York Times Dealb%k*, (April 15, 2013), http://dealbook.nytimes.com/2013/04/15/dish-network-makes-25-5-billion-bid-for-sprint-nextel/.

57 "Sprint and Softbank Announce Completion of Merger," *Sprint Newsroom*, (July 10, 2013), http://newsroom.sprint.com/news-releases/sprint-and-softbank-announce-completion-of-merger.htm.
58 Munson, Ben, "Dish Network Sweeps H Block Spectrum Auction," *Wireless Week*, (March 3, 2014), http://www.wirelessweek.com/news/2014/03/dish-network-sweeps-h-block-spectrum-auction.
59 Gompa, Neal, "Dish Secures Spectrum for 150Mbps LTE Wireless Broadband to Rural Homes in the US," *ExtremeTech*, (March 5, 2014), http://www.extremetech.com/electronics/177897-dish-secures-spectrum-for-150mbps-lte-to-rural-homes-in-the-us.
60 Zacks Equity Research, "FCC Starts Allocating Spectrum to AWS-3 Auction Winners – Analyst Blog," *Yahoo Finance*, (April 13, 2015), http://finance.yahoo.com/news/fcc-starts-allocating-spectrum-aws-221310690.html;_ylt=A0LEVjlFxVxV6zsAYwYnnIlQ;_ylu=X3oDMTByNXM5bzY5BGNvbG8DYmYxBHBvcwMzBHZ0aWQDBHNlYwNzcg--.
61 Atkinson, Claire, "Dish's Ergen Set to Launch a Wireless Triple Play," *New York Post*, (May 14, 2015), http://nypost.com/2015/05/14/dishs-ergen-set-to-launch-a-wireless-triple-play/.
62 See Dish Wireless, https://www.dishwireless.com/home.
63 Marek, Sue, "Dish's Hopes for a 2024 Turnaround Look Bleak," *Fierce Network*, (March 1, 2024), https://www.fierce-network.com/wireless/dishs-hopes-2024-turnaround-look-bleak.
64 Suciu, Peter, "DirecTV: How Can Satellite TV Survive in 2022?", *1945*, (July 14, 2022), https://www.19fortyfive.com/2022/07/directv-how-can-satellite-tv-survive-in-2022/.
65 Jewett, Rachel, "No Deal: The Dish and DirecTV Deal Is Off," *Satellite*, (November 22, 2024), https://www.satellitetoday.com/finance/2024/11/22/no-deal-the-dish-and-directv-deal-is-off/.

Part II
The Future of the Streaming Media

3 The Future of Television Delivery Systems

Internet Protocol Television

Internet protocol television, or IPTV, will be the delivery mechanism for all television, starting in this century and into the foreseeable future. The ubiquitous nature of the Internet, coupled with its versatility, makes the Internet the perfect powerhouse delivery system for television in the future.

Internet Protocol television is defined as "multimedia services such as television/video/audio/text/graphics/data delivered over IP based networks managed to provide the required level of Quality of Service (QoS)/Quality of Experience (QoE), security, interactivity and reliability."[1] That definition, from the International Telecommunications Union, suggests that IPTV is a multifaceted system capable of providing everything that the 21st century television viewer is looking for – an immersive, all-encompassing television experience. The viewer wants to be able to experience his or her television, regardless of whether it comes from a traditional content provider; an Internet-based content provider such as YouTube, Hulu, Netflix, or any of the other channels currently available, on the drawing board, in the mind of someone at this time, or not even yet envisioned; or social media rooms such as Meta, LinkedIn, X, or any other new or future social media sites.

The viewer also wants to be able to use his or her television experience to find information about the program (s)he is watching through the websites and fan rooms of the stars or the websites of the content providers. The viewer wants to be able to receive information and/or make purchases of items (s)he might see on a program using clickable product-placement links that take the viewer directly to a website that has the information and purchasing options the viewer needs or desires. IPTV gives the viewer those options, while delivering the same variety of programming that today's cable and direct-to-home (DTH) satellite industries do, plus an almost unlimited number of additional television/video/social media/advertising/etc. choices. In other words, IPTV can do everything that today's television systems can do, plus everything else that the viewer wants and will want in the future. Further, IPTV can deliver all the above in high, ultra-high (UHD or 4K), and super-high (SHD or 8K) definition television, and holographic television, making immersive television experiences of the future (discussed later in the book) possible.

DOI: 10.4324/9781003625384-6

In their book, *IPTV and Internet Video*, Wes Simpson and Howard Greenfield make five basic arguments for why IPTV is growing and will continue to grow until it is the dominant delivery system, not only in the U.S., but around the world. Those five arguments are listed here.

1. Because broadband IP networks reach so many households in developed countries, video service providers can use these networks to launch video services without having to build their own networks.
2. IP can simplify the task of launching new video services, such as interactive programming, *video-on-demand* (VOD), and targeted, viewer-specific advertising. (emphasis Simpson and Greenfield)
3. The cost of IP networking continues to decline due to the massive volume of equipment produced each year and the existence of worldwide standards.
4. IP networks can be found in every country in the world, and the number of users with high-speed Internet connections continues to grow at a rapid pace.
5. IP is the perfect technology for many other applications, including data transactions (such as e-mail or banking), local area networking, file sharing, Web surfing and many others.[2]

Let us look at each one of these arguments in more depth. First, the developed world, specifically, North America, Europe, and Oceania/Australia, accounts for the largest portion of Internet penetration in the world. In North America alone, Internet penetration stands at 92% of the population as of 2024. The penetration rate was 79.4% for Oceania/Australia and 91.6% for Europe in the same period.[3] The Internet usage in these regions is the driving force for all forms of Internet development. Because the penetration rate is so high in these countries – and growing rapidly in the rest of the world – new content providers and distributors have a ready-made distribution system to deliver their programming to viewers in a cost-effective manner. The content providers and distributors no longer need to establish over-the-air local affiliates like the networks, or convince cable providers to carry their offerings like the cable industry of today. They simply have to upload their content to the Internet, and they are ready to go. However, *uploading* and *monetizing* programming on the Internet are two different things and will be addressed in a later section. Nevertheless, the ability to reach large numbers of viewers through the various forms of IPTV – whether through over-the-top (OTT) set-top boxes (STBs), connected television (CTV) sets, or mobile phones and tablets – is becoming easier and easier and more and more cost effective. This will only continue in the future.

Second, IPTV makes it possible for the new media technologies to flourish. Without IPTV, there would be limited Netflix, no Roku, and no need for Google Chromecast, Amazon Fire TV, or Apple TV. All video would be available only on computers and those smartphones and tablets with Internet capability. The Internet is the distribution channel through which all streaming media get to the viewer – therefore, the critical role IPTV plays in the development and explosion of the new media technologies is clear. Additionally, IPTV provides advertisers with the ability to deliver directly to the viewer those advertisements – and only those advertisements – that appeal to the viewer and that will make the strongest impact on them. Traditional media cannot deliver advertising in such a strategically targeted manner. For traditional media, advertising is much like a shotgun blast – you try to cover the widest possible area in hopes of hitting your target. IPTV advertising gives you the accuracy of a rifle shot, needing only a narrow window to reach the intended target. Advertising over IPTV gives the advertiser the best possible opportunity to reach the intended audience in the most cost-effective manner.

Third, as Chris Anderson points out in his book, *FREE: The Future of a Radical Price*, the three technologies that most directly impact the development of and the ability to deliver IPTV – computer processing power, digital storage, and bandwidth – have continuously become cheaper.[4] This development, he says, is based upon the notion of Moore's Law, which states that the number of transistors that can be placed onto a given integrated circuit, or "chip," doubles every two years.[5] The more transistors that are available per chip, the higher the computing processing power. Anderson points out that the same occurrence exists for digital storage and bandwidth, although, both double faster than the two-year window stated originally by Moore in 1965.[6] Anderson recognizes that, now, computing processing power actually doubles every 18 months, while digital storage doubles every year, and bandwidth increases the fastest, doubling every nine months.[7] (While not all aspects of Moore's Law still apply fully today, the overall point of the law is still relevant.)

The increase in bandwidth makes it possible to have all the different streaming services in both high definition and UHD (4K) television, while the increase in storage makes possible the numerous smartphones, laptops, and tablet computers capable of storing and replaying full length movies and television programs.[8] Anderson says:

> Never in the course of human history have the primary inputs to an industrial economy fallen in price so fast and for so long…. In a world where prices always seem to go up, the cost of anything built on these three technologies [computer processing power, digital storage, and bandwidth] will *always* go down. And keep going down, until it is as close to zero as possible (emphasis Anderson's).[9]

The continual drop in the price of computer processing power, digital storage, and bandwidth makes IPTV both viable and cost effective.

Fourth, as Simpson and Greenfield so accurately put it, the Internet is in every country and on every continent in the world (although, for North Korea, the number of Internet users is miniscule and only a guess, because there is no hard data for that country).[10] For television content providers and distributors, the explosive growth in Internet usage throughout the world opens new opportunities to reach a global audience, not just those viewers in the markets served by over-the-air broadcast television, cable systems, or DTH satellite providers. With IPTV delivery, a content provider can reach the television viewer wherever (s)he is anywhere in the world because the signal is delivered through the Internet. Likewise, with television delivered through the Internet, advertisers can target viewers directly, regardless of the country or area of the world in which they reside. IPTV opens new possibilities for global revenues for all content providers and distributors, whether they are the traditional content providers or the new content providers and distributors.

The fifth argument for the explosion of IPTV is self-explanatory. For a number of years, the Internet has been available for the various uses mentioned above. What IPTV does is to allow the viewer to do all those activities simultaneously from wherever (s)he is experiencing television. No longer will the viewer need to have a notebook computer, a smartphone, or a tablet computer at the ready while watching a program to be able to chat, e-mail, purchase a product seen on a program, etc.

With a CTV, the viewer can do all the abovementioned activities, while at the same time continuing with the television program (s)he is watching, all on the television screen. While watching a television program, the viewer will be able to watch an advertisement, click on the product right on the television set and go straight to a website where (s)he can get more information about the product and immediately purchase it. The viewer can then go to her/his bank's website and transfer money from one account to another to cover the amount of the transaction if the viewer does not have enough money in the account (s)he used to make the purchase. All this can be done without ever leaving the program the viewer is watching or needing a second device to carry out the transactions. All activities are carried out immediately, right there on the viewer's television set because the set is connected to the Internet.

Internet Protocol Television Development and Future

The first television program was delivered over the Internet in 1994. In that year, *ABC's World News Now* was telecast over the Internet, using the CU-SeeMe video conferencing software.[11] The term "IPTV" first appeared on the scene when the Precept Software company developed a video product to use over the Internet called IP/TV. IP/TV was a Windows and Unix based application that was compatible with multicast backbone (MBONE), an experimental backbone for IP multicast traffic across the Internet that was developed in the early 1990s. The IP/TV application was able to transmit both single and multisource audio and video traffic, with quality that was as good as DVDs.[12]

What IPTV products can offer that cable and DTH satellite companies cannot is the potential for complete interactivity within the television landscape and across all other platforms. IPTV is the driving force behind all the new and developing television technologies available today and in the future. IPTV's versatility makes it the system for delivering television in the future. IPTV has the capability to deliver television through wired broadband connections, over Wi-Fi and cellular connections, and even over the air (potentially) through ATSC 3.0. It has the capability to deliver television today through a high definition or an UHD signal, and, in the next few years, through a SHD (8K) signal. In addition, IPTV will be able to deliver television in a holographic 3D television format, currently being developed in the U.S. and around the world.[13] IPTV can provide the viewer traditional "lean back" passive television viewing, or can provide her/him with a fully immersive, fully interactive, "lean forward" experience that, until recently, had been the domain of the science fiction writer. As has so often been the case with technological developments throughout history, today's IPTV is science fiction becoming science fact.

Further, IPTV has the capability to deliver all the television choices to a variety of devices and screens. IPTV can deliver television to the traditional television set through OTT STBs such as Roku, Apple TV, Chromecast, and Amazon Fire TV, a video game console such as the Xbox Series X|S, or a Blu-ray DVD player, or directly, through a CTV set. It can deliver a television signal to the traditional personal computer through wired, wireless, or cellular connections. IPTV also has the capability to deliver television to mobile devices such as smartphones and tablet computers, and notebook computers so that the viewer-on-the-go can watch her/his favorite television program.[14]

IPTV can also provide the capability to multitask while watching television. As the viewer watches a favored program (s)he can surf the web; check e-mail; connect with friends, neighbors, family, and other viewers; find out more about the star of the program or a supporting cast member; purchase a product seen on television in an advertisement or through product placement; search for other programs the viewer might enjoy; or play a video game – all simultaneously. In other words, IPTV allows the viewer to do most anything (s)he would like without having to use multiple devices or stop doing one thing to do another.

But IPTV provides the viewer with an even more exciting opportunity – to watch any television program produced by any company and shown on any content provider anywhere in the world at any time and on any device. IPTV gives the viewer the opportunity to follow his/her favorite program no matter where in the world the viewer is, no matter where the program originates or is distributed. For instance, an American viewer, living in Santiago, Chile, could watch a program that originated in the U.K. and is telecast on the BBC on his or her tablet computer. That same BBC program could also be watched by a Vietnamese man at home on his CTV set, while his neighbor, who happens to be Thai, is watching that same program on his or her smartphone while traveling in South Africa. All three viewers are sharing a common experience. While each is a native of and living in a different country, they can enjoy the same program on different television technologies, in different locations around the world at the same time. Only with IPTV is that possible.[15]

William Cooper, the founder and principal consultant at independent interactive television consultancy informitv, and Graham Lovelace, founder of Lovelace Consulting, which specializes in convergent media, put it this way in their groundbreaking report *IPTV Guidex*:

> Exploiting the full potential of digital delivery, this new form of distribution [IPTV] will fundamentally affect the way television is viewed, change channels of distribution and disrupt the traditional broadcasting business, as

> the conventional boundaries of television and telecommunications industries collide and collapse. The transition from four or five terrestrial networks to multichannel television will continue with an exponential expansion of channels and a proliferation of programmes available on demand.
>
> The choice of channels and programmes will further explode as viewers roam beyond the national borders of broadcast television and access live and recorded programmes from around the world, reflecting every conceivable interest. Viewers will further benefit from increasing control, watching what they want, when they want, where they want, on the device of their choice.[16]

Cooper and Lovelace wrote those words in their report in 2006, just as the current television explosion was beginning. Their words were prophetic for the television viewers as well as the television professionals of today.

Additionally, IPTV makes it possible to drive advertising to the viewer in ways that are only being explored today. Addressable television advertising is a major topic at conferences around the world as the possibility of reaching the viewer directly with the advertising (s)he *wants* to watch, instead of *has* to watch, becomes a reality. IPTV makes it possible to deliver one advertisement to one viewer who is watching a television program, while delivering a second advertisement to a second viewer who is watching the same program at the same time, and a third advertisement to a third viewer. Each advertisement can be tailored to the viewer's likes and dislikes so that the advertisement is virtually certain to influence the viewer.[17]

Finally, IPTV makes possible the development of future technologies that are on the horizon or even the drawing boards of today's start-up companies and the traditional major players in television. The further refinement of virtual reality (VR) and augmented reality (AR) systems, as well as other futuristic ideas such as holographic, interactive television and VR/AR contacts or implants, will be possible because of IPTV.

Further, because IPTV can be delivered through any of the mechanisms available today (wired, Wi-Fi, and cellular), the viewer could watch television no matter where (s)he might be. In addition, the viewer, because of the interactive nature of IPTV, could also chat with others while watching television, shop online – or even in a store – for a product that is currently being advertised during the television program or that the viewer sees being used by one of the characters on the program. IPTV also allows the travelling viewer using VR/AR glasses/headsets to watch her/his favorite television program anywhere in the world, or watch a local program made in the country where (s)he is currently staying. The viewer could use the glasses to chat with a friend about the program (s)he is watching, check out the latest local products and shop for them, or get directions to a restaurant.

The possibility of having IPTV available on their VR/AR glasses as they travel allows viewers to interact with wherever they are. The viewer can have advertisements for products (s)he would be interested in knowing about shown to the him/her on the local television program (s)he might be watching. For instance, imagine an American viewer is traveling to Ireland. She has tweeted and put in her Facebook status that she is heading to Dublin for a week. One of her Facebook or X friends mentions a place to stay. Because her friend has previously visited Ireland, he follows an Irish travel agency on Facebook. Now, that Irish travel agency can contact our American viewer with suggestions for where she might want to stay, places to go, things to see and do, etc.

On her flight over, our viewer continues to get, through her glasses, information and advertisements for "all things Ireland," even on her favorite television program. Upon arriving, her glasses introduce her to local television, where she selects a program and begins to receive advertisements for local products, services, and stores that will interest her. She selects the things she wants to shop for and gets directions to shops that sell those products, allowing her to compare prices. Based on her shopping, she receives recommendations for additional products that she might like as well as information on where to buy them. She receives all this information because she is connected to the 21st century television universe through IPTV.

Summary

There is no doubt that IPTV and the future of television go hand-in-hand. As mentioned earlier, the move to an all-IP infrastructure was, seemingly, on almost everyone's lips as far back as the National Association of Broadcasters (NAB) 2015 convention. When you have the broadcasters(!) constantly talking about the need to move to an all-IP infrastructure, is there really any doubt that IPTV is the future of the television universe?

The versatility of IPTV makes it an excellent delivery system for 21st century television. IPTV can be delivered over a wired connection, through Wi-Fi, or through a cellular connection. It can deliver high definition, UHD (4K), and SHD (8K) television and holographic television, either through a traditional scheduled day of programming, or in an on-demand format. IPTV can deliver completely addressable, interactive advertising through the use of dynamic ad insertion.[18] It can deliver a wide range of differentiated and undifferentiated promotional content designed to attract the viewer to those television programs that (s)he wants to watch as well as the products and services the viewer/consumer desires.[19] As such, IPTV will be the delivery mechanism for the future of television.

ATSC 3.0

ATSC 3.0 – or what is now known as "NextGen TV" – is the latest iteration of a television system from the Advanced Television Systems Committee (ATSC), a part of the Advanced Television Committee. Its purpose is to establish technical standards for advanced television (not traditional analog television). The ATSC is responsible for the development of the standards for HDTV (high-definition television) and SDTV (standard-definition television) (both digital standards for television; the analog standard was the National Television System Committee (NTSC) standard from the early 1950s), and is developing the next standard for over-the-air (OTA) television – ATSC 3.0.[20] In addition to the broadcast community, other organizations represented in the ATSC include the broadcast equipment, motion picture, consumer electronics, computer, cable, DTH satellite, and semiconductor industries.[21]

While it has moved beyond the development stage, at this time ATSC 3.0 has not yet achieved complete rollout nationwide, even though the expectations were that the ATSC would have had a 3.0 standard ready to begin its rollout sometime in 2017. However, there is still work to be done before ATSC 3.0 is "ready for prime time." The original digital television standard is more than 30 years old today, and television/video technology has progressed dramatically since that time. For the broadcasters, the opportunities that ATSC 3.0 provides, offer the possibility of allowing the industry to compete into the future alongside the streaming media.

Although this book will not delve into the engineering aspects of ATSC 3.0, suffice it to say that the new system – should it be fully developed and fully implemented throughout the country – will provide broadcasters the ability to offer what is being called "a wireless, data-agnostic Internet Protocol (IP) pipeline."[22] The new system would make it possible for broadcasters to compete directly with their linear and streaming media counterparts by being able to provide their content not only through the television set, but also on smartphones, tablets, and computers.[23] As an early example of the hoped-for expectations of ATSC 3.0, in May 2015 Phil Kurtz wrote in a *TV NewsCheck* article:

> But just as important, having the ability to use the big stick – supplemented by [single frequency network] SFN sites, if needed – to blanket a TV market with wireless internet services opens up business models few broadcasters have previously considered." Kurtz continued, "One might be delivering navigation data, traffic conditions, maps and other pertinent travel data to drivers zipping down the highway. Another could involve distributing educational materials to students, schools, and remote campuses. The opportunities are only limited by the creativity of broadcasters to find ways to use this new IP transport capability in commercially profitable ways.[24]

Kurtz wraps up with the supportive statement, "Yes, ATSC 3.0 will be OTA IPTV – on steroids."[25]

ATSC 3.0 – if ever fully deployed and implemented – promises the delivery of "stunning" 4K and later 8K video, including high dynamic range (HDR) and movie-quality sound and added voice clarity. It is anticipated that it will provide two-way interactivity (something that has been desired in the television world for decades but never achieved), delivered both over the air and through Internet connections. Further, ATSC 3.0 promises to deliver Internet content on-demand in an enhanced way, data delivery to cars (much as Kurtz described earlier), and emergency alerts – to name just some of the most prominent of the enhanced offerings.[26]

It has been a decade since work began on ATSC 3.0, and yet it is still not the default standard in the U.S. In fact, for most of the country, the system is still in the roll-out and testing stage, where the signal is available, but not the expected choice for viewers. David Bloom of *NextTV* described ATSC 3.0 in a 2023 article just before the NAB convention that year as "...like a TV tech version of *Waiting for Godot*, where an unspecified *something* [emphasis Bloom's] is imminently arriving to make everything better, yet never quite materializes before we fade to black."[27]

ATSC 3.0 has faced a myriad of challenges throughout its development and implementation. Even today, ATSC 3.0 only reaches about 75% of the total television market in the U.S., with that percentage coming from only 70 out of the 210 markets in the country. Then there is the problem of the literally thousands of potential configurations of the new standard (the NAB itself says there are 40,000) – the ability to receive the signal depends on what configuration the viewer has. That problem also complicates the delivery of the ATSC 3.0 signal to cable customers, thus making it difficult for the cable companies. Additionally, much of what is being offered by the ATSC 3.0 promise is already available on other devices, including STBs and CTV sets. Further, there is the cost to the consumer for ATSC 3.0 when/if it comes to fruition. Although ATSC 3.0 is now backwards-compatible with the original ATSC 1.0 (it was not in the early days), the viewer will still need to purchase either a converter box or a new ATSC 3.0-capable television set to get the full benefits of the ATSC 3.0 system, especially those Internet-oriented aspects of ATSC 3.0. Without the new set or converter box, the new standard offers very little to the television viewer.[28]

There are other problems as well. One of these problems is that, although the proponents of ATSC 3.0 tout its ability to show programming in 4K, virtually all programming on television is still being shown in HDTV, not 4K. The question then becomes, why should consumers spend additional money for a new television set or an antenna and converter box, when all they will be able to receive is the same programming they already get from their current television sets.[29]

A second problem is the digital rights management (DRM) requirements that are part of ATSC 3.0. At this time, unless a television set has tuners with the latest DRM requirements built in (they came out only in March 2024), those sets will be blocked from delivering shows with the latest DRM requirements. Additionally, with ATSC 3.0, it will be possible for broadcasters to prevent viewers from recording programs for later playback. Under the current system (ATSC 1.0), broadcasters are prohibited from preventing viewers from making those recordings. It would be a real "dealbreaker" for most, if not virtually all, viewers if they could not record shows to watch later.[30]

Finally – and this has been mentioned earlier in this section, are the continuing delays in getting ATSC 3.0 to the entire country a case of "too little, too late." The NAB is so concerned that is has been urging the Federal Communications Commission (FCC) in the strongest possible words that, without the FCC's intervention, ATSC 3.0 is in peril of not making it as the new standard.[31] At the 2023 NAB convention, FCC Chair Jessica Rosenworcel announced support for the new system, but no time frame was set for the switchover from ATSC 1.0 to the new 3.0 standard.[32]

Even so, the changeover to ATSC 3.0 – if it ever comes about (and that is still in doubt) – is no longer the only way to watch free television content. As is discussed in the next chapter, free ad-supported streaming television (or FAST) channels are available for those with CTV sets. These channels provide the opportunity to watch older television programming on numerous different channels. These FAST channels are available on both CTV-delivered choices such as The Roku Channel, Samsung TV Plus, and Vizio's WatchFree Plus, as well as stand-alone choices such as Tubi, Pluto TV, and others.[33]

Despite all these concerns, supporters of ATSC 3.0 believe that the system is the solution that will allow broadcasters to compete on a level playing field with all the other current and future television players. Certainly, those who are involved with the development of ATSC 3.0 are in favor of the system, along with many of the local station group owners. They are desperate for ATSC 3.0 to be that "real thing" that gives them a reason to exist as something other than a hyperlocal independent television station in the 21st century television universe. Just like Phil Kurtz' description of ATSC 3.0 as "OTT IPTV – on steroids," Harry Jessell of *TV NewsCheck* fame wraps up his arguments for ATSC 3.0 by saying "No, free TV of the future will not be free, but it's a bargain that will pay dividends for generations to come."[34] At this point, the jury is still out on ATSC 3.0, so the best that can be said is simply, "We willl see...".

Over-the-Top Set-Top Boxes

OTT STBs provide alternative ways of delivering video content to homes. The OTT STB has a long and distinguished history of providing major step forwards for television, only to see it ultimately replaced by new developments and technologies. Today's OTT STBs deliver a variety of video content to viewers through their attachment to CTVs. OTT STBs must be connected to the Internet in some way, either directly through a digital subscriber line (DSL) or some other connection, or through Wi-Fi.

History of Over-the-Top Set Top Boxes

The history of STBs in general goes back to the earliest days of television. In the wake of the television freeze of 1948–1952, the FCC divided the U.S. into geographical, non-overlapping areas, or markets. In each of these markets, the FCC placed set numbers of channels, so that each channel would not interfere with their competitors in that market. The FCC had the choice of placing very high frequency (VHF) band channels (over-the-air channels 2–13), ultra high frequency (UHF) channels (over-the-air channels 14–83 at that time), or an intermixture of VHF and UHF channels in each of the markets that they established. Early television manufacturers, though, had placed only VHF tuners in their television sets, because the two major networks of the time, NBC and CBS, had their affiliates primarily on the VHF band. ABC, the weakest of the three networks during the early days of television, had come later to television and so their affiliates were relegated to the UHF band primarily. In intermixed markets and in UHF-only markets, television audiences had no way to receive the UHF channels directly over the air through their sets.[35]

The initial remedy for the inability to watch UHF channels directly through the television set was the UHF channel converter box – one of the original STBs for television.[36] Viewers who lived in UHF-only or intermixed markets were able to purchase these boxes from vendors so they could watch the UHF television channels. To use the UHF converter box, the viewer hooked it into the back of the television set, tuned the set to channel one (a channel that was unused and had been given to FM during World War II for field telephones[37]), selected the correct channel to be viewed (the boxes had a rotating dial marked with each of the 14–83 channels that could be selected depending on the channel[s] that were available in the market), and programming would appear on the television set. The UHF-converter box was not inexpensive, costing upwards of $30–50 to purchase during a time when a new automobile could be bought for less than $2000.[38] However, for those viewers living in a UHF-only market, it was the only way to watch television during the 1950s and early 1960s.

The UHF converter box remained a staple of UHF viewing until the mid-1960s. In 1962, in an effort to relieve the problems of UHF viewing, the U.S. Congress passed the "All-Channel Receiver" bill into law. This law required all television set makers to include both VHF and UHF tuners on their television sets.[39] Once the bill became law, the sets were modified to receive all VHF and UHF channels directly through the television set, thus eliminating the need for the UHF converter box.

A second early form of STB was the antenna tuning box.[40] This box was part of the home antenna system for viewers who lived in rural areas and on the fringes of the television markets. These boxes were connected to tall antennas that were attached to the outside of the home and were needed to pick up signals that were too weak to be received by a home television set's built-in antenna (the "rabbit ears" antenna). The boxes had a compass dial, and by turning the dial, the antenna would move in the direction of the television signal's origination. The antenna would then pick up the station's signal and deliver it to the television set for viewing. The further from the station a home was, the taller and more powerful the antenna system needed to be.

The antenna tuning box came as part of the antenna system itself and was not an additional cost. However, the antenna system was expensive to purchase and a necessity for those audiences who wanted to watch television and had no other way of receiving the signals due to distance from the station, or lived in mountainous regions where the mountains blocked the station's signals to the home.

Beginning in the mid-1970s, a third form of STB became a staple in many television households – the cable converter box.[41] Because television sets of the time were not manufactured with the ability to view cable offerings, cable companies turned to the STB to deliver the channels to their subscribers directly. Once cable went from simply retransmitting local and distant over-the-air signals to delivering cable only content (early HBO, WTBS [or rather WTCG-TV], CNN, ESPN, etc.), its rise was stratospheric. Audiences who originally saw no need for a "pay-TV service" when it was merely a retransmission device. found new reasons to consider cable due to its ability to differentiate itself from over-the-air television. When cable moved beyond offering only the three networks plus PBS and the occasional independent over-the-air television stations the cable business boomed.

The cable converter STB operated much in the same manner as the UHF converter box. The cable from the local system's headend was plugged into the back of the converter box. A second cable then ran from the converter box to the back of the television set. The television set was tuned either to channel three or channel four, depending on the set-up of the box that the cable company supplied as part of the installation and subscription (it was not a separate purchase like the UHF converter box). Once the installation was complete, turning on the television provided the viewer with the ever-growing number of cable-only channels. The viewer merely had to turn the dial on the box to select a favorite channel. Cable converter STBs originally provided as many as 23 channels per box. That number was expanded to 40 before the boxes were finally phased out.

The cable converter box remained a staple until the development of the "cable-ready" television set, a TV that was designed to play signals sent directly to the set from the cable headend without the need for an intermediary device. With the advent of the cable-ready television set, the cable converter box – just like the UHF converter box before it – became obsolete.

Along with the cable STB providing a multitude (at that time) of viewing options, another juggernaut of an STB came along – the videocassette recorder, better known as the VCR. The VCR was introduced in 1975 by the Sony Corporation in the form of its Betamax VCR. The original Betamax was the first commercial consumer player/recorder machine, and to purchase one, you also had to purchase a 19" Sony television set – at a combined cost of $2295! The Betamax machine was an excellent player, providing high-quality television viewing for the owner. While its quality was the best of the VCRs, its non-standard size limited the tape's use to the Betamax machine alone. Further, the original Betamax machine would only record for one hour and had only the one-hour standard-play mode.[42]

The next year, JVC introduced its version of the VCR, the original VHS, or video home system. First introduced in Japan in 1976, it was quickly sold in the U.S. the next year. The JVC VHS system used a standard ½ inch in diameter videotape in its cassette, making it possible for numerous other companies to make videocassettes for the players. Further, unlike the one-hour record mode of the Betamax, the VHS recorder could record up to two hours on a single tape in standard mode, depending on the make and model of the VCR, and up to four hours in the original long-play mode, which was first included on RCA's version of the VHS recorder. The VHS machine was significantly less expensive than the Sony Betamax, and could be purchased as a stand-alone product, without having to be coupled with an expensive television set. The quality of the VHS image was not as good as the Sony Betamax, but the trade-off was the relatively inexpensive price to purchase a set.[43]

As it turned out, the consumer was willing to accept a lower quality picture for a less expensive machine, and the VHS system – whether from JVC or any of the other brands of the time – became the de facto home viewing and recording device for the television home audience until the development of the digital video recorder (DVR). The VCR was used to watch purchased movies and, toward the end of its life, purchased television programs. Television viewers also rented movies – Blockbuster and numerous other companies made fortunes renting videotapes of favorite movies in their stores. Additionally, audiences taped their favorite television programs for later viewing and even for keeping and replaying.

Finally, audiences, if they had a camera and videocassette recorder system, or, later, a camcorder (camera and recorder all in one), could shoot home movies and watch them immediately after recording. There was no need to send the movies off to be processed as was needed with film; now there was the immediacy of playback, of recording two hours of shaky, fast panning, but ultimately unforgettable and priceless tapes of the kids growing up, of the parents growing old, and of the neighbors, friends, and extended family joining in with the fun. For more than 20 years, the VCR was the high-tech STB in the average family household.

The second system to come on the scene about the same time as the videocassette system was the videodisc player, originally called a "Reflective Optical Videodisc" or "Laser Optical Videodisc." Originally developed and marketed by MCA/Phillips as the DiscoVision, the first videodisc player designed specifically for the consumer was the Magnavox Magnavision VH-8000 VLP (which stood for – in the U.S. – video long play).[44] The videodisc player was first marketed in Atlanta, Georgia, on December 15, 1978, two years after the VHS videocassette recorder and four years before the compact disc or CD, which is based on Laserdisc technology.[45] As the name suggests, the videodisc player was a play-only device and, while there was some user interest in developing a record mode, it was never added to the player.

The videodisc player came in two styles – a stylus model (not unlike a record turntable) and an early laser model. The stylus model was the less expensive of the two and was short-lived. Both the stylus and the laser models provided high-quality video playback of recorded discs, which were about the same size as an LP (album) record. Both players played in standard speed mode only and, depending on which model you chose, could play 30 minutes or 60 minutes on one side. For a movie then, the viewer would have to manually turn the disc over to finish the movie. Movies lasting longer than two hours would have to be placed on three discs for the 30-minute-a-side player, and on two discs for a 60-minute-a side player, unlike a VHS cassette which could hold a two-hour or longer movie on one cassette in long-play mode. The players as well as their videodiscs were expensive to purchase and, while there were attempts at videodisc rentals by companies that also sold the players and discs, neither gained mainstream popularity in the U.S. American homes simply preferred the ease, the recording ability, and, especially, the much lower cost of the VCR. However, it was the development of the videodisc player that ultimately led to the development of the compact disc, as mentioned earlier, and later, the digital video disc or DVD.

The first DVD players appeared in Japan at the end of 1996 and moved to the U.S. a few months later in early 1997.[46] When the DVD player came to the U.S., it was originally limited to seven major cities across the country. The original cost of the DVD player started at $1000 and went higher – much like the original Sony VCR, except one did not have to buy a television set to go with the player.[47] Just three years later, DVD player prices had dropped to less than $100 at discount retailers. By 2003, the price of a DVD player was less than $50 at those same discounters. So fast was the adoption rate of the original DVD players that just six years after the initial introduction into the U.S., there were approximately 1000 different models of DVD players produced by more than 100 manufacturers.[48]

The DVD players at first were not a complete substitute for the VCR in that the DVD players were not also recorders. In fact, during the early days of the DVD player and before the development of the DVR, companies took advantage of the DVD player's lack of recording ability by making hybrid machines with both a DVD player and a VCR built into a single machine. While these hybrid machines were available, they were often expensive in comparison to the DVD player, and, with most households already owning VCRs, they were considered an unnecessary luxury.

As the quality of televisions progressed, consumers wanted new and better DVD quality. The result was the blu-ray DVD. It was first released in 2006 and had the ability to supersede the original DVDs of the time. The blu-ray DVD (and player) was one of two competing systems, the other being what was termed HD-DVD. Both formats were released in 2006, although the HD-DVD format (at the time nicknamed "red-ray" as opposed to blu-ray) was released a few months before the blu-ray. The HD-DVD competition was short-lived as the system was discontinued just two years later in 2008.[49]

Blu-ray's future seemed positive until the advent of connected television sets, STBs, and, especially, digital downloads from Netflix and other streamers.[50] However, the blu-ray DVD (now 4K blu-ray DVD) may remain as an alternative source of program delivery for at least the near future and become a format that endures, much as vinyl records and CDs have seen a resurgence in the last few years. The DVD industry may be helped by the fact that the streamers, like Netflix, Disney+, Max, and others, have started purging their offerings, which could end up on DVDs.[51] Whether or not this happens is yet to be seen.

When people hear the term "set top box," the first thing they usually think of is the TiVo DVR. TiVo was developed by Jim Barton and Mike Ramsey. The two originally intended to create a home network device, but decided to create the first iteration of the current device that records digitized video onto an internal hard drive. The first experimental trials of their new device occurred in the San Francisco area in 1998.[52]

In January the following year (1999), TiVo was first exhibited at the Consumer Electronics Show, where it was announced that the initial TiVo machines would ship at the end of March. Originally, the TiVo device digitized and compressed analog video signals from a variety of sources, including the television's antenna, cable signals, and signals being received through DTH satellite systems. Additionally, the TiVo system was also integrated into the STBs of both cable companies and DTH satellite companies.[53]

Following the success of the TiVo DVR system, companies such as Panasonic and Sony, among others, began making stand-alone DVR machines. These machines were more versatile than the TiVo machine because they could record to a hard drive like the TiVo machine did, but they could also record directly to a

DVD. Additionally, these DVR machines could play DVDs, and thus were the first true DVD/DVR system, capable of replacing the VCR and finally making it obsolete.[54] However, these DVR machines could not play the later-developed HD blu-ray DVDs and, while they could record in digital format, they could not record in high definition, so with the move to digital, high definition television, these DVRs became obsolete. They could still play standard definition DVDs and any programs that had been previously recorded to their hard drives on high-definition television sets, but at a lower quality.

The Over-the-Top Set Top Box Today

There are currently several different forms of STBs available to consumers today. These include the stand-alone STB, the blu-ray digital video player, and the videogame console.

The Stand-Alone Set Top Box

When the term "cord-cutting" first started to be mentioned – referring to those people who decided to turn off their cable or satellite subscription in favor of watching programming over the Internet – the most likely device for cord-cutting was the stand-alone STB. Stand-alone STBs are exactly what the name suggests – they are separate boxes that the consumer can connect to the television set through an HDMI (High-Definition Multimedia Interface) for the purpose of bringing programming from the Internet to the consumer's television screen. The STB is then connected to the Internet either through a direct, wired Internet connection, or, today, most often through a Wi-Fi connection that can receive the signal from the consumer's wireless router.

Once connected, the STB has built-in software that allows it to display the specific programming from the Internet it has been designed to receive. The stand-alone STB serves as the interface between these programming services and the consumer only, in that the consumer must still pay for the service if payment is required (such as the monthly fee for subscription video-on-demand [SVOD] channels). Using stand-alone STBs viewers can watch user-generated video on YouTube, and movies and original programming on Netflix or Amazon Prime Instant Video, for example. Additionally, viewers can watch network television programs from sites such as YouTubeTV, Hulu+LiveTV, Philo TV, Fubo TV, and many others, as well as a variety of niche program channels providing specialized programming.

ROKU

Roku is the top-selling stand-alone STB in the U.S. As of February 2023, Roku has sold some 41 million devices in the U.S. Roku's customers stream more than 40 billion hours of programming, and Roku devices are sold in 20 countries, primarily in Canada, Europe, Mexico, and Latin America.[55] Roku's products include its Roku Players, Roku Streaming Sticks, and Roku TVs – made by a variety of different television manufacturers. It also has its own FAST channel called – appropriately enough – the Roku Channel, with a revolving selection of original series, movies, TV shows, 24/7 live news in the U.S. and Canada, and popular childrens' entertainment – all completely free to those who have a Roku device or a Roku TV. Viewers can also choose from thousands of entertainment options on-demand, with no subscriptions, purchases, or rentals required. Plus, Roku customers in the U.S. can add more than 50 premium subscriptions, including Paramount+, Discovery+, AMC+, STARZ, and MGM+. Roku also has an agreement with Spectrum Cable for its Spectrum TV service, which offers 250 live channels and 30,000 on-demand TV shows and movies for subscribers to Spectrum's home Internet service.[56]

Roku's current line-up of streaming players includes a variety of different streaming sticks and boxes, with the top-end device including a sound bar for cinematic Dolby sound. All of the current generation Roku players are capable of streaming in high definition, and all but the lowest-end products stream 4K and include HDR to the consumer's television set.[57]

All current generation Roku players are capable of delivering more than 5,000 channels of streaming entertainment programming, including both free and premium (pay) channels.[58] The 5,000+ channels include not only movie and television channels (such as Netflix and YouTubeTV), but also Internet-available channels that provide news, sports, childrens', tech, web TV, lifestyle, international, and spiritual (and religious) television programming. Additionally, all current generation Roku boxes have access to more than a quarter million movies and television episodes. Every Roku device can alert subscribers when new movies are available and provide search opportunities.

In January 2014, Roku moved away from being a strictly OTT-STB company, introducing Roku TV, an internal streaming system designed to be built into the television sets that Roku licenses to TV manufacturers. Currently, Roku has nine different television manufacturers that install the Roku TV system. Additionally, Roku has begun marketing its own branded Roku TVs to the public, making it possible to buy a television set either from Roku directly or from one of the set manufacturers Roku licenses its streaming system to.[59]

While Roku is the industry leader, there are other STB makers available to the television consumer.

ANDROID TV/CHROMECAST

In 2014, Google introduced its first streaming system, originally called Google TV, now called Android TV, along with the Google Chromecast.[60] Android TV is an internal system designed to let the consumer's television operate as a smart television set. Further, for those with Android-based mobile smartphones, there is an app that will allow the consumer to use the smartphone as the Android TV remote control. Android TV has the capability for voice search, using Google's voice recognition software. Android TV makes it possible for the viewer to "cast" his or her favorite entertainment apps from Android and iOS devices, Mac and Windows computers, and the Google Chromebook to the television set running Android TV. In addition to casting, Google's Chromecast allows the viewer to voice-control with Google Assistant and "smart home control" those devices connected to Google's smart home system. The Chromecast product is a dongle for a television set, while Android TV is an internal system. The Chromecast dongle also comes in a 4K model as well as a simple high-definition model.[61]

While the idea of the original Google TV was trumpeted with fanfare when it was released in May 2010, the early results were less than sparkling. Google TV was hit with a major problem when the three major broadcast television networks – ABC, CBS, NBC – refused to allow their Internet programming to be streamed over Google TV.[62] The consumer could still watch the networks using his or her cable, satellite, or over-the-air system, but could not watch the programming online. In addition, the price for the Logitech Revue STB was $259, significantly higher than the Roku and other stand-alone boxes. Logitech and Google have since parted ways.[63]

Today, Android TV supplies its operating system to a variety of different television set manufacturers, and to streaming devices for some of the largest manufacturers, including Nvidia and Xiaomi.[64] Android TV is available worldwide and is most popular in Asia and Africa. In addition, its Chromecast is supported in only 11 countries.[65]

APPLE TV

Apple TV was originally introduced in 2007 as an interface device designed to stream video from a computer to a television set. It was going to be named "iTV" to go along with its other "i" products but became Apple TV when concerns over the "iTV" brand sprang up due to the British independent broadcaster ITV holding the rights to the name in the UK and threatening to take legal action. The original Apple TV was introduced with a 40 GB hard drive, but within a couple of months of the introduction, Apple began selling a 160 GB hard drive model, and ultimately discontinued the 40 GB model. The original Apple TV was an expensive device, ahead of its time, and did poorly in the market.[66]

In September 2010, just four months after Google introduced Google TV, Apple reintroduced a reinvented Apple TV to compete not only with Google TV, but also with Roku and the other stand-alone STBs. Apple's new Apple TV box was smaller than the original and cost much less than Google TV and was about on par with the other stand-alone boxes.[67]

Apple TV competes more directly with Roku, Chromecast, and Amazon Fire TV in that it does not have an internal system driving a smart television set. Rather, Apple TV is an internal system add-on to most television sets, even including its rivals Roku, Google TV, and Amazon Fire TV. It can also be an add-on to both the Sony Playstation and the Microsoft XBox. Additionally, like the others, Apple TV has external devices that can be attached to a television set.[68]

Like the Android devices, Apple TV devices can also be used as the focal point of a smart home. Using voice commands through its assistant Siri, Apple TV can control smart devices connected to it such as lights, thermostats, security (cameras and sensors), and the like. It becomes the foundation, then, of a smart home.[69]

Apple TV is available in more than 100 countries worldwide and has sold more than 26 million devices in the U.S. and 53 million worldwide.[70]

AMAZON FIRE TV

Amazon's Fire TV grew out of Amazon's move into tablets with the Fire and the Fire HD. Amazon introduced the Fire TV on April 2, 2014, years after the other major players introduced their products and two major players (Boxee and Sezmi) had left the OTT-STB space.[71]

Like everything else Amazon does, its Fire TV has come a long way since those first two devices. Today, Amazon has an entire line of Amazon Fire TV branded television sets running its Fire TV internal operating system. These sets are designed to compete with LG, Samsung, and other major brands, with top-of-the-line quality, but at a lower price point. In addition, Amazon has licensed its operating system to run on Insignia, TCL, and Hisense brand television sets as well. Amazon's Fire TV operating system competes directly with Roku's and Android's systems, forming the foundation of the smart portion of the television, on which a myriad of apps can be run (including apple TV).[72] Like the others, Amazon also has a variety of external devices designed to connect to television sets.[73] Amazon Fire TV is available in more than 100 countries worldwide and seven default languages and has sold more than 30 million devices[74] and over 200 million sets globally.[75]

Videogame Consoles

One of the more interesting features of the later videogames consoles is their ability to serve as STBs. Each console, whether it is Microsoft's Xbox Series X or S or Sony's Playstation 5, is more than just a videogame player. Today, gaming has moved from the solo game disc to be purchased, played, and then – when the gamer gets tired of it – returned for credit toward a new or updated game, to the multiplayer, world-wide competition of the online, or cloud, game world. Today, gamers can play directly against their friends, neighbors, classmates, colleagues, or even complete strangers across the globe online. Additionally, there are online, world-wide tournaments for certain games, and even "professional" gamers who can make a living winning tournaments with cash prizes.[76]

As the gaming world moved to the web, it was natural that game consoles moved beyond what they were originally designed to do. Even before the widespread development of online gaming, the Xbox One and the Playstation 4 allowed the consumer to enjoy DVDs in addition to playing game discs – it was a natural add-on. Today, both companies have added functions to their game consoles that allow the consumer to enjoy blu-ray DVDs and online premium video sites such as Netflix and Vudu; Sony has also developed its own Playstation store where consumers can rent and/or purchase Sony Pictures movies and television programs as well as myriad games.[77] Further, both the Xbox series and the Playstation 5 work well with many of the current 4K television sets through the use of an HDMI 2.1 connector.[78]

Finally, both videogame consoles can serve as a streaming device, much like the Roku and Amazon Fire TV devices.[79]

While none of the three major players in this market offer the extensive options of the stand-alone STB, they are certainly acceptable substitutes for the STBs, especially for gamers who enjoy watching DVDs or streamed movies. With the continual development of online gaming, the game console is moving closer and closer to becoming a true STB plus game console.

The Future of Set-Top Boxes

The STB has existed since the beginning of the television era. From the earliest days when the first STBs were used to turn an antenna so a household could receive an over-the-air signal, the STB has had a distinguished, multifaceted place in the television world. STBs have given consumers in rural locations the ability to watch television. They have given viewers in UHF-only and intermixed markets the ability to receive UHF signals before their sets had UHF tuners. They provided early cable subscribers with the ability to watch the various cable channels through their converter boxes before TVs became cable ready. STBs gave consumers the ability to watch commercially recorded programs on their videocassette players, and then record programs from the television to watch later on their VCRs. These same VCRs made it possible for consumers to watch their jerky, out-of-focus, fast-pan-until-everyone-is-seasick home videos on their television sets immediately, rather than having to send their Super 8mm film off for processing. STBs have led the way in the new television technology universe, giving consumers the ability to stream programming from the Internet to the television set. Just as television has come a long way, so has the STB.

However, the STBs days are numbered. With the continuing development and increasing diversification of the connected television, the need for an STB ultimately will no longer exist. The use of smart television sets had overtaken the stand-alone STB as the default entry point for watching television by the end of 2023.[80] Nevertheless, the time frame for total obsolescence is somewhere in the near-distant to distant future. Much of the resilience is in the global market, with the global STB market growing over the next ten years by a compound annual growth rate of 4.1%, rising from $25.01 billion in 2023 to $37.38 billion by 2033.[81] Most of these boxes are spread across OTT, IPTV, Cable, and DTH satellite boxes, with the largest percentages being located in Europe and the Asia-Pacific regions.[82] In the area of videogame consoles, more and more younger gamers, especially, are playing video games on their cell phones, their tablets, and their laptop computers rather than on game consoles hooked to television sets. In fact, as of March 2024, only 36% of gamers played using game consoles and worldwide that percentage was only 24%. By far and away, the most popular device for playing video games in the U.S. was the mobile phone.[83] Further, the cloud gaming market is expected to see enormous growth over the next few years, going from $5.0 billion in 2023 to $143.4 billion in 2032, a compound annual growth rate of 46.9% during that time period.[84]

The winners in the STB industry, ultimately, will be companies such as Roku, Amazon, Google, and WebOS who have developed and continue to refine and improve their internal STB software platforms for smart television sets, and those systems like the Xbox Series X and Series S and the Playstation 5 that can provide a wide variety of different options through the console, including the ability to offer cloud gaming and OTT television options.

Throughout its long and distinguished history, the STB has continued to be a transitional device, helping to take the television viewer ever farther into the continually evolving universe that is television. While the long-term future does not bode well for the stand-alone STB industry, the STB is expected to remain viable as it morphs into new and different roles within the television universe and even smart-home of the future. Ultimately, though, the STB, in all its forms, will find a favored place in the museums of television history.

Summary

Overall, the future of the television delivery system is bright. As mentioned earlier, IPTV is the future of television. As long as the Internet continues to exist and function – and at this time articles discussing what comes after the Internet (metaverse, artificial intelligence (A.I.), Web3, and others) still have, at their core, the Internet[85,86,87,88] – IPTV will continue to deliver television to viewers whether by wire or wirelessly through Wi-Fi, cellular, or other, future innovations. IPTV is truly the backbone of today's television and will be the backbone of the myriad changes and advancements in the television of the future.

ATSC 3.0 certainly has a place in this future of television – if it can ever fully get off the ground. At this point, despite all the hype you can find on the new broadcast standard, ATSC 3.0 is still a long way off. There are very few reasons, if any, to upgrade to one of the few television sets that have ATSC capability or to buy a tuner box just to watch programming over ATSC 3.0 – if any exist in the market where the viewer lives.[89] In April 2025, the FCC released a public notice for comments on the NAB's petition for rulemaking asking for the turnoff of ATSC 1.0 (the current television standard viewers watch today) in the top 55 markets by February 2028 and the rest of the country by 2030.[90] However, already there are challengers to that turnoff, including the Consumer Technology Association, low power TV broadcasters, and Multichannel Video Programming Distributors (MVPDs) (because the change to ATSC 3.0 will require costly infrastructure changes to the MVPDs as well as requiring viewers to purchase new television sets because for them ATSC 3.0 is not backward compatible with the current system).[91] Further, the major players in the television set world either do not offer ATSC 3.0 built into their sets or are only offering the standard on high-end sets. This lack of choice will either force the consumer to spend (potentially) a lot of money on top-end sets or to buy low-end sets not offering the new standard. Of course, if the FCC decides in favor of the ATSC 1.0 turnoff dates, the likelihood of all television manufacturers offering ATSC 3.0 compatible sets by 2028 in the U.S. is highly likely, but consumers who have bought televisions in the three years (at the time of writing in 2025) leading up to the turnoff will likely be very unhappy with having to scrap that almost-brand-new television set and spend more money on an ATSC 3.0 compatible one. Either that or they will have to buy a tuner box that will convert the signal so that viewers can watch programming on their current, non-ATSC 3.0 television sets.

As mentioned in the previous section, STBs have had a long and distinguished life. From the earliest days of television right through to today, STBs have been a part of television. However, just like previous generations of STBs have disappeared over time as television technology has advanced and improved, many of today's STBs will go the way of their predecessors. Stand-alone boxes are being replaced by television sets that have the box software built into the set itself. External Roku boxes are today being included in a variety of television sets and are needed only when a person is traveling and the television set in the hotel room does not have streaming software built in. The same goes for Android and Apple TV boxes – both are now built into many smart TVs or can be included as an additional add-on through an app. Videogame consoles, too, while still popular, are being replaced by cloud gaming that can be placed on a variety of devices. These devices will go the way of previous STBs.

Nevertheless, we are likely to see certain types of STBs stick around in the near future, and they may occasionally make short-term reappearances as new television technologies are developed and an STB is needed to facilitate the move from current technology to new technology (for example, as the ATSC 3.0 tuner boxes just mentioned). As a transitional device, the STB will remain important to the development of television.

Notes

1 "IPTV Standardization on Track Say Industry Experts," *ITU-T Newslog*, (October 27, 2006), (May 7, 2024), www.itu.int/ITU-T/e-flash/028-nov06.html#008.
2 Simpson, W. and H. Greenfield (2007), *IPTV and Internet Video*, (Massachusetts, United Kingdom: Elsevier), 2.
3 Duarte, Fabio, "Countries With the Highest Number of Internet Users (2024)," *Exploding Topics*, (May 7, 2024), https://explodingtopics.com/blog/countries-internet-users.
4 Anderson, Chris (2009), *FREE: The Future of a Radical Price*, (New York: Hyperion), 77, 78.
5 Kanellos, Michael, "Moore's Law to roll on for another decade," *c/net*, (February 10, 2003), http://news.cnet.com/2100-1001-984051.html.
6 Anderson, *FREE: The Future of a Radical Price*, 77, 78.
7 Anderson, *FREE: The Future of a Radical Price*, 77, 78.
8 Anderson, *FREE: The Future of a Radical Price*, 91.
9 Anderson, *FREE: The Future of a Radical Price*, 78.
10 Duarte, Fabio, "Countries with the Highest Number of Internet Users (2024)."
11 "What is IP television?" *The Economic Times*, (November 27, 2006), http://articles.economictimes.indiatimes.com/2006-11-27/news/27425252_1_iptv-service-internet-protocol-television-boxes-with-broadband-internet.
12 "IPTV," *Wikipedia*, http://en.wikipedia.org/wiki/IPTV#cite_note-3.
13 For more information on the AT&T acquisition of DirecTV, see Chapter 2: The Future of the MVPD.
14 See the section on Connected TVs in Chapter 5: The Future of Television Viewing.

15 See the section on the iWorld in Chapter 5: The Future of Television Viewing.
16 See Chapter 10: The Future of U.S. Television in the Global Television Market.
17 Cooper and Lovelace (2006), *IPTV Guide*, http://iptv-report.com/guide/request/download/IPTV-Guide.pdf, 4, 5.
18 For more information, see Chapter 7: The Future of Television Advertising.
19 For more information, see Chapter 9: The Future of Television Content Search & Promotion.
20 Rouse, Margaret, "Advanced Television Systems Committt," *WhatIS.com*, (2011), http://whatis.techtarget.com/definition/Advanced-Television-Systems-Committee-ATSC.
21 "About ATSC," *ATSC*, http://atsc.org/about-us/about-atsc/.
22 Kurtz, Phil, "Call It What It Is: ATSC 3.0 Is OTA IPTV On Steroids," *TVNewsCheck*, (May 7, 2015), http://www.tvnewscheck.com/playout/2015/05/call-it-what-it-is-atsc-3-0-is-ota-iptv-on-steroids/.
23 Kurtz, "Call It What It Is: ATSC 3.0 Is OTA IPTV On Steroids."
24 Kurtz, "Call It What It Is: ATSC 3.0 Is OTA IPTV On Steroids."
25 Kurtz, "Call It What It Is: ATSC 3.0 Is OTA IPTV On Steroids."
26 Lehane, Scott, "ATSC 3.0: Everything You Need to Know About the Broadcast Industry's 'NextGen' Technology Standard," *Next/TV*, (May 9, 2024), https://www.nexttv.com/news/atsc-3-0-nextgen-tv.
27 Bloom, David, "Is This Thing Going to Happen or What? Broadcast Enters NAB 2023 Still Waiting for the ATSC 3.0 Train to Arrive (Bloom)," *Next/TV*, (April 9, 2023), https://www.nexttv.com/news/is-this-thing-going-to-happen-or-what-broadcast-enters-nab-2023-still-waiting-for-the-atsc-30-train-to-arrive.
28 Scott, "ATSC 3.0: Everything You Need to Know About the Broadcast Industry's 'NextGen' Technology Standard."
29 Morrison, Geoffrey and Ty Pendlebury "Why is ATSC 3.0 Taking So Long?", *C|Net*, (September 14, 2023), https://www.cnet.com/tech/home-entertainment/why-is-atsc-3-0-taking-so-long/.
30 Morrison and Pendlebury, "Why is ATSC 3.0 Taking So Long?"
31 Morrison and Pendlebury, "Why is ATSC 3.0 Taking So Long?"
32 LaFayette, Jon, "FCC, NAB Set Initiative to Finish Shift to ATSC 3.0," *NABAmplify*, April 18, 2023), https://amplify.nabshow.com/articles/nabshowdaily-fcc-nab-atsc3/.
33 Morrison and Pendlebury, "Why is ATSC 3.0 Taking So Long?"
34 Jessell, Harry A., "TV Next-Gen TV Benefits Well Worth the Cost," *TV NewsCheck*, (May 22, 2015), http://www.tvnewscheck.com/article/85584/nextgen-tv-benefits-well-worth-the-cost?ref=search.
35 Head, Sydney W. and Christopher H. Sterling (1990), *Broadcasting in America*, (Boston: Houghton Mifflin), 65–68.
36 Sterling, Christopher H. and John M. Kittross (1978), *Stay Tuned: A Concise History of American Broadcasting*, (Belmont, California: Wadsworth), 324–325.
37 Head and Sterling, *Broadcasting In America*.
38 Sterling and Kittross, *Stay Tuned: A Concise History of American Broadcasting*.
39 Longley, Lawrence D., "The FCC and the All-Channel Receiver Bill of 1962," *Journal of Broadcasting*, xiii (Summer 1969), 293–302, http://transition.fcc.gov/Bureaus/OSEC/library/legislative_histories/612.pdf.
40 I remember as a child that my grandmother had one of the personal tall antennas attached to her home in Mississippi. The nearest television stations in a major market were in Memphis, TN. Every time I wanted to watch TV, I had to turn the tuning dial on the tuner box until the signal would come in well enough for me to see the picture.
41 "Cable Converter Box," *Wikipedia*, http://en.wikipedia.org/wiki/Cable_converter_box.
42 http://www.cedmagic.com/history/betamax-lv-1901.html.
43 See http://www.jvc.com/company/index.jsp?pageID=2 and http://www.cedmagic.com/history/vbt200.html.

44 http://gizmodo.com/5316154/magnavox-magnavision-model-8000-discovision-laserdisc-player-reviewed.
45 http://www.blam1.com/discovision/DiscoVision_History.htm.
46 "DVD Player History," *Pavtube*, (April 10, 2008), http://www.pavtube.com/dvd/dvd_player_history.html.
47 "DVD Player History," *Pavtube*.
48 "DVD Player History," *Pavtube*.
49 "Blu-ray," *Wikipedia*, https://en.wikipedia.org/wiki/Blu-ray.
50 Richtel, Matt and Brad Stone, "Blu-ray's Fuzzy Future," *The New York Times*, (January 5, 2009), https://www.nytimes.com/2009/01/05/technology/05bluray.html.
51 Weprin, Alex, "Why the Dying DVD Business Could Be Headed for a Resurrection," *The Hollywood Reporter*, (November 10, 2023), https://www.hollywoodreporter.com/business/business-news/dying-dvd-bluray-business-resurrection-cds-vinyl-1235639108/.
52 "History," *TiVo*, http://www.tivo.com/jobs/questions/history-of-tivo/index.html.
53 "History," *TiVo*, http://www.tivo.com/jobs/questions/history-of-tivo/index.html.
54 http://www.estcctv.com/profession-news/history-of-digital-video-recorder.
55 Cullen, Edward, "Top 6 Streaming Devices to Launch Your OTT App On," *Vodlix*, (February 1, 2023), https://vodlix.com/blog/top-6-streaming-devices-to-launch-your-ott-app-on.
56 https://www.roku.com/.
57 https://www.roku.com/products/players.
58 Cullen, "Top 6 Streaming Devices to Launch Your OTT App On."
59 https://www.roku.com/products/roku-tv.
60 Cullen, "Top 6 Streaming Devices to Launch Your OTT App On."
61 https://store.google.com/us/product/chromecast_google_tv_compare?hl=en-US&pli=1.
62 Abell, John C., "Google TV Growing Pains: Networks Block Web TV Shows," *Wired*, (October 22, 2010), http://www.wired.com/business/2010/10/google-tv-growing-pains-networks-block-web-tv-shows/.
63 Quain, John R., "Google TV Is Dead. Long Live Google TV?", *Fox News.Com*, (November 22, 2011), http://www.foxnews.com/scitech/2011/11/22/google-tv-is-dead-long-live-google-tv/.
64 https://www.android.com/tv/.
65 Cullen, "Top 6 Streaming Devices to Launch Your OTT App On."
66 http://www.apple.com/appletv/.
67 http://www.apple.com/appletv/.
68 https://tv.apple.com/.
69 https://www.apple.com/tv-home/.
70 Cullen, "Top 6 Streaming Devices to Launch Your OTT App On."
71 http://www.amazon.com/dp/B00CX5P8FC?tag=mh0b-20&hvadid=7000460244&hvqmt=e&hvbmt=be&hvdev=c&ref=pd_sl_4y8l3tehwg_e.
72 https://www.amazon.com/b?ie=UTF8&node=18067453011.
73 https://www.amazon.com/Amazon-Fire-TV-Family/b?ie=UTF8&node=8521791011.
74 Cullen, "Top 6 Streaming Devices to Launch Your OTT App On."
75 https://www.aboutamazon.com/news/devices/amazon-updates-the-fire-tv-lineup-with-new-qled-sizes-a-200-smart-tv-and-availability-in-new-countries.
76 Hruby, Patrick, "So You Wanna Be a Professional Video Game Player?" *ESPN-PAGE2*, (October 11, 2007), http://sports.espn.go.com/espn/page2/story?page=hruby/071008.
77 https://www.playstation.com/en-us/ps-plus/?smcid=pdc%3Aen-us%3Acorporate-about-us%3Aprimary%20nav%3Amsg-store%3Asubscribe-to-ps-plus.
78 Morrison, Geoffrey, "Best TV for PS5 and Xbox Series, X, Series, S for 2024: LG OLED, Hisense, Vizio," *CNET*, (May 29, 2024), https://www.cnet.com/tech/home-entertainment/best-tv-for-ps5-and-xbox-series-x-series-s/.

79. https://agoodmovietowatch.com/cord-cutting/best-streaming-services-on-playstation/.
80. Fletcher, Bevin, "Smart TV Apps Surpass Set-top Boxes as Entry Point for TV Viewing," *StreamTV Insider*, (November 29, 2023), https://www.streamtvinsider.com/video/smart-tv-apps-surpass-set-top-boxes-entry-point-tv-viewing.
81. Pangarkar, Tajammul, "Set-Top Box Statistics: Essential Devices in the Television Sector," *market.us*, (January 12, 2024), https://scoop.market.us/set-top-box-statistics/.
82. Pangarkar, Tajammul, "Set-Top Box Statistics: Essential Devices in the Television Sector," *market.us*, (January 12, 2024), https://scoop.market.us/set-top-box-statistics/.
83. Clement, J., "Video Gaming Worldwide – Statistics & Facts," *Statista*, (June 3, 2024), https://www.statista.com/topics/1680/gaming/#topicOverview.
84. "Cloud Gaming Market to Soar to USD 143.4 Bn by 2032 | Driven by Technological Advancements and Growing Demand for High-Quality Gaming Experience," *yahoo!finance*, (February 19, 2024), https://finance.yahoo.com/news/cloud-gaming-market-soar-usd-121200504. html?guccounter=1&guce_referrer=aHR0cHM6Ly93d3cuZ29vZ2xlLmNvbS8&guce_referrer_sig=AQAAALr3ePqDnzfzjmaMAzrkIpJql qxuq1KPC84l3yUmwhXdFrRGyOVaCSoUQbtC077CZpvboa5WnvjGZZCe8Qnq SGlr0V3wp8uVTIwjp2SxpCEKakaYHZ3nauTPKFwXr6id21QxOVQgw97tXbw_ QTyymkGJcjKFXyl4rHkMmrrMUaih.
85. Marr, Bernard, "Here's What the Future of the Internet Will Look Like," *Forbes*, (May 9, 2023), https://www.forbes.com/sites/bernardmarr/2023/05/09/heres-what-the-future-of-the-internet-will-look-like/.
86. Totino, Vincent, "What Comes After The Internet?" *LinkedIn*, (January 31, 2022), https://www.linkedin.com/pulse/what-comes-after-internet-vincent-totino/.
87. Crawford, Hal, "What Comes After the Internet? Welcome To 'the Metaverse'," *The Spinoff*, (August 11, 2021), https://thespinoff.co.nz/tech/11-08-2021/what-comes-after-the-internet-welcome-to-the-metaverse.
88. Ma, Adrian, "The Next Phase of the Internet is Coming: Here's What You Need to Know About Web3," *The Conversation*, (February 27, 2023), https://theconversation.com/the-next-phase-of-the-internet-is-coming-heres-what-you-need-to-know-about-web3-192919.
89. Newman, Jared, "ATSC 3.0: The Future of Broadcast TV Spent Another Year Stuck in Neutral," *PCWorld*, (January, 30, 2025), https://www.pcworld.com/article/2592581/atsc-3-0-another-year-stuck-in-neutral.html.
90. Kurz, Phil, "April Brings Good Omen for ATSC 3.0's Future," *tvtech*, (May 5, 2025), https://www.tvtechnology.com/opinion/april-brings-good-omens-for-atsc-3-0s-future#:~:text=Proponents%20of%20ATSC%203.0%20received%20three%20pieces,future%20of%20NextGen%20TV%20and%20ancillary%20services.&text=Broadcasters%20backing%20the%20standard%20say%20they%20cannot,in%20markets%20are%20dedicated%20to%20NextGen%20TV.
91. Kurz, "April Brings Good Omen for ATSC 3.0's Future."

4 The Future of Television Programming

Since the emergence of television, audiences have been forced to watch their favorite programs according to an inflexible, highly scheduled rotation, and given the chance to watch a program only once a week at the specified time the program has been scheduled. Further, audiences who missed an episode or even worse, several episodes, have had to wait until the program went into reruns or into syndication to be able to watch the missed episode or episodes. The audience had no input, let alone any choice, as to when the program would air. The lack of input or choice forced audiences into the practice of what is known as "appointment viewing." Audiences, simply put, were subject to the whims of the television programmers.

The arrival of cable television as a viable alternative to over-the-air (OTA) broadcast television provided audiences with additional opportunities to watch their favorite programs. While the audiences were still subject to the programmers, at least the cable networks proliferated to the point that, once a program went into syndication, the opportunities for multiple viewings of a particular episode or even an entire series became possible. Cable channels could offer multiple airings of a particular episode (called "doubling" or "tripling" or "encore presentations"), multiple airings of a series over a number of seasons (depending on the terms of the contract), and even deliver back-to-back episodes of a program throughout a given day (called "marathons" – the earliest form of binge-watching). Still, the programmer scheduled the programs for particular time slots and the audience was forced to watch, though the audience may have had more than one scheduled opportunity to do so.

The development of the digital video recorder (DVR) and, later, the HD DVR, left viewers with a desire for video-on-demand (VOD) by giving the viewer the opportunity to record programs and play them back at the viewer's leisure. Later, the DVR/HD DVR made (and continues to make) it possible for the viewer to record, pause, rewind, and fast-forward (until reaching "real time") live television. No longer did the viewer have to take what the programmer provided him or her at the time the programmer scheduled it. The beginning of the VOD era was underway.

VOD has changed the relationship between the viewer and the programmer. Just as cable transformed television viewing from a one- to several-opportunities-to-view system, VOD is remaking the television industry again, this time even more drastically, by altering the relationship between the viewer and the television programmer. VOD moves the control of viewing a program from the programmer

DOI: 10.4324/9781003625384-7

to the viewer by making programming available to the viewer whenever, wherever, and – today – on whatever platform the viewer wishes to watch.

The development of VOD in the U.S. took a back seat to the development of VOD in Europe. Testing of the use of VOD came as early as 1994 in England, through the Cambridge Digital Interactive Television Trial. The trial included a VOD component delivering a form of interactive television to a small number of homes, schools, and businesses between 1994–1996.[1]

Following the trial in the mid-1990s, a number of English television companies worked to further develop and refine VOD, culminating in a joint project by the British Broadcasting Corporation (BBC), ITV, and Channel 4 called "Kangaroo" in 2008. The program was developed to deliver more than 10,000 hours of TV programming in a VOD format. The project was designed to provide viewers with the opportunity to watch recently aired programs as well as older programs that were in the three companies' archives.[2] However, the program was blocked by an agency of the British government and never got off the ground in its original form.[3]

Video-On-Demand

VOD in the U.S. began as subscription television, a form of OTA, scrambled-signal television that viewers – for a fee – could watch by leasing a converter box to unscramble the signal. The service was designed to provide special events such as championship boxing matches and major concerts to those people who were willing to pay extra for the service. While subscription television was popular in certain parts of the country, the service, as it was originally developed, never truly caught on nationwide.

However, what success that subscription television did have served as the forerunner of the original pay-per-view services that began in the late 1970s and early 1980s. Pay-per-view services, like those for subscription television, were originally designed primarily to deliver major sporting events to homes as well as large venues such as stadiums and theatres, along with the occasional major concert or theatre presentation. It was expensive for venues to host pay-per-view events, so customers were charged high prices. For instance, when a major championship boxing match was shown on pay-per-view, those in attendance would have the opportunity to see the entire night's card of fights, shown without commercial interruption. The lack of commercials allowed the viewer to watch what went on in each fighter's corner between rounds, including often hearing the instructions of the trainers to their fighters as the pace of the rounds ebbed and flowed. The events were exciting and often well-attended, but the prices for the time were expensive.

Pay-per-view moved from the arena to the home, with the introduction of pay-per-view movies on the cable systems in the U.S. in the mid-1980s. Pay-per-view allowed viewers to watch movies uncut and with no advertising interruptions without having to take a premium cable service such as HBO or Showtime. For a one-time payment viewers could select a favorite movie to watch one time or – as is done today – for an entire 24-hour or longer period. Often, the movies delivered by pay-per-view were as recent, or even more recent, than those shown on the premium pay cable services.

VOD has grown out of pay-per-view to encompass not only all the traditional types of pay-per-view, but the various modern forms of VOD, such as subscription video-on-demand (SVOD), advertising-driven video-on-demand (AVOD), and transactional video-on-demand (TVOD). Each of these forms will be discussed later in the section.

VOD can be defined as a:

> real time Digital Cable and Telco TV service that allows users to select and watch video on their TV immediately after making a selection. Viewers can fast forward, rewind and pause programming. VOD is also used as an overarching term to describe any video content that can be accessed and viewed at any time (on demand).[4]

Today VOD goes further. With the continuing development of Internet protocol television (IPTV), VOD has expanded to include all video that can be accessed through the Internet and viewed over a multitude of different platforms such as smartphones, tablets, notebooks, desktop computers, and connected television (CTV) sets. The different video content that can be viewed varies, from user-generated videos and original professionally produced programs such as those on the branded channels of YouTube to time-shifted OTA and original television programs such as those on Hulu/Hulu+ to movies and original programs such as those seen on Netflix and Amazon Prime Instant Video. In fact, the new definition of VOD might be "the ability of the viewer to watch a program or video of her/his choice whenever, wherever, and on whatever platform the viewer chooses."

Types of Video-On-Demand

Subscription Video-On-Demand

As the name suggests, SVOD is subscription based. Generally, the viewer pays a monthly (or, depending on the service, a yearly – often discounted) subscription fee for the right to watch everything the service offers. SVOD grew out of the DVD rental industry, dominated by Blockbuster throughout the end of the last century, when Reed Hastings began Netflix's streaming service in 2007.[5] At that time, Netflix had a total of 1,000 movies available to stream.[6] From that small start, Netflix – as well as the SVOD industry as a whole – has grown into a multibillion-dollar industry,[7,8] one that offers a myriad of options to its subscribers. As an industry as a whole, the U.S. SVOD market is expected to surpass the $1 trillion mark in market capitalization by 2030.[9] Today there are numerous SVOD streaming services, led by Netflix, Amazon, and Disney+. Each of these offers movies, original programs, and additional streaming options to their subscribers.

Today, SVOD platforms face the challenges of rising costs to pay for original content[10] and a viewership that frequently turns over (called "churn"), choosing to sign up for short periods of time (a free trial time period), binge watch the program they signed up for, then cancel the subscription before the free trial period runs out.

Churn rates among SVOD platforms in the U.S. range from a low of 8% for Amazon Prime Video to nearly 43% for Discovery+.[11] These rates bring into question the long-term viability of many of the current SVOD platforms to remain subscription-based only in the future. In fact, the three largest and most powerful SVODs in the U.S. – Netflix, Amazon Prime Video, and Disney+ – have realized the potential difficulties of holding onto their subscribers in the future and have taken the step of adding an AVOD (see below) tier to their platforms. In fact, Amazon simply converted its entire original SVOD tier over to AVOD and added a separate, more expensive, SOVD tier at the beginning of 2024. Subscribers who had been accustomed to Amazon Instant Video being strictly SVOD and without commercials suddenly found themselves having to proactively resubscribe to a new, higher-priced SVOD tier to continue receiving the programs without commercials.[12] Netflix and Disney+ gave their original subscribers the choice of whether or not to switch to the lower-priced service with advertisements or stay with the pure SVOD service. Half of new subscribers to the Disney+ service have subscribed to the ad tier,[13] while Netflix has seen its ad tier grow to 40 million subscribers in those countries where it is offered. That is slightly more than a quarter of all of Netflix's subscribers worldwide.[14]

Advertising-driven Video-On-Demand

Like SVOD, AVOD is, on the surface, self-explanatory. Like SVOD, AVOD platforms are VOD; unlike SVOD, traditionally AVOD platforms have been free to subscribe to, with advertising taking the place of subscription costs.[15] The earliest service to offer its platform in an AVOD format was YouTube in 2006. After it had been purchased by Google, the platform began to monetize its content through advertising. It became one of the first and now largest AVOD providers today.[16] AVOD came about as an alternative to SVOD platforms when those platforms began raising their prices to fund the exorbitant costs of original programming. As those costs grew, viewers turned to AVOD platforms because of their lower costs and because – as has always been the case – people are conditioned through decades of broadcast and then cable and direct to home (DTH) satellite television to watch commercials, even those that are not particularly interesting or relevant to them. The trade-off of a lower cost with limited commercial interruptions has been particularly inviting to many viewers – as can be seen by the numbers for Disney+ and Netflix earlier.

Of the major AVOD platforms today, none is larger than YouTube. As of February 2025, YouTube attracted more than 2.7 billion viewers to its platform each month.[17] That's 2.7 billion sets of eyeballs available for advertisers every month. The ability to monetize a personal channel on YouTube has made millionaires out of a myriad of influencers on such channels, including the popular MrBeast (217 million subs), PewDiePie (111 million subs), Dude Perfect (60 million subs), and Jenna Marbles (19.7 million subs).[18] Other top AVOD platforms include Tubi and Crackle, which are pure AVOD,[19] and Hulu, Paramount+, and Peacock, which are hybrid models, being primarily AVOD, but with a higher-priced SVOD tier as well.[20]

Transactional Video-On-Demand

Transactional VOD is actually one of the oldest forms of VOD, originating more than a quarter century ago, when cable and DTH companies began offering pay-per-view options to their customers. At the time, it was first called pay-per-view and offered everything from uncut movies to major sporting events such as championship boxing matches.[21] Pay-per-view was eventually separated into pay-per-view (for the major events) and what was, at that time, called near video-on-demand (NVOD).[22] The cable and DTH satellite companies added what they called video-on-demand to go with their NVOD offerings. Today, those VOD offerings are grouped under the umbrella of TVOD.

TVOD, today, is a monetization model where customers rent or buy a piece of content they want to watch rather than having to subscribe to an SVOD platform. Examples would be iTunes, Google TV, and Amazon Prime Video (not to be confused with its SVOD/AVOD hybrid service Amazon Instant Video). In all three cases, the viewer can purchase a piece of content to own (called "electronic sell-through") or rent the particular piece of content for a stated period of time with limitless views during that time (called "download to rent"). In the case of all three platforms – iTunes, Google TV, and Amazon Prime Video – no subscriptions are needed to purchase or rent a piece of content. Additionally, TVOD programming, because the content is downloaded to rent or bought through electronic sell-through, comes free of commercials.[23]

Premium Video-On-Demand

Premium video-on-demand (PVOD) is a monetization model where an over-the-top (OTT) provider offers early access to certain content for a higher price. A good example of this type of model is when Disney+ offered the live-action movie *Mulan* as a premium choice for three months before the movie became available to the full subscriber base at no additional cost. Those who wanted to watch the movie before the average subscriber paid the premium price of about $30 for the privilege of being able to say they had seen the movie first. Generally, PVOD is an additional offering from an SVOD provider. Therefore, viewers who wish to enjoy the PVOD availability must first be a subscriber to the SVOD service. PVOD became extremely popular during the pandemic when watching movies at the theatre was out of the question.[24]

While PVOD can bring in additional revenue to an SVOD provider, it can also cause viewers to choose the PVOD service instead of watching the content in a theatre, if they are released simultaneously or even overlapping, thus cannibalizing box office revenue.[25]

Future of Video-On-Demand

The television viewer of today demands, and will continue to demand, the ability to watch her/his favorite television program anywhere, anytime, and on any platform. As such, the day of the programmer scheduling television shows into daily time slots is coming to an end. For that reason, VOD will become the mechanism for delivering all television to the viewer. With television moving to all IPTV, television programs are available through wired, Wi-Fi, and cellular connections. This change in delivering television to the viewer makes VOD the viewing mechanism of choice.

Just because full VOD will become the mechanism of choice for viewers watching their favorite television programs does not mean that there will be no scheduled programs. Live sporting events will still have their start and stop times. Live television programs will also start and stop when they are scheduled. As such, viewers will be able to watch their favorite live programs when they are telecast, but they will also be able to stream those programs afterwards whenever they choose, should they be busy, away from the delivery platform, or out of range of a signal (something that will become less and less likely in the future).

What *will* change dramatically will be scripted programs on television – those programs that today are recorded for playback at a scheduled time during the week. Programs produced by the various content producers, recorded, and serialized will no longer need to be scheduled by the content providers – viewers will choose when they want to watch their favorite programs, whether they watch an individual episode at a time, or spend hours binge-watching an entire season or even an entire series in a single sitting. The control for television programming will shift, then, from the programmers to the viewers. The viewers will decide when they want to watch a program, where they want to watch it, and on what platform they want to watch it, not the television programmers. Programs, though, will still have a release date and time – it just will not matter when it is, other than to note the program's availability.

Traditionally, VOD was a subscription-based service, with viewers having to subscribe to cable, DTH satellite television, or IPTV-based telephone video service, then having to pay a second, separate charge for on-demand content. The on-demand service was limited to a single viewing or a specified period of one or more days for watching the program the viewer had selected. Want to watch the program past that specified period and the viewer had to pay a second charge. Generally, VOD was limited to viewing on a traditional television set, although cable, DTH satellite companies, and the IPTV-based telephone video services began to allow on-demand viewing of programs over other platforms through the use of mobile phone and tablet apps.[26]

Today and in the future, VOD works and will work in a very different way. First, because television is viewed almost completely over some type of IP connection, televisions come with complete Internet connectivity. Today's CTV sets operate using apps for all programming, including the linear channels that are located on the apps of channel-aggregator (vMVPD) sites such as YouTube TV, Hulu+ Live TV, Fubo TV, Philo TV, and others, as well as apps for the major streaming services, giving the viewer the opportunity to watch the programs (s)he wants, whether linear or streaming programming.

Second, because the IPTV television sets use apps to replace the traditional channels, television viewers today and in the future make, and will make, their viewing choices by selecting the app that corresponds to the content provider they wish to watch. For instance, if viewers want to watch a program on ABC, they simply select the ABC app. The app will deliver them directly to the ABC programming site, where the viewers have available to them the entire library of television programs that are running or have ever run on the ABC network. They then select the program and episode they want to watch, and it is immediately available to them. It may be a current program that viewers choose to watch. But just as easily, it could be a program from the earliest days of the network, or any program in between. The viewers will have the ability to choose. Today, only a portion of this scenario is possible. Viewers using the ABC network app can choose to watch current season programming but must navigate and subscribe to Hulu/Hulu+ to watch previous seasons.[27] However, the ABC app and the ABC website can both deliver not only the current seasons of ABC programming, they can also deliver the current seasons of all the ABC (actually, Disney-owned) channels such as FX and Freeform.[28]

Third, VOD provides versatility in viewing possibilities that is not currently possible. Today, television is still driven by schedules and appointment viewing – at least on linear channels. VOD places the decision-making for programming into the viewer's hands. Using VOD, the viewer can make decisions about whether and when (s)he wants to watch a program. If the program is shown live, the viewer has the option to watch the program at its scheduled time. Not only does this choice apply to events such as the NFL, NBA, or MLB season games, college football and basketball games, golf tournaments, and the like, but it also applies to those programs shown live such as *Dancing with the Stars* and *The Voice*. Additionally, the viewer can also choose to do or watch something else during the time slot, preferring to watch the live event "on demand" at a time of his or her choosing. The same is true if the viewer wanted to watch a local newscast or other local program. However, today, to watch a program on a linear channel on-demand, the viewer must proactively set the program to record for on-demand viewing. This can be done days – or in some cases, weeks – ahead of time, but must still be done.

Additionally, it is up to the viewer to choose when (s)he will watch a current program running on a content provider such as a network or a cable channel such as HGTV or USA television. In the future, the term "current" when describing a scripted program will have no meaning outside the mind of the individual viewer. When everything is on-demand, there are no "new seasons," no "second seasons," and no reruns. Current may be, for one viewer, when the content provider first releases a program, while for another viewer current may be one or more weeks, months, or years later.

Fourth, VOD has removed the need for the digital video recorder (DVR). Television delivered in true VOD will have no need for recording a program to watch later or to save permanently, because the program the viewer wishes to watch will always be available through the content provider's website. Further, recording of a program for, say, use in a classroom setting will also not be necessary because the instructor will simply select the program using any of the multitude of television platform devices and show the program to the class through a "smart classroom" setup that many educational institutions already make available either through a permanent classroom setup or a portable one. DVD players and DVRs will only be necessary to watch older recorded programs that the viewer may have purchased. However, with the diversity of content providers available today, and the ever-growing number of ones that will populate the future television universe, there is no need to watch older DVDs when those programs are immediately available 24 hours a day, seven days a week, for the viewer to watch. DVDs and their players/recorders will be relegated to the same nostalgia niche that vinyl records are today, and where CDs are headed.

Finally, the VOD of television in the future makes it possible for the viewer to watch his or her favorite program anywhere (s)he is in the world. Because all television is available all the time on any platform, television viewers will have the ability to watch their favorite programs wherever they might be, so long as country laws permit viewing of the website. At this time, Netflix is in over 190 countries,[29] Amazon Prime Video is in over 200 countries and territories,[30] and YouTube is not allowed in only five countries around the world (of which China is the only one of consequence that the viewer might visit either for work or leisure).[31] Streaming television is virtually ubiquitous around the world. Additionally, for those U.S. domestic services such as YouTube TV which can only be viewed in the U.S., using a virtual private network (VPN) makes it possible to appear to be in the U.S. while traveling abroad.[32] So, for all these examples, assuming no legal restrictions in the country, a person from the U.S. traveling in Vietnam would be able to watch his or her favorite television program while in Hanoi or Ho Chi Minh City as long as (s)he had some form of Internet connectivity. A more interesting example would be a person from the U.S. who is able to watch his or her favorite Argentinian television program while in Hanoi or Ho Chi Minh City. A third example would be a German citizen traveling to India, who could watch the Greek version of *American Idol.* With VOD, time zones do not matter, hemispheres do not matter, and schedules do not matter. The viewer will be able to watch his or her favorite television program anywhere (s)he is. All that does matter is the ability to receive an Internet signal in some way.

Summary

VOD, as the delivery system for television programming in the future, provides exciting opportunities for both the television viewer as well as the television content provider. For the television viewer, VOD provides the opportunity to take control of her/his viewing preferences. The viewer can choose what programs to watch, when to watch them, where to watch them, and the platform to watch the programs on, no matter where in the world the viewer is at the time. Further, VOD in the future brings the viewer the entire libraries of the different content providers so that (s)he can watch the newest releases, current programs, or classic shows going back to the earliest days of recorded television.

For the content provider, VOD requires a completely different way of considering television. The programming department of the content provider will take on new responsibilities, very different from the current decision-making on a specified number of programs to fill certain hours of the television day and the ordering of them in a fashion designed to drive the maximum number of eyeballs to the provider's television channel. Instead, the programmer will be responsible for overseeing a vast inventory of programs, of keeping search results current, and of working with the now-necessarily-enhanced promotions department to fashion the best promotional strategies possible to keep viewers informed of the newest programs that are added to the content provider's inventory.

Additionally, because VOD makes all programs available to all viewers all the time, the content provider's entire inventory will now be a valuable commodity. Even the oldest of the classic programs will be vehicles for advertisers to reach audiences interested in reliving their former days of watching television, or new viewers who find they like the classic programs of early television. Westerns such as *Bonanza* or *Gunsmoke* would likely be fascinating to television audiences who have never had the opportunity to see a television Western. Whereas those programs now reside on linear channels, with VOD those programs would revert to the inventories of the original content providers who could then sell advertising on the programs.[33]

The move to all VOD has already begun. While content providers still operate on the traditional system of schedules and appointment viewing, even they are seeing the value in VOD. Look for full conversion from schedules and appointment viewing to all VOD by the end of the next decade at the latest.

Free Ad-Supported Streaming Television

Free ad-supported streaming television, or "FAST," is the latest entrant into the OTT television environment. FAST, by definition, describes digital channels that are subscription free and stream ad-supported content over connected TVs and connected TV devices. Like linear channels, content plays on a pre-set schedule with planned and scheduled ad breaks. FAST simulates linear television but is delivered through Internet Protocol (IP) and is a one-to-one distribution model that allows advertisers to use addressable advertising to reach each viewer with advertisements specifically designed for her/him.[34,35] FAST has come about because of the rising costs of SVOD services. Today, there are more than 1,000 FAST channels available in the U.S. FAST makes it easy to watch with no contracts, no fees, and no worries about sharing passwords.[36]

Viewers looking for FAST channels can find them on platforms such as Roku, Pluto TV, and Rakuten TV, along with certain television manufacturers such as Samsung, LG, and Vizio that have their own lineups of FAST channels built into their software. Many FAST channels are niche and are focused on very specific topics such as health or food.[37] Many, if not most, FAST providers offer both the pre-set schedule of FAST programming with anywhere from limited to extensive AVOD offerings, thus allowing viewers the best of both services. Outside of the television manufacturers' own offerings, FAST platforms can be downloaded to any connected TV set, streaming device such as a Roku or Amazon Fire stick, mobile device, or web browser.[38] The FAST world is continually expanding, with additions such as channels from around the world and in a variety of languages. *CNET* says, "FAST TV is tucked in between the worlds of cable TV and subscription-based streaming, and it's a billion-dollar industry that's changed how we watch TV."[39]

virtial Multichannel Video Programming Distributors

vMVPD is streaming's version of cable television. It is a service designed to help users watch the same television channels through their Internet connections instead of having to have cable service. As such, it is a type of OTT platform like the different VOD and FAST services. As cable rates have exploded, more and more people are turning to vMVPDs to watch the programs they enjoy, while not having to pay the exorbitant rates that cable companies charge.

Typically, vMVPDs will aggregate content from the local broadcast channels in the viewer's market, along with a selection of the most popular cable channels. However, those cable channels will be curated so that instead of hundreds of channels like the cable companies offer, the vMVPDs generally will offer only 60–80 different channels, some more and some less.[40] Additionally, vMVPDs provide viewers with the ability to watch on-demand video content such as films and other features like an electronic programming guide to the channels, times, and programs on the service as well as unlimited cloud-based DVR for recording programs for later viewing (or rewatching, bingeing, etc.)[41] with, often, extended time periods before the program is removed from the viewer's DVR library (six months or more). Once a program is marked for recording, all subsequent showings of episodes of that program will also be recorded and stored in the viewer's library. As long as the program continues to run in syndication, the various episodes of the show are there permanently or until the program quits airing at all or the viewer decides to unmark the show for recording.

Other important features of vMVPDs include no annual contracts (so the viewer can subscribe and cancel at any time without penalty), no additional hardware to add for the service itself,[42] and the ability to watch programs on personal computers, tablets, and mobile phones anywhere an Internet connection can be received. vMVPDs do charge (usually) a monthly rate like the cable companies do, but their pricing is generally substantially less than cable rates, and the no-contract feature makes vMVPDs very attractive to viewers because they can quit a service or change services easily and without penalty.

While vMVPD platforms have been around since 2010, when Philo TV began as a dorm room experiment at Harvard University,[43] it was the 2015 Consumer Electronics Show (CES) convention introduction of Dish Network's Sling TV platform that gave the vMVPD its momentum. Today, YouTube TV is the fourth largest subscription television service with 8 million subscribers, moving past Dish Network into that fourth position. Only Comcast, Charter, and DirecTV are larger.[44] It is also the fastest growing of all the subscription TV services, and the only one of the top four that is gaining subscribers, not losing them.

As television of the future becomes IPTV, the vMVPD will continue to grow and be a powerful alternative to the linear pay-TV services of today. This is already evidenced by the fact that DirecTV, Comcast, and Charter all have their own version of the vMVPD that competes with YouTube TV and the other vMVPDs of today. As discussed in Chapter 2, the future of cable is not cable; it is the backbone of IPTV, and the vMVPD is, and will be, the provider of traditional television in the future.

Notes

1. Cambridge iTV Trial, http://koo.corpus.cam.ac.uk/projects/itv/.
2. Sweney, Mark, "Broadcasters to Launch Joint VoD Service," *The Guardian*, (November 27, 2007), http://www.guardian.co.uk/media/2007/nov/27/bbc.itv.
3. Ramsey, Fiona, "SeeSaw Selected as Name of Video-on-demand Service," *BrandRepublic*, (May 13, 2008), http://www.brandrepublic.com/news/808546/SeeSaw-selected-name-video-on-demand-service/.
4. "What is VOD?" *Music Choice*, http://www.musicchoice.com/Advertising/pdf/AboutVOD.pdf.
5. Anderson, Nate, "Netflix Offers Streaming Movies to Subscribers," *arstechnica*, (January 16, 2007), https://arstechnica.com/uncategorized/2007/01/8627/.
6. Anderson, "Netflix Offers Streaming Movies to Subscribers."
7. Netflix, Inc., *Stock Analysis*, (June 13, 2024), https://stockanalysis.com/stocks/nflx/market-cap/.
8. Durrani, Ana, "Top Streaming Statistics In 2024," *Forbes*, (June 13, 2024), https://www.forbes.com/home-improvement/internet/streaming-stats/.
9. Durrani, "Top Streaming Statistics In 2024."
10. Westcott, Kevin, Jana Arbanas, Chris Arkenberg, and Jeff Loucks, "Streaming Video at a Crossroads: Redesign Yesterday's Models or Reinvent for Tomorrow?" *Deloitte Insights*, (March 20, 2024), https://www2.deloitte.com/us/en/insights/industry/technology/digital-media-trends-consumption-habits-survey/2024/customization-and-personalization-lead-the-svod-revolution.html.
11. "Research: Prime Video Lowest US SVoD Churn Rate, *Advanced Television*, (May 31, 2024), https://advanced-television.com/2024/05/31/research-prime-lowest-us-svod-churn-rate/.
12. Heydari, Anis, "Commercials May Be Here to Stay on Streamers Like Amazon Unless You Open Your Wallet," *Canadian Broadcasting Corporation*, (February 2, 2024), https://www.cbc.ca/news/business/cheap-ad-free-streaming-is-probably-gone-1.7102266.
13. Barr, Aaron, "Disney+ Beefs Up Ad Tier With More Targeting, Measurement Features," *Marketing Dive*, (October 30, 2023), https://www.marketingdive.com/news/disney-plus-ad-supported-tier-targeting-measurement-features/698101/.
14. Whitten, Sarah and Alex Sherman, "Netflix Ad-supported Tier Has 40 million Monthly Users, Nearly Double Previous Count," *NBC News*, (May 15, 2024), https://www.nbcnews.com/business/business-news/netflix-ad-supported-tier-40-million-monthly-users-rcna152463.
15. "Advertising-Based Video On Demand (AVOD)," *SymphonyAI*," https://www.symphonyai.com/glossary/media/avod-advertising-based-video-on-demand/.
16. "Advertising-Based Video On Demand (AVOD)," *SymphonyAI*."
17. "YouTube Statistics 2025 (Demographics, Users by Country & More)," *GMI Research*, (Feb 4, 2025), https://www.globalmediainsight.com/blog/youtube-users-statistics/#4_Which_YouTube_Channel_has_the_most_subscribers_in_2025.
18. Rawat, Shivam, "15 Top YouTube Influencers in 2025," *Tagbox*, (February 27, 2025), https://taggbox.com/blog/youtube-influencers/.
19. "What is AVOD? And How is it Different to SVOD & TVOD?", *Little Dot Studios*, (October 23, 2023), https://blog.littledotstudios.com/en-gb/news-views/what-is-avod.
20. Halpert, Scott, "Understanding AVOD Part 2: Business Models and List of Top AVOD Platforms," *penthera*, (September 6, 2022), https://www.penthera.com/post/avod-educational-series-part-2-business-models-and-list-of-top-avod-platforms.
21. Wadgaonkar, Pratik, "TVOD – Definition, Types, Pros and Cons and More," *Gumlet*, (February 1, 2024), https://www.gumlet.com/learn/what-is-tvod/.
22. NVOD, or near-video-on-demand, was a service offered by cable and DTH satellite services where customers could rent a movie for a short period of time, usually 48 to 72 hours. The service is called "near" because when a customer rented a movie, the

movie would usually be delivered on four consecutive channels, with the movie beginning at the top or bottom of the hour for two consecutive hours. Therefore, the viewer had to wait until the time reached the top or bottom of the hour to watch the movie from its beginning, instead of beginning the movie immediately at any time (VOD). As such, the service became known as NVOD to distinguish it from true VOD.

23 Wadgaonkar, "TVOD – Definition, Types, Pros and Cons and More."
24 "PVOD (Premium video on demand)," *AppsFlyer*, (n.d.), https://www.appsflyer.com/glossary/pvod/.
25 "PVOD (Premium video on demand)," *AppsFlyer.*
26 See for example, Comcast's Xfinity app, Dish Network's app, and AT&T's U-verse app for smartphones and tablets. These are just three examples of how the cable, DTH satellite, and telephone companies are incorporating apps into their delivery plans for today and into the future.
27 https://abc.com/browse.
28 https://abc.com/browse.
29 "Company Profile," *Netflix*, https://ir.netflix.net/ir-overview/profile/default.aspx#:~:text=Netflix%20is%20one%20of%20the,variety%20of%20genres%20and%20languages.
30 "Prime Video Offerings," *Video Central – Amazon*, https://videocentral.amazon.com/home/help?topicId=GWKF2YM3PC5WLAZ8&ref_=avd_sup_GWKF2YM3PC5WLAZ8#:~:text=Prime%20Video%20Subscription,and%20a%20compatible%20connected%20device.
31 "Countries That Have Blocked YouTube," *Wikitubia*, https://youtube.fandom.com/wiki/Countries_that_have_blocked_YouTube.
32 Garland, Ian, "How to Watch YouTube TV From Abroad with a VPN in 2025," *comparitech*, (updated January 16, 2025), https://www.comparitech.com/blog/vpn-privacy/watch-youtube-tv-abroad-vpn/.
33 See Chapter 7: The Future of Television Advertising and Chapter 9: The Future of Television Content Search & Promotion.
34 "Free Ad-Supported Streaming TV (FAST)," *smartclip*, https://smartclip.tv/adtech-glossary/free-ad-supported-streaming-tv/.
35 For more information on addressable advertising, see Chapter 7: The Future of Television Advertising.
36 Jackson, Kourtnee, "FAST TV: What It Is and Why It Should Matter to You," *CNET*, (November 18, 2023), https://www.cnet.com/tech/services-and-software/fast-tv-what-it-is-and-why-it-should-matter-to-you/.
37 "Free Ad-Supported Streaming TV (FAST)," *smartclip.*
38 Jackson, Kourtnee, "FAST TV: What It Is and Why It Should Matter to You."
39 Jackson, Kourtnee, "FAST TV: What It Is and Why It Should Matter to You."
40 "vMVPD (Virtual Multichannel Programming Distributor," *AppsFlyer*, (n.d.), https://www.appsflyer.com/glossary/vmvpd/.
41 "vMVPD (Virtual Multichannel Programming Distributor," *AppsFlyer.*
42 Although, if the viewer is watching an vMVPD on a television set, the set must be a connected TV set or have some form of set-top box (STB), such as a Roku box or stick or Amazon Fire stick connected to the set.
43 "Philo (Company)," *Wikipedia*, https://en.wikipedia.org/wiki/Philo_(company).
44 Kundu, Kishalaya, "YouTube TV Surpasses Dish to Become the Fourth Largest Pay-TV Provider in the US," *TechSpot*, (February 8, 2024), https://www.techspot.com/news/101812-youtube-tv-surpasses-dish-become-fourth-largest-pay.html.

5 The Future of Television Viewing

The chapter focuses on a variety of receiving platforms that are integral to the future of television. The chapter looks at connected or "smart" television sets, virtual reality (VR) and augmented reality (AR), and second-screen devices or what I call the "iWorld," the variety of possibilities that exist in the universe of mobile telephones, tablet computers, and the latest in VR and AR devices. It is referred as the "iWorld" because of the impact that two Apple products – the iPhone and the iPad – have had on the entire category.

Connected Television

If Internet protocol television (IPTV) is the way viewers will receive their television experiences in the future, and broadband, Wi-Fi, and cellular are the delivery systems for IPTV, then the connected television (CTV) set is the mechanism by which the viewer enjoys his or her home television viewing experiences. The connected or "smart" TV is a television set that is connected to the Internet through one of a variety of methods. CTV sets can be connected to the Internet through a direct wired broadband connection, through Wi-Fi, or through a cellular connection.

Television sets connected to the Internet have led to a phenomena known as "cord-cutting," "cord-shaving," and, more recently, "cord-nevers." Cord-cutting is used to describe the decision of television viewers who are fed up with the programming delivered by the linear television sources and what they see as constantly increasing cable or direct-to-home (DTH) satellite rates, and so have turned to the Internet for all their television viewing. These cord-cutters spend their time watching programming that is available to them through the Internet. Often, these cord-cutters watch movies and other programming streamed through Netflix, iTunes, Amazon, and other such sources, including the streaming aggregator sites such as YouTube TV and Hulu+ Live TV that are direct competitors to cable and satellite companies. They also turn to advertising-driven video on demand (AVOD) and free ad-supported streaming television (FAST) channels, which function as niche linear TV, and watch YouTube, which has moved from strictly user-generated content (UGC) to a myriad of channels of professionally produced programming.[1] In 2014, 7.3% of all U.S. households were cord-cutters.[2]

DOI: 10.4324/9781003625384-8

By year-end of 2023, that percentage had risen to 35.9% of U.S. households, and is estimated to rise to 44.1% by the end of 2027 – and that represents cord-cutters only.³ As the number of cord-cutters increases, the number and percentage of traditional pay TV households continues to shrink. In 2023, that percentage was only 45.6%, with estimates showing cable and DTH satellite services down to only 34.9%, or just over one third of all U.S. television households.⁴ In fact, cord-cutting has become so prevalent it is no wonder that SVB MoffettNathanson senior analyst Craig Moffett said that "'We are watching the sun beginning to set' on the pay TV business."⁵

Cord-shavers are viewers who still want to watch some programming from the traditional television sources but have chosen to make watching programming through the Internet a major part, or even the bulk, of their television viewing. These viewers reduce their television viewing costs by moving to the most basic cable television package or eliminating it altogether if they have the capability to receive over-the-air (OTA) signals.⁶ Cord-shaving was considered to be a major threat to linear TV back in the mid-2010s,⁷ but cord-shaving has given way to simply cutting the cord, with the availability of alternative virtual Multichannel Video Programming Distributor (vMVPD) streaming choices.

Cord-nevers, then, are those viewers who have never had any form of linear pay-television. Because of the continuing explosion of costs for both cable and DTH satellite services, cord-nevers have chosen instead to spend their viewing money on subscription streaming services such as Netflix and Amazon Prime Instant Video for movies and original programming. For network programming, cord-nevers choose YouTube TV or Hulu/Hulu+ Live TV, preferring to pay the subscription fee for either aggregator to receive the programming from broadcast and cable networks. Long-term, it is the cord-cutters and cord-nevers who pose the biggest threat to traditional pay-television companies, who worry their CEOs, and who have helped bring about the newest streaming offerings.⁸ By the end of 2022, cord-cutters and cord-nevers represented 53% of U.S. households, and estimates place that percentage at 75% by 2026.⁹

One interesting aspect of cord-cutting and cord-shaving has been a resurgence in the sale of external antennas capable of receiving OTA television signals. It seems that cord-cutters and cord-shavers, especially millennials and Gen-Xers, still want to receive local and possibly network programming for news and information at the very least.¹⁰ One would think that, as the number of U.S. households cutting the cord or never using one increases, the number of antennas sold would also increase, beyond the current 30% of U.S. households owning antennas.¹¹

Today there has been a major shift in the CTV industry – a shift from the hybrid connection of an over-the-top set-top box (OTT-STB) to a direct connection between the television itself and the Internet. Television makers have contracted with major OTT-STB makers to install the software necessary to allow their television sets to connect to the Internet without the need for an STB. Like the STBs themselves, the CTV is designed with the ability to connect through a wired broadband connection or home Wi-Fi system.

WebTV, Roku, and Amazon are three of the major companies supplying CTV makers with the software they need to build and further develop CTV sets. Surprisingly, Apple has not moved into the CTV set business. Apple already makes its own OTT-STB called "Apple TV"; for CTV sets, Apple TV is an available app with its own programming lineup of shows. In addition to the contracts the OTT-STB companies have with the TV set manufacturers, both Amazon and Roku have introduced their own branded lines of CTV sets to compete directly with the major players such as Samsung, LG, Vizio, TCL, and others.

Future of Connected Television

Charles F. Kettering, noted inventor, engineer, founder of Delco, and philanthropist of the early to mid-1900s,[12] said, "The opportunities of man are limited only by his imagination."[13] To adapt that statement to the CTV industry, "The future of the connected television set is limited only by the imagination of the television industry." In other words, the future of the CTV industry is, for the foreseeable future at least, very bright. While CTV sets have been around for a decade, the full extent of the industry is just now being realized.

Ultra-High Definition TV/Super-High Definition TV

Today, the ultra-high definition (UHD or 4K) CTV set is the de facto set that the viewer has in her/his home. Purchasing a good or even mediocre set these days requires a purchase of a 4K television, and the competition among the different set manufacturers and, now, the branded streamer sets is so fierce that the prices have been driven so low as to be easily in the price range of any consumer. For instance, a quick check of the prices on the Best Buy website shows that a 43" Insignia (a Best Buy brand) 4K television set costs $149.99. Larger sets on that website, show 55" 4K television sets as low as $229.99 and 65" 4K sets for as low as $299.99.[14] Those size sets would have been as much as five times as expensive less than a decade ago, and the number of different brand choices would have been limited. On the other end of the spectrum, Best Buy sells a 42' gaming 4K television set with a bendable design for $2,149.99, so for special sets, the price can still be steep.[15] While the linear networks still primarily deliver their programming in high definition, more and more streaming services are delivering their programming in 4K.

While 4K is still the de facto connected television set today, super-high definition (SHD or 8K) is the expected successor to today's UHD (4K) TV. The 2015 Consumer Electronics Show (CES) convention could be considered as at least one of the "coming out parties" for the SHD television sets.[16]

8K television produces a pixel resolution of 7680 by 4320, or a resolution approximately 4 times that of 4K, and 16 times the resolution of high definition television (HDTV).[17] In both the 2014 and 2015 National Association of Broadcasters' (NAB) conventions, Japan's NHK research lab demonstrated 8K television on a variety of different screen sizes.[18] Additionally, Japan made available

8K television for the 2020 Olympics in Tokyo designed to drive a "new round of resolution increases" according to the research firm HIS.[19] While only about 2,700 8K television sets were expected to be shipped worldwide during 2015, by the time of the Olympics some 911,000 units were expected to be shipped across the globe.[20] While 911,000 units worldwide is a meager number, consider those units to be a vanguard for the 8K industry. Further, virtually all the sets shipped during the period were 65″ or larger because 8K is better viewed on the largest screen possible.[21] The need for a larger screen for viewing 8K has driven the development of ever larger screens for home use. Today, offerings of 8K television sets generally start at 65″ and larger. 8K sets today are produced by the major television set manufacturers, Samsung, LG, and Sony, and the price for these sets ranges from about $1,500 at the very low end to $10,000 on the high end.[22]

The big question then becomes, what happens to 4K television? While some see 4K as a standard for the foreseeable future, it is more likely that 4K will ultimately be the steppingstone to 8K, a transitional format much like 720p HDTV was the steppingstone to full 1080p HDTV. The major question as to when the changeover from 4K to 8K will happen depends not on the price or quality of the television set, but rather the timeframe required for the content providers to switch to producing programming in 8K. The linear media continue to produce their programming in HDTV with only a smattering of 4K-produced programming, including sporting events. Today's major streamers such as Netflix and Amazon are beginning to stream their newest programs in 4K, but until there is a dramatic move to 4K production of television programs, the audience will really not know what it is missing. Therefore, it is the content providers, not the consumers or the television set manufacturers, who will decide when 8K adoption will replace the 4K television set.

Nevertheless, the future of CTV is bright. CTV had a 10.9% growth in 2023 and a 13.8% growth in 2024, and demand still has not caught up with supply.[23] One major reason for the continued success of the CTV set is its versatility. Because the "smart" TV platform is driven by an Internet connection, it has the ability to deliver the programming using apps rather than channels and channel numbers like the TV set of bygone days. This versatility, then, allows the connected television set to make available to the viewer a myriad of different streaming services including subscription video-on-demand (SVOD), AVOD, FAST, and now gaming services, along with its own FAST channels.

Additionally, one of the major growth areas in CTV is advertising spend. Advertisers are finally beginning to recognize just how valuable CTV advertising can be. CTV advertising makes it possible for advertisers to target highly specific audiences with remarkable precision. They are also able to leverage the data analytics and audience segmentation capabilities that are critical now and especially into the future of television, as the television universe becomes ever more fragmented and larger.[24] As the audiences for streaming television continue to grow ever larger and the audiences for linear television continue to shrink, the need for reaching highly precise audiences with advertising that speaks to them and motivates them to action becomes ever more critical to the continuing success of television, especially among the younger demographic audiences.[25]

Holographic Television

Not here yet, but on the distant horizon is the holographic television, a set that will render the 3D idea of the past obsolete and usher in a new era of unparalleled lean-forward television experiences. A release from the Massachusetts Institute of Technology, or MIT, has reported that their researchers are in the process of producing a form of 3D television from holograms that will make previous 3D TV seem as quaint as black and white television would be to today's teenager. According to the release, members of MIT's Object-Based Media Group, led by head researcher Michael Bove, presented a system "that can capture visual information using off-the-shelf electronics, send it over the Internet to a holographic display, and update the image at rates approaching those of feature films (24 frames per second)."[26] What is different from previous research on holographic TV is that the MIT team is the first to get refresh rates approaching motion picture film speed, and they were able to accomplish their work using only a single data-capture device – a Kinect camera designed for the Xbox 360 game system.[27]

According to the MIT release, there is a significant difference between holograms and 3D movie images in theatres. The old 3D movies may give an audience perceived depth, but it is from only one perspective. In other words, people sitting anywhere in the theatre get exactly the same image. What is different about a hologram is that whenever you move around a hologram, you get multiple perspectives of the image from all angles and sides just as you would if you were walking around a real person.

A standard 3D movie camera captures light bouncing off of an object at two different angles, one for each eye. But in the real world, light bounces off of objects at an infinite number of angles. Holographic video systems use devices that produce so-called diffraction fringes, fine patterns of light and dark that can bend the light passing through them in predictable ways. A dense enough array of fringe patterns, each bending light in a different direction, can simulate the effect of light bouncing off of a 3D object.[28]

Holographic images were used by CNN as far back as its 2008 Presidential election night coverage. A hologram of reporter Jessica Yellin was "beamed" from Chicago to CNN's New York City election headquarters for a report. Anchor Wolf Blitzer discussed the election for a few minutes with a holographic Yellin as she appeared to be in studio.[29]

The development of consumer-level holographic television is still a number of years away. Many of the problems associated with holographic television are technical – the technology simply has not been fully developed at this time. However, there are companies around the world that are working on the technology, such as Japan's National Institute of Information and Communications Technology (NICT) and "Project Echo," a Danish/Swedish collaboration.[30,31]

Project Echo has developed what it terms "directional pixel technology," which can be described as possibly the most serious first step toward consumer level holographic television to date. The technology has the ability to deliver simultaneous, multiple 2D, or 3D views, including what can be termed as "look-around" capability in high quality and without the need for or use of special glasses (as is required by current 3D programs) or other possible accessories to experience (no longer "watch") the content.[32]

Japan and Korea are two of the world leaders in the development of holographic productions. While not yet ready for television, in Japan young people enjoy the performances of Hatsune Miku, a holographic singer who appears on stage to large and enthusiastic crowds.[33] In Korea, the K-pop group KDA's performances include both live singers and hologram singers on stage at the same time.[34] An additional example is the hologram in a box (my term for the scene).[35] While none of these examples are designed for the television of today, they show what can be done now and presage the future possibilities. Realize that the holographic television of the future is not simply 3D television of the early 2010s brought back. These 3D televisions were bound to a single screen and needed special glasses to create the 3D image. Holographic television creates a true 3D character that is not bound to a single screen, and does not require special glasses to view. Indeed, combining wall-sized television sets with an interactive floor (see Chapter 1 for a discussion of both), holographic television can provide the viewer with an almost true-life experience.

The completion and production of 3D, holographic capabilities of massive-sized CTV sets will make television the immersive experience that viewers in the latter half of the 21st century will come to expect. Expect the first generation of immersive sets by 2050 at the latest, and likely sooner.

The combination of connected TV, 4K or 8K TV, and holographic TV will ultimately provide the viewer with a television experience (s)he has never been able to have before – a truly lean-forward, immersion television experience where the viewer can, if (s)he so chooses, become a part of the program (s)he is watching. With the continuing development and refinement of the technology, a connected, SHD, holographic television room with television sets forming the walls of the room, and the programming delivered over the Internet at speeds of gigabits or even terabits per second, will provide the viewer with a television experience unlike any other. From passive, lean-back, one-screen viewing, to full immersion, four-wall holographic participation, the television viewer will have an experience that will seem as normal to her or him as it seems fantastic to consider today.[36] Think of the Enterprise's holodeck on the television series *Star Trek: The Next Generation* – this will be the ultimate future of holographic television.

Virtual Reality and Augmented Reality

Today, if you talk to professionals working on the cutting edge of 21st century television, most will tell you that the next iteration of television – at least until holographic television is ready – will be VR and/or AR television. The two terms are not the same, although both suggest a way of watching television that is much closer to a "lean-forward" experience than the traditional "lean-back" passive viewing of today.

Notice the difference in the terms when discussing lean-forward versus lean-back. Lean-forward is described as an "experience"; lean-back is described as "viewing," and therein lies the major difference in 21st century television. The future of television is in the ability – if the viewer chooses it – to become involved from a physical and a sensorial perspective, rather than just the continued passive viewing the consumer has today.

Virtual Reality

Chris Woodford, in an article on VR, provides an interesting set of examples in his opening:

> You'll probably never go to Mars, swim with dolphins, run an Olympic 100 meters, or sing onstage with the Rolling Stones. But if **virtual reality** (emphasis original article) ever lives up to its promise, you might be able to do all these things – and many more – without ever leaving your home.[37]

For television, VR can make it possible for the viewer to "experience" the thrill of being on pit row of a NASCAR race, on the 50-yard line of the Super Bowl, or in the audience at a game show or reality show or even a drama or sitcom.

So what is VR? *Virtual Reality Site* defines VR as "a three-dimensional, computer generated environment which can be explored and interacted with by a person."[38] Chris Woodford in his article defines VR as, "A believable, interactive 3D computer-created world that you can explore so you feel you really are there, both mentally and physically."[39] Jonathan Strickland, in his article, defines VR as "using computer technology to create a simulated, three-dimensional world that a user can manipulate and explore while feeling as if he were in that world."[40] Finally, the *Merriam-Webster* dictionary defines VR as "an artificial environment which is experienced through sensory stimuli (as sights and sounds) provided by a computer and in which one's actions partially determine what happens in the environment."[41]

Regardless of which definition you choose, they all include similar elements of VR. According to these definitions, VR is: 1. Believable, 2. Interactive, 3. Immersive, 4. Something you can explore, 5. Computer-generated, and 6. Multi-sensory. Let us look at each element in more detail.

1. Believable: The user must feel as if (s)he is actually in the world that has been created. A person in a VR experience must continually believe that the virtual world that the person is involved with is real and that (s)he is intrinsically part of that world.
2. Interactive: VR is an experience. As the user moves through the VR environment, the environment must move and change with him or her. The user must be able to direct her or his movement within the VR environment and have that environment react to each movement or activity. Further, the response to the user's actions must make sense even if that response only makes sense in the virtual environment.
3. Immersive: This element is, probably, the most important of the six. In a VR environment, the user be completely involved in that virtual world as if that world is reality – because it is reality for the user while (s)he is within that

environment. Without total user immersion, VR can become disjointed and completely unbelievable, defeating the purpose of VR.
4 Something you can explore: The user must be able to move around, look up and down, forward and backward, and side to side, and watch the VR environment logically change as (s)he does so. When watching the Super Bowl in a VR environment (in real time, or as a later experience), the user must not only be able to watch the game from end zone to end zone, but must also be able to notice who is beside, in front of, and behind her/him. The user must be able to see the peanut vendor, the cheerleaders, the jumbo scoreboard, and fully accept the environment. As the user gets up and moves down an aisle, the environment must allow her or him to notice the different angles, people, reactions, etc., that would exist in the real world.
5 Computer-generated: Whether using a television set, a smartphone with software, or some other set of devices, VR must be delivered at some stage through a computer user interface to reach the user.
6 Multi-sensory: VR should engage all the user's senses, especially sight, sound, and touch. Today's VR equipment includes the typical headset for sight and sound, and specialized gloves that help to create the sense of touch when exploring the VR environment. Future generations of VR will need to create a full sensory experience, including all senses, without the need for headsets, gloves, and other apparatus.

Virtual Reality and Television

As mentioned at the beginning of this section, VR is potentially the next step in the development of the future of television because it creates the immersive, interactive fully lean-forward experience that the television viewers of the future will crave. Edward Miller, head of visuals for the 360-degree video app, "Immersive. ly," says, "We need to think beyond 16:9. Television and game are converging and we need to start looking at the new tools we've got."[42] Gene Munster, a Piper Jaffray technology analyst says, "Envisioning the next 10 years, it seems less likely that the television will be the centerpiece of the living room with the evolution of virtual reality and augmented reality."[43]

They may be right. Already companies like Immersive.ly and NextVR continue to develop VR experiences, both real time and non-real time. From NASCAR races[44] to a pro-democracy protest in Hong Kong[45] to participation in a *Game of Thrones* episode[46] to a professional soccer match, hockey game, and flyover of the Golden Gate Bridge,[47] software and hardware companies have demonstrated the capabilities of the future of VR television. While the best-known of the headsets is the Meta Quest, there are more than a dozen companies making VR headsets, including Apple's Vision Pro and a variety of Playstation VR headsets as well.

The question now is how much of an impact VR will have on television and how soon will that impact will be felt. A lot will depend on at least two aspects – what big name companies will be investing in VR television, and how quickly VR can move into the mainstream. As for the big-name companies, the major players are already turning out headsets and upgrading their quality and possibilities. As far as a timeframe, Edward Miller of Immersive.ly believes that VR is still at a "wow effect" point, much as films were in the early 1900s.[48] However, all speculation on when VR will begin to supplant traditional television viewing will be understood through the lens of what happened with 3D television.[49] While there is currently great excitement for the potential of VR television, it will be up to the manufacturers to produce VR equipment that the viewer will want to wear, and to be able to convince the viewer that VR television is the next thing in television. Ultimately, though, the true VR television experience is still only the stuff of science fiction. In the late 2010s, VR was the rage – now, it seems as if the excitement has cooled tremendously. Whether or not VR becomes the next "television" is still in question.

Augmented Reality

Where VR creates an entirely new virtual world for the user, AR leaves the user in the real world while adding to that physical world. *Mashable* defines AR as "a live, direct or indirect, view of a physical, real-world environment whose elements are augmented by computer-generated sensory input such as sound, video, graphics, or GPS data."[50] *WhatIs.com* says, "Augmented reality is the integration of digital information with live video or the user's environment in real time. Basically, AR takes an existing picture and blends new information into it."[51] Finally, the *Financial Times* states that "Augmented reality (AR) refers to the technology that offers a real-time view of one's immediate surroundings altered or enhanced by computer generated information.[52] Notice that, in each case, AR keeps the user in her or his real world setting, and adds to that setting a variety of computer-generated alternatives. AR does not move the user into a separate, virtual world, but provides additional information or stimuli to the user's physical environment to assist the user or make the user's environment and/or real-life experience more pleasurable, exciting, or, at the least, different.

Augmented Reality and Television

Augmented reality is already in use in television today – at least in a relatively simple form. When the viewer is watching a football game and sees the yellow line-to-gain marker that is computer generated, that is a form of AR. When the viewer watches a professional golf tournament like The Masters or The Open Championship and sees the computer-generated tracker line of a drive off the golfer's club – that is also a form of AR. In both cases, the physical world that the viewer is watching is augmented by some information that is computer generated and not located in the physical world.

Advertisemnts can also be part of AR. When the viewer watches a soccer match in Europe on television, (s)he sees computer-generated advertisements for sponsors magically appear on the field of play – that is a form of augmented reality. Advertisements for the USA Network's program, *Dig*, are coming to life for the network using AR.[53]

AR is such a part of television – especially live television – that the viewer does not even stop to consider what (s)he is watching. In one sense, the AR used today in television is helping pave the way for the VR of tomorrow. In the future, as AR content in television becomes more and more complex and an integral part of all television, AR will make television viewing more interesting, entertaining, and informative, and will serve as a transition point for the move from traditional television viewing to VR television viewing/experiencing.

Second-Screen Devices (The iWorld)

"Second-screen devices" is the term that is used to describe any form of alternative screen, most especially to describe television on mobile smartphones, tablets, and personal computers, along with the world of apps that are available on the devices.

Smartphones

While most people date the true smartphone to the introduction of the original iPhone in 2007, smartphones in one form or another have been around since 1993 when IBM introduced the Simon. Compared to the sleek smartphones of today, the Simon was big, heavy, clunky, and expensive. It did, though, combine a cell phone, data services, and even a fax machine.[54] Despite the development of the IBM Simon, in the early days of the consumer mobile phone, the favored aspect of the phone was a desire for it to be small and light – think the Motorola Star-Tac, which was one of the early, small, lightweight mobile phones. Consequently, it was one of the most popular and most desired, despite its high cost for that time. For doing business, the Palm Pilot and other personal digital assistants (PDA) were the preferred equipment choices.

It was not until the Canadian company Research in Motion (RIM) developed the Blackberry in 2002 that the smartphone became an important piece of mobile phone technology. The original Blackberry, the 5810, gave mobile phone users – usually businessmen – the ability to surf the web, access their e-mail, and talk on the phone. The one drawback to using the Blackberry as a mobile phone was that the user had to plug in a headset to be able to talk on the phone. It took RIM two years to produce a headset-free smartphone, the 6210, which entered the market in 2004.[55] RIM has since rebranded and is now named "Blackberry," after its famous phone.

Another early smartphone that must be mentioned is the Palm Treo 600, which combined the abilities of the Palm Pilot with a mobile phone developed by device manufacturer Handspring. Handspring was a competitor in the industry until it was bought out by Palm. The Treo 600 was the first smartphone to feature the possibility to purchase both GSM (Global System for Mobile Communications) and CDMA (Code Division Multiple Access) models. Despite its popularity, the Treo 600 came out about the time Palm's influence in the market began to decline.[56]

The iPhone

It was in 2007 that the mobile phone market saw the introduction of the smartphone that not only revolutionized the mobile phone industry then, but continues to do so even today – Apple Corporation's original iPhone. The iPhone has become the icon of the mobile phone world, producing record sales every time a new edition is released. The iPhone was announced in January 2007 and released on June 29th of that year. It came in two memory sizes with two different prices, 4GB for $499 and 8GB for $599. The original iPhone came in black only and had a metal-back casing. It provided the smartphone world with the first fully touchscreen phone, eliminating the keyboard that the Blackberry and other smartphones of the day had, and allowing the screen of the iPhone to cover practically the entire front surface of the phone.[57] The elimination of the physical keyboard in favor of a touchscreen keyboard gave the world something it had not seen before in a mobile phone – a screen large enough to watch movies and stream videos comfortably.

By September 29th, Apple had sold its 1,000,000th iPhone.[58] With its ability to make phone calls, surf the web using its Safari browser, send and receive e-mails and text (but not multimedia messaging service [MMS]) messages, and operate as an iPod with its syncing ability to the iTunes store, the iPhone took the smartphone from a phone designed strictly for someone in the business world, and became the smartphone icon against which all other smartphones are measured. With the development of its iOS 2.0 operating system, Apple introduced apps to the iPhone, another of its groundbreaking revolutions.[59]

The current Apple iPhone is the iPhone 17 With its variety of sizes, its power, and its technology, as well as its (for many) staggering price, the Apple smartphone has come an amazingly long way from that first iPhone introduced just 18 years earlier.

Android Phones

In the fall of 2007, Google, desiring to compete with Apple, introduced the Android operating system for mobile phones. Unlike the Apple iOS system, the Google Android operating system was developed as an open system. Because the Android system is an open system, third-party developers can produce apps for a variety of mobile phone companies needing different requirements. While the Apple operating system is a proprietary system and third-party developers must write software code that is specific to the Apple mobile phone equipment, the Android system can run on virtually any mobile phone regardless of the phone's specifications. This ability to run on a variety of mobile phones has allowed Google's Android system to become the most popular operating system worldwide, commanding almost 71% of the global market compared to a little over 28% for Apple's iOS system. In the U.S., however, Apple's iOS leads the way with almost 59%, compared to Android's almost 41% share of the mobile phone market. Both those percentages have remained fairly consistent for the past decade. Young people in the U.S. – those younger than 35 – tend to favor the iPhone, whereas those 35 and older tend to favor the Android by a slight majority. Worldwide, Android dominates in all age categories.[60]

The major cell phone manufacturer using the Android system and operating in the U.S. is Samsung. Samsung is second only to Apple in mobile phone popularity across the country, with 27% of mobile users choosing the Samsung Galaxy line of smartphones. No other phone company (other than Apple, of course) comes even close to reaching double digits in popularity.[61]

Tablet Computers

Introduced in 2010, the iPad was not the first tablet computer, but it was the first truly successful consumer tablet computer in terms of market share and how it has revolutionized the computer world. However, the iPad is just one of a number of tablet computers vying for market share today. Chief among its rivals are the Galaxy Tab from Samsung, the Surface and Surface Pro from Microsoft, and the Kindle Fire from Amazon (although the Fire does not compete fully as a true tablet computer).

The tablet computer world is dominated by the Apple iPad, which has 43% percent of the U.S. tablet market as of March 2024, with Samsung second at 25%, and Amazon third at 20%. No other tablet comes close to double figures.[62] Worldwide, the Apple iPad leads the way as well with a 32% market share. After that, only the Samsung Galaxy Tab line of tablets reaches double figures with 21.7% market share. The next three companies after Samsung are all Chinese tablet makers, but only Huawei comes close to double figures at 9.7% market share.[63]

Development of Tablets

The tablet computer itself really only dates back to just after the turn of the millennium when, in 2002, Microsoft introduced the Microsoft Tablet PC. The Microsoft Tablet PC was designed primarily for business use, especially for those business people that Microsoft called the "corridor warriors." Microsoft defined these corridor warriors as "...the workers that spend most of their time in the office, but significant amounts of that time is spent taking notes during meetings or otherwise away from the desk."[64] As it turned out, the Microsoft Tablet PC was minimally successful because it was expensive and it had usability problems that kept it from being a product that the general public would want to buy. As such, it had very limited saleability.[65]

It was Apple in 2010 that gave the world the first general use tablet computer when the original Apple iPad went on sale, the Wi-Fi only version on April 3rd and the Wi-Fi + 3G model April 30th. The original iPad came with three data storage sizes – 16 GB, 32 GB, and 64 GB, each having a Wi-Fi only and a Wi-Fi + 3G model, for a total of six variations. Whereas the Microsoft Tablet PC was designed for the businessperson needing a device for meetings, the iPad gave the user not only the ability to use it in meetings to take notes, but also to enjoy a multitude of other options. Those options included listening to music through its built-in iPod capability; reading e-books, newspapers, and other forms of periodicals; watching movies, television programs, and YouTube – all in HDTV – as well as home videos; viewing personal photographs; playing games from the App Store on a larger and more enjoyable screen than the iPod or the iPhone; downloading free and purchased apps from the Apple App Store; and surfing the web through its built-in Safari browser. In addition, as the iPad caught the fancy of the general public, developers began turning out apps designed specifically for the iPad's larger size, allowing the user to receive the full benefit of the iPad's large screen. At the time of its launch, there were only 12 apps designed specifically for the iPad, but the device could also run the more than 150,000 iPhone apps that were available from the Apple App Store.[66]

One year later on March 2, 2011, Apple released its iPad2, an improvement over the original iPad. The iPad2 was sleeker than its predecessor – it was 33% thinner and 15% lighter, had a more powerful dual-core processor and upgraded mobile phone capability (4G instead of 3G and quad-band instead of tri-band), and boasted new features such as both a rear-facing camera that could produce 720 HD video as well as a front-facing camera for video-chat for the first time.[67]

One cannot discuss the iPad without mentioning the iPad mini, currently on its seventh generation. The iPad mini is somewhat larger than its 7″ competitors, running at 8.3″ – a noticeable difference when compared directly to the 7″ tablets, its 8.3″ screen makes the iPad mini less of a sharp rectangle than its competitors.[68] The original iPad mini was launched in 2012, with the second generation released the next year. What was expected to be the latest generation was launched in 2021, and there was some question as to whether or not there would be an iPad mini 7. Apple did, in fact, release an iPad mini 7 in October 2024.[69]

Of the other tablet computers, the largest percentage runs the Google Android operating system. Because the Android system is an open system, numerous companies run the Android system. Of these, the best-known is Samsung with its Galaxy Tab line of tablets, but others include Google's own Nexus brand of tablets (and smartphones as well), Sony, Toshiba, Acer, Lenovo, and HTC, among others.[70] Over the past decade, Android has made major inroads. In Q1 of 2015, Android had an 18.1% market share whereas the iPad's market share was 74.3%.[71] As of May 2024, for the U.S. market, the Android-operating tablet market percentage was 42.2%, compared to the iPad's 57.57%.[72] For the worldwide market during Q1 of 2015, Google commanded 30.7% of the market compared to iOS at 65.5%.[73] As of May 2024, the worldwide market share for the Android system was 44.58% while the iPad iOS system's market share was 55.23%.[74] Note that by May 2024 for the U.S. market Android and iOS commanded 99.77% of the market share and worldwide the two commanded 99.81% of the market share, effectively making the market for the operating system for tablets a duopoly.[75]

Tablets and TV

In the television world of the future, the tablet computer will actually only play a minor role in the mobile viewing environment. Tablet computers have the capability to deliver high resolution HDTV, UHDTV, and will deliver SHDTV to the viewer anytime (s)he wants to watch, and pretty much anywhere the viewer chooses. Through the tablet computer's ability to deliver a signal via Wi-Fi or mobile phone capability, the tablet can give the viewer the complete freedom to watch her/his favorite program while on the go, or even in the viewer's own home if (s)he is somewhere other than in front of a television set. However, so can the smartphone, which is equal in power and smaller, lighter, and easier to carry. This can be seen in that the number of tablets shipped worldwide has consistently decreased year-over-year since the highs in 2013 and 2014.[76]

Additionally, tablet users are more likely to be highly educated, have higher household incomes, and be in their 30s and 40s or younger.[77,78] These demographic groups will be the force championing the tablet as a television viewing device as the younger generations come into a world dominated by IPTV and the second screen.

Apps and Television

Apps are the driving force of television today and in the future, regardless of the hardware chosen by the viewer. Already, apps such YouTube and YouTube TV, Netflix, and Amazon Instant Video drive television viewing on tablets and smartphones, and apps also drive much of the alternative television program viewing on CTV sets today. Additionally, Comcast, Time Warner, and many of the other cable companies are making it possible for subscribers to watch their favorite programs anywhere through the development of specialized subscriber apps for tablets and smartphones. DirecTV and Dish Network have done the same.[79]

YouTube TV and Hulu+Live TV apps make it possible for viewers to watch streamed television network programs. Even the broadcasters are seeing the benefits of apps for smartphones and tablets. In addition to being on the aggregator platforms, the networks have developed their own apps, for news and sports, and even their own SVOD apps such as Paramount+ and Peacock.

2015 marked the year that the television viewer had the opportunity to experience the beginnings of at least one aspect of 21st century television – app-driven streaming of real-time programming from the networks and the premium cable channels. CBS introduced its "CBS All-Access" streaming service.[80] ABC, NBC, and Fox all followed suit either with new services or expanded services.[81,82,83] HBO – now called "Max" – introduced its "HBO Now" stand-alone service to complement its HBO Go service. HBO Now was (and in its Max version is) for viewers who want a TV Everywhere service without having to subscribe to the cable service along with a TV Everywhere service. HBO Now was first available only for Apple products, then moved to Google's Play Store and to Amazon.[84] Showtime did the same with its "Showtime-Anytime" service.[85] Several of the cable channels such as A&E and USA made their programming available through streaming services as well.[86] While generally denying that they have any plans to drop their affiliates, such moves by the networks, especially, make that next step a likely foregone conclusion. 2015 may well be remembered as the year that linear television began its move from 20th century television to 21st century television.

Local television stations are using apps to drive viewers to their sites, which they have specially designed with text and video content. While the stations originally did not include their local newscasts, they have since included their newscasts in real time along with providing video clips of the major stories of the day – both local and national – as well as weather, sports, and traffic information and reports. As far back as March of 2011, Jacques Natz, director of digital media content at Hearst Television, announced that the day of the deadlines is over. "You have to provide the info on the spot when it happens and mobile is often the way to do it."[87] He was exactly right, and his view has certainly come true.

The Future of Apps

As the television universe continues to change, the app has become the new channel for watching television. Networks, both the broadcast networks and cable networks/channels, will ultimately turn from channel locations to apps to make it easier for viewers to find the programs they want to watch. Currently, every time the viewer travels from one market to another, (s)he must find a television station listing in a hotel room to find out what channel to watch to see his or her favorite program. With the app-delivered television set, the viewer can find that favorite program simply by turning on the set and selecting the correct app. Want to watch an original program on Netflix? Simply select the Netflix app. Prefer to watch the latest episode of *The Chosen?* Choose The Chosen app (yes, there is one.) If *ESPN Sportscenter* is your favorite program to wake up to, simply select the ESPN app on the TV screen. With apps there is no scrolling up and down the television channels looking for that favorite program, which will be especially important once the broadcast networks have dropped their local affiliates and have chosen to deliver their programming directly to the viewer.

In addition to being the new channel selector, apps on television sets in the future will also deliver social media choices so the viewer can interact with friends and others who are viewing the same programming. With the ability to interact directly with their friends, family, and others, the "watercooler effect" moves from happening the next day to happening simultaneously with the viewing of the program. Further, social media apps allow viewers to attend virtual viewing parties with others, even if programming is delivered on-demand. Today, the only way to get social media on your television set is to "cast" it from your mobile phone, tablet, or computer. That will change in the near future.

Today, connected television sets come with at least one web browser app that allows the viewer to access the World Wide Web while watching television. In the near future, (s)he will be able to select her/his preferred browser and load it onto the set. Viewers will be able to check e-mail, take telephone or videophone personal or conference calls through the television set using Voice over Internet Protocol (VoIP) or other services, order a product that is seen on the screen from a local or Internet retail site, check on the baby that is sleeping on the other side of the house, change the thermostat to control the temperature, change the level of the blinds or open or close the drapes – pretty much whatever needs to be done, all while the viewer is watching that favorite program. In that way, the app-driven television set will become one of the focal points, if not the major focal point, of the "connected home" within the Internet of Things (IoT) ecosystem.

The app-driven CTV set is already a staple in viewers homes, with the CTV penetration rate across the U.S. standing at **88%** at the end of 2023.[88] Virtually all of today's set manufacturers include a wide range of apps that allow the viewer to do many of the things listed above. Further, smart TVs also have voice-recognition for turning on the set and adding text where necessary, such as listing a web address in a browser, and movement-recognition for scrolling through and selecting apps.[89] These sets are the vanguard of a revolution that will change the entire way the world interacts with the magnificent technology that is television.

Screens, Screens Everywhere

Today, it seems as if there are televisions everywhere. Not only are they in virtually every home in the U.S. and around the world, but televisions are also in restaurants and bars, airport concourses, covering giant areas on the sides of high-rise office buildings in major cities, even on long-distance airline flights, as well as long-distance buses and trains. Viewers can watch content on their home television sets, as well as their smartphones, tablets, and portable and desktop computers (as has just been discussed).

The future will offer the viewer the luxury of everything being a screen. In the future, not only will all the current television screens be available, but also screens not considered today (except in certain unusual circumstances). Expect in the future for the bathroom mirror to also be a television screen so that the businessperson can prepare for the day physically, but also have the latest news, weather, stock market news, etc. Not only that, but the mirror in the hall, the full-length mirror on the bedroom door, even the windows throughout the home could also serve as screens – even to the point of negating the need for the traditional television screen.[90]

But screens will not be just in viewers' homes and on public transportation. While this book will not explore the development of the autonomous automobile, screens everywhere certainly includes the almost guaranteed car-windows-as-screens scenario. Given that the driver and all others are passengers in the automobile (autonomous, remember!), the need to pass the time becomes more important the longer the travel time and/or distance. The businessperson on the way to the office who has a distant commute or is stuck in rush-hour traffic can pass the time catching up on the events of the day – for example, what the financial markets are doing – or enjoying a tranquil scene to relax her/him instead of having to deal with the tenseness of the morning traffic. Likewise, a person/couple/family needing to travel several hours on the interstate highways to reach her/his/their destination could enjoy watching a movie to pass the time and arrive more relaxed and ready for all the destination has to offer.

The future of screens everywhere is real and will be available to the consumer sooner rather than later.[91]

Future of Second Screen Devices

It is virtually impossible to try to predict where and when we will encounter the next trend in second screen devices because as soon as one makes a future prediction, Google, Apple, or someone else makes that prediction a reality. Nevertheless, here are some ideas regarding what to expect.

Smartphones

In the short run, the smartphones of today will continue to grow in size as the smartphone and tablet come close to merging into a single technology (think Samsung Galaxy Fold) which allows the user to do almost everything (s)he would like to do. Already, smartphones can do many of the things that computers, cameras, and tablets did just a few years ago – the near-future will see the uses increasing significantly.

Longer term, it is possible, and even likely, that smartphones give way first to wearables, and then to some form of tactile-driven device, and, possibly, some form of VR/AR. Smartphones, then, will become quaint artifacts of a previous generation, although the move to wearables was dealt a setback after the failed widespread adoption of Google glasses. Today, the more likely development of wearables that can add to, or (later) replace, the smartphone is seen in the smart watches from Apple, Samsung, LG, and others. It is difficult to put a timeframe on these developments, although AR glasses with phone capabilities are becoming a reality, as both start-ups and established companies, such as Ray-Ban, bring their AR glasses to market.

In the longest term – mid-21st century or later – wearables will likely be replaced by implants under the skin or the side of the head, making the need for any type of device that would function as a mobile phone or, potentially, even a television set obsolete. Such implants would make interacting with holographic television easier or could even allow a person to interact with the content (s)he is watching in the same way that VR users interact in their own VR world, without the need for visuals others can see.[92]

Second, that tablet computers will be a part of the television landscape in the future is not in dispute. What role they will play is the question that will have to be answered. Earlier in the current decade it was thought that tablets would replace laptops, notebooks, ultrabooks, netbooks, desktops, and all other outdated forms of computers. However, given the evolution of the personal computer (non-desktop), the tablet's use in the future may be in question. While the iPad and the Galaxy Tab are still popular to certain groups, the number of tablets shipped worldwide has been steadily decreasing for the last decade.[93] Tablets, when they were first introduced, were alternatives to computers. Today, there are numerous different iterations of hybrid portable computers that can be used as tablets, while still providing the users with a built-in keyboard, touchscreen, and more computing power and alternatives than the tablet can currently offer. Further, as smartphones continue to grow in size, especially with the continuing introduction and improvements to the foldable smartphone (such as the Samsing Galaxy Fold) to the point of rivaling the small tablets, the ability to watch television content on a smartphone will become easier. At that point, there may be little need for the tablet.

Third, apps will continue to deliver all 21st century television programming from the content provider directly to their audiences. Gone will be the days of the television channels, even for those who would "cut the cord" and purchase an antenna; in its place will be the content provider app.

Fourth, VR and AR television will become the screen of choice as a supplement to traditional television for the younger generations and will be the vanguard for the coming holographic-designed, fully lean-forward experience that will be television in the future. Already, demonstrations of what VR technology can offer the viewer – including real-time events – makes real a way of experiencing television that only a few years ago would have been the stuff of daydreams and science fiction. Today's VR and AR developments make it possible to believe that the Enterprise's holodeck can and will be developed and made available sometime in the relatively near future. VR and AR technologies will make it possible for viewers to interact with television programs of the future in ways that will make television a completely immersive experience – if the viewer so chooses that immersive experience. While there is no idea of the time frame for such technology, it will certainly be available to television viewers before the year 2100. Children born in 2010 or later will almost certainly be able to enjoy the total immersive experience of the future of television.

The continual development of second-screen technologies, along with improvements in CTV set technology, will take the television viewer of the future from the passive "lean-back" television viewing of today to an interactive, immersive "lean-forward" television experience that will define the coming television universe.

Notes

1 Perez, Sarah, "Nielsen: Cord Cutting And Internet TV Viewing On The Rise, *Techcrunch*, (February 9, 2012), http://techcrunch.com/2012/02/09/nielsen-cord-cutting-and-internet-tv-viewing-on-the-rise/.
2 Fetto, John, "One Million More Households Became Cord-cutters Last Year," *Experian Marketing Services*, (March 6, 2015), http://www.experian.com/blogs/marketing-forward/2015/03/06/one-million-households-became-cord-cutters-last-year/.
3 "Less Than 50% of US Households Now Subscribe to Pay TV, as Cord-Cutting Jumps More Than Expected," *eMarketer*, (March 7, 2023), https://www.emarketer.com/press-releases/less-than-50-of-us-households-now-subscribe-to-pay-tv-as-cord-cutting-jumps-more-than-expected/.
4 "Less Than 50% of US Households Now Subscribe to Pay TV, as Cord-Cutting Jumps More Than Expected," *eMarketer*.
5 Spangler, Todd, "Cord-Cutting Hits All-Time High in Q1, as U.S. Pay-TV Subscriptions Fall to Lowest Levels Since 1992," *Variety*, (May 12, 2023), https://variety.com/2023/tv/news/cord-cutting-all-time-high-q1-2023-pay-tv-losses-1235610939/.
6 Perez, Sarah, "Diary Of A Cord Cutter In 2015 (Part 3: Using An Over-The-Air DVR)," *TechCrunch*, (February 20, 2015), http://techcrunch.com/2015/02/20/diary-of-a-cord-cutter-in-2015-part-3-using-an-over-the-air-dvr/#.04k2i7:ijSs.
7 "Forget Cord Cutters, Cord shavers Threaten Pay TV," *WSJ VIDEO*, (October 10, 2014), https://www.wsj.com/video/forget-cord-cutters-cord-shavers-threaten-pay-tv/14230C68-B48F-4867-9BDC-B7334CC9492A.

8 Kurz, Phil, "'Cord Shaving' Rather Than Outright 'Cord Cutting' Likely Among Many Cable-TV Broadband Subscribers This Year, Says, Report," *Broadcast Engineering*, (February 22, 2012), http://broadcastengineering.com/ott/Report-cord-shaving-Cable-TV-subscribers-02222012/.
9 Reese, Thomas, "Cord Cutting Statistics 2025 – Market Trends & Latest Data," *evoca.tv*, (June, 20, 2025), https://evoca.tv/cord-cutting-statistics/.
10 Maglio, Tony, "Why Do So Many Millennials Have a TV Antenna?", *IndieWire*, (April 17, 2024), https://www.indiewire.com/news/analysis/who-uses-tv-antenna-study-1234974892/.
11 Maglio, Tony, "Why Do So Many Millennials Have a TV Antenna?".
12 *Encyclopedia of World Biography*, http://www.bookrags.com/biography/charles-f-kettering/.
13 "Charles Kettering Quotes," *SearchQuotes*, http://www.searchquotes.com/quotation/The_opportunities_of_man_are_limited_only_by_his_imagination._But_so_few_have_imagination_that_there/109235/.
14 Best Buy Website, https://www.bestbuy.com/site/searchpage.jsp?id=pcat17071&st=4k+television+sets (retrieved June 26, 2024).
15 Best Buy Website, https://www.bestbuy.com/site/lg-flex-42-class-oled-4k-uhd-smart-webos-tv-with-bendable-design/6525170.p?skuId=6525170, (retrieved June 26, 2024).
16 As mentioned in an earlier chapter, I attended the 2015 CES convention and had the opportunity to witness the demonstrations of 8K television sets by many of the major television set manufacturers.
17 Michael, Andrew, "What Is Ultra High Definition?" *Ultra HDTV*, (May 27, 2015), http://www.ultrahdtv.net/articles/what-is-ultra-hd/.
18 I also have attended numerous National Association of Broadcasters' (NAB) conventions, including the 2014 and 2015 conventions in Las Vegas, NV, where I had the opportunity to witness the NHK exhibition of 8K television.
19 McDonald, Andrew, "8K TV Shipments to Pass 900,000 Units," *TBIvision*, (July 14, 2015), http://tbivision.com/news/2015/07/8k-tv-shipments-pass-900000-units/456791/.
20 McDonald, Andrew, "8K TV Shipments to Pass 900,000 Units," *TBIvision*.
21 McDonald, Andrew, "8K TV Shipments to Pass 900,000 Units," *TBIvision*.
22 Best Buy Website, https://www.bestbuy.com/site/searchpage.jsp?id=pcat17071&st=8k+television+sets, (retrieved, June 26, 2024).
23 Troha, Ryan, "Unveiling CTV Trends, Challenges, and Future Outlooks," *Mindgruve*, (March 25, 2024), https://mindgruve.com/blog/strategy/unveiling-ctv-trends-challenges-and-future-outlooks.
24 Troha, Ryan, "Unveiling CTV Trends, Challenges, and Future Outlooks," *Mindgruve*.
25 For more information and a deep dive into the future of advertising, see Chapter 7: The Future of Television Advertising.
26 Hardesty, Larry, "3-D TV? How About Holographic TV?" *MIT news*, (January 24, 2011), http://web.mit.edu/newsoffice/2011/video-holography-0124.html.
27 Hardesty, Larry, "3-D TV? How About Holographic TV?" *MIT news*.
28 Hardesty, Larry, "3-D TV? How About Holographic TV?" *MIT news*.
29 Welch, Chris, "Beam Me Up, Wolf! CNN Debuts Election-night 'Hologram,'" *CNN Tech*, (November 6, 2008), http://articles.cnn.com/2008-11-06/tech/hologram.yellin_1_hologram-video-cameras-point-and-shoot?_s=PM:TECH.
30 "New Projection-Type Holographic 3D Display Technology Enables Free Design of Display Size, Visual Angle," *AZO Optics*, (October 14, 2016), https://www.azooptics.com/News.aspx?newsID=23021.
31 Press Release, "Realfiction Will Demonstrate LCD, OLED, and microLED Based 3D Display Technology at CES 2024," *Realfiction*, (November 29, 2023), https://view.news.eu.nasdaq.com/view?id=bbd52d7de682f51ce173fe749180e732c&lang=en&src=micro.
32 "Project Echo," *Realfiction*, (n.d.), https://www.realfiction.com/what-is-dpt.

33 See Hatsune Miku "World is Mine" video on YouTube, https://www.youtube.com/watch?v=jhl5afLEKdo.
34 See KDA Performance At The Worlds 2018, https://www.youtube.com/watch?v=POGzo9TKEUw>).
35 https://x.com/portalgraph/status/1895642035803345029.
36 See Chapter 11: Final Thoughts and Future Visions.
37 Woodford, Chris, "Virtual Reality," *ExplainThatStuff!*, (Last updated, May 27, 2015), http://www.explainthatstuff.com/virtualreality.html.
38 "Virtual Reality," *vrs.org.uk*, http://www.vrs.org.uk/virtual-reality/what-is-virtual-reality.html.
39 Woodford, Chris, "Virtual Reality," *ExplainThatStuff!*.
40 Strickland, Jonathan, "How Virtual Reality Works," *howstuffworks*, http://electronics.howstuffworks.com/gadgets/other-gadgets/virtual-reality.htm/printable.
41 "Virtual Reality," *Merriam-Webster Dictionary*, http://www.merriam-webster.com/dictionary/virtual%20reality.
42 Cuthbertson, Anthony, "Forget Reality TV, Virtual Reality TV Is the Future of Broadcast Television," *International Business Times*, (February, 25, 2015), http://www.ibtimes.co.uk/forget-reality-tv-virtual-reality-tv-future-broadcast-television-1489400.
43 McDuling, John, "Forget TV Sets, Apple's Next Big Thing Could Be Virtual Reality," *Quartz*, (May 19, 2015), http://qz.com/407659/is-apple-virtual-reality-going-to-be-a-thing/.
44 Goff, Leslie Jaye, "Virtual Reality TV: Live Via a Headset Near You," *Multichannel News*, (Amrch 26, 2015), http://www.multichannel.com/news/tv-apps/virtual-reality-tv-live-headset-near-you/389210.
45 Cuthbertson, Anthony, "Forget Reality TV, Virtual Reality TV is the Future of Broadcast Television."
46 Sydell, Laura, "Path to Television's Future May Be Paved in Virtual Reality," *NPR – All Things Considered*, (March 10, 2014), http://www.npr.org/2014/03/10/288712948/path-to-televisions-future-may-be-paved-in-virtual-reality.
47 I had a chance to witness these demonstrations at the 2015 NAB convention in Las Vegas in April of that year.
48 Cuthbertson, Anthony, "Forget Reality TV, Virtual Reality TV is the Future of Broadcast Television."
49 3D television was thought to be a serious competitor to the current HDTV. Today, 3D television is not even mentioned other than as an initially failed product.
50 "Augmented Reality," *Mashable*, http://mashable.com/category/augmented-reality/.
51 "Augmented Reality (AR)," *WhatIs.com*, http://whatis.techtarget.com/definition/augmented-reality-AR.
52 "Definition of Augmented Reality," *Financial Times*, http://lexicon.ft.com/Term?term=augmented-reality.
53 Gonzalez, Sandra, "Ads for USA Network's 'Dig' Come to Life Using Augmented Reality," *Mashable*, (February 9, 2015), http://mashable.com/2015/02/09/dig-augmented-reality-ads/.
54 Reed, Brad, "A Brief History of Smartphones," *PCWorld*, (June 18, 2010), http://www.pcworld.com/article/199243/a_brief_history_of_smartphones.html.
55 Reed, Brad, "A Brief History of Smartphones."
56 Reed, Brad, "A Brief History of Smartphones."
57 Reed, Brad, "A Brief History of Smartphones."
58 Snow, Shane, "The History of the iPhone," *Mashable.com*, (June 25, 2010), http://mashable.com/2010/06/25/history-of-the-iphone-infographic/.
59 Snow, Shane, "The History of the iPhone."
60 Howarth, Josh, "iPhone vs Android User Stats (2024 Data)," *Exploding Topics*, (June 14, 2024), https://explodingtopics.com/blog/iphone-android-users.

61 Pao, Pallavi, "Ranked: The Most Popular Smartphone Brands in the U.S.," *Visual Capitalist*, (April 3, 2024), https://www.visualcapitalist.com/charted-americas-preferred-smartphone-brands/.
62 Bashir, Umair, "Tablet Ownership By Brand in the U.S. as of March 2024," *statista*, (May 22, 2024), https://www.statista.com/forecasts/997209/tablet-ownership-by-brand-in-the-us.
63 Laricchia, Federica, "Tablet Shipments Market Share by Vendor Worldwide from 2nd Quarter 2011 to 1st Quarter 2024, *Statista*, (May 17, 2024), https://www.statista.com/statistics/276635/market-share-held-by-tablet-vendors/.
64 Olavsrud, Thor, "Tablet PC: Coming to an Office Near You?", *Datamation*, (November 6, 2002), http://www.datamation.com/netsys/article.php/1495701/Tablet-PC-Coming-to-an-Office-Near-You.htm.
65 Bright, Peter, "Ballmer (and Microsoft) Still Doesn't Get the iPad," *ars technica*, (July 31, 2010), http://arstechnica.com/microsoft/news/2010/07/ballmer-and-microsoft-still-doesnt-get-the-ipad.ars.
66 "iPad Available in US on April 3," *Apple Press Info*, (March 5, 2010), http://www.apple.com/pr/library/2010/03/05iPad-Available-in-US-on-April-3.html.
67 "Apple Launches iPad 2," *Apple Press Info*, (March 2, 2011), http://www.apple.com/pr/library/2011/03/02Apple-Launches-iPad-2.html.
68 "iPad mini," *Apple*, https://www.apple.com/ipad-mini/specs/.
69 Rogerson, James, "iPad mini (2024): Price, Release Date, AI, and Everything You Need to Know," *Techradar*, (October 16, 2024), https://www.techradar.com/news/ipad-mini-2022.
70 Bell, Donald, "Best Android Tablets," *c|net*, (March 19, 2012), http://reviews.cnet.com/best-tablets/best-5-android-tablets?tag=contentBody;page.
71 "Tablet Operating System Market Share United States Of America May 2023 – May 2024," *statcounter*, (May 2024), https://gs.statcounter.com/os-market-share/tablet/united-states-of-america.
72 "Tablet Operating System Market Share United States Of America May 2023 – May 2024," *statcounter*.
73 "Tablet Operating System Market Share Worldwide May 2023 – May 2024," *statcounter*.
74 "Tablet Operating System Market Share Worldwide May 2023 – May 2024," *statcounter*.
75 "Tablet Operating System Market Share Worldwide May 2023 – May 2024," *statcounter*.
76 Laricchia, Federica, "Worldwide Tablet Shipments From 2nd Quarter 2010 to 1st Quarter 2024," *statista*, (May 17, 2024), https://www.statista.com/statistics/272070/global-tablet-shipments-by-quarter/.
77 Pew Research Center, "The Tablet Revolution: Who Tablet users Are," *Journalism.org*, (October 25, 2011), http://www.journalism.org/analysis_report/who_tablet_users_are.
78 Elad, Barry, "Tablet Statistics 2024 – By Website Traffic, Countries, Demographics, Screen Resolution, Provider, Lifespan and Usage," *Coolest-Gadgets*, (January 15, 2024), https://www.coolest-gadgets.com/tablets-statistics.
79 Comcast has its "Xfinity" app; for Time Warner, it is "My TWC" or "TWC TV" apps; for Cablevision it is their "Optimum" app. DirecTV's and Dish Network's apps go by their names. Some companies have apps for all platforms; others are just for the Apple App Store or the Google Play Market; still others are optimized for the iPad only. See the companies' websites for more information.
80 Friedman, Wayne, "CBS All Access Expands to Most of U.S.," *MediaPost*, (June 17, 2015), http://www.mediapost.com/publications/article/254239/cbs-all-access-expands-to-most-of-us.html.
81 Gowan, Michael and Kevin Ohannessian, "How to Watch Live TV Online," *Tom's Guide*, (February 14, 2015), http://www.tomsguide.com/us/watch-live-tv-online,news-17512.html.

82 Banks, Alicia, "NBC Launches Live Streaming Service 'TV Everywhere,'" *The Wrap*, (December 16, 2014), http://www.thewrap.com/nbc-launches-live-streaming-service-tv-everywhere/.
83 "Watch on Fox Now," *Fox*, http://www.fox.com/fox-now.
84 Morran, Chris, "HBO Now Finally Launching on Android," *Consumerist*, (July 16, 2015), http://consumerist.com/2015/07/16/hbo-now-finally-launching-on-android/.
85 Axmaker, Sean, "Showtime Launches a Streaming Service and 'Ex Machina' and 'It Follows' Debut on VOD," *The Spokesman-Review*, (July 17, 2015), http://www.spokesman.com/stories/2015/jul/17/showtime-launches-a-streaming-service-and-ex/.
86 Gowan, Michael and Kevin Ohannessian, "How to Watch Live TV Online."
87 Whitney, Daisy, "Stations' Mobile Apps Showing Promise," *TVNewsCheck*, (March 15, 2011), http://www.tvnewscheck.com/article/2011/03/15/49813/stations-mobile-apps-showing-promise.
88 Stoll, Julia, "Internet-connected TV Penetration Rate in the United States from 2014-2023," *statista*, (June 6, 2023), https://www.statista.com/statistics/294654/connected-tv-penetration-rate-usa/.
89 http://www.samsung.com/us/2012-smart-tv/.
90 See the section on screens in Chapter 11: Final Thoughts and Future Visions.
91 Esser, Ralf and Wanja Alexej Giessen, "Future of Screens: The Screen is Dead, Long Live the Screen!" *Deloitte Center for the Long View*, (n.d.), file:///C:/Users/aycockfa/Downloads/gx-tmt-future-of-screens.pdf.
92 See Brain-Computer Interfaces in "What Type of Electronic Gadgets Will Replace Smartphones in Future?" *Blackview* Blog, (January 30, 2024), https://www.blackview.hk/blog/tech-news/what-will-replace-smartphones.
93 Elad, Barry, "Tablet Statistics 2024 – By Website Traffic, Countries, Demographics, Screen Resolution, Provider, Lifespan and Usage," *Coolest-Gadgets*, (January 15, 2024), https://www.coolest-gadgets.com/tablets-statistics.

6 The Future of Cloud and Artificial Intelligence

The Cloud

The *Oxford Dictionary* defines cloud computing as "the practice of using a network of remote servers hosted to the Internet to store, manage, and process data, rather than a local server or a personal computer."[1] *Dictionary.com's 21st Century Lexicon* defines cloud computing as "a type of computing based on sharing computing resources rather than having local servers or personal devices to handle applications."[2] Considering only the term, "cloud," a good definition for the term is "a metaphor for the Internet (based on how it is depicted in computer network diagrams) and is an abstraction for the complex infrastructure it conceals."[3]

Looking at the definitions of cloud and cloud computing above, there are several important aspects to the cloud.

First, a cloud must be tied to the Internet. Two of the three definitions specifically state the use of the Internet as defining the cloud and cloud computing. One of the definitions of cloud defines it as a metaphor for the Internet itself, a good way of considering the cloud these days.

Second, while *the* cloud at its ultimate may be metaphorical for the Internet, *a* cloud is a subset of the Internet. In other words, there are many clouds that are part of the largest cloud, the Internet itself.

Third, a cloud is restricted to a specific group that can access that particular cloud, but is not necessarily available for everyone to access. While the Internet can be accessed by anyone who has the appropriate technology, the user of a particular cloud has to have an individual way of connecting to it that others cannot use.

Fourth, the source of a cloud *generally* is not local. In other words, it most often is not internally connected within a company, but rather connected externally through the Internet.

Fifth, the specific group of people who are allowed access to a particular cloud can access that cloud from anywhere there is an Internet connection. That access, then, is not limited, except where governments deny the possibility to connect to the Internet. A businessperson from Florida with access to a particular cloud hosted in California can connect to that cloud even if (s)he is in France, Japan, Australia, or anywhere else in the world where that businessperson can connect to the Internet.

DOI: 10.4324/9781003625384-9

Despite the current definitions of the terms "cloud" and "cloud computing," in reality, precursor forms of the cloud have been around for a number of years. Using the definitions in the earlier paragraph, the following are not technically clouds, but are the forerunners of today's clouds.

1. Servers tying together all computers in an organization. An office at a university is connected to a series of servers that the university owns and operates. On one or more of those servers is located the software that a person uses every day, and the different work files that (s)he produces. The person does not have to use a browser to connect and produce her/his work, but, at the same time, the software and work files are not on her/his specific computer. Further, that person is not able to work on her/his files at home or on the road unless (s)he downloads them and cannot upload the files back to the server without being in the office. However, if the organization (s)he works for creates its own private cloud, that person can access her/his work from anywhere using the employer's cloud.
2. A home that has several computers tied to a specific server. Much like the previous example, this one is, technically, not a cloud for the same reasons. There is no need to go to the Internet to connect to the server to access the software and files that are available. While a homeowner might say that (s)he has a private cloud with this arrangement, in reality, it is not a true cloud.

Types of Clouds

Most often known as deployment models, there are three major types of clouds in use today as identified by the National Institute for Standards and Technology (NIST) of the U.S. Department of Commerce (DoC). They are the public cloud, the hybrid cloud, and the private cloud.[4] Each of these types of clouds is designed for specific purposes, and with each one, the sphere of users generally becomes smaller.

The public cloud is designed and implemented for open use by the general public. The public cloud is generally made available to all users interested in making use of the public cloud by a service provider. Often these services are available free of charge, although some are designed as pay-per-use. The public cloud generally exists at the location of the cloud provider.[5] Examples of public clouds today include Microsoft OneDrive, Google Drive, Apple's iCloud, or Amazon's cloud. The public is free to make use of Google Drive, free to join Apple's iCloud, and free to join Amazon's or Microsoft's cloud as well. While a person may have to buy a song or a book to have a use for Apple's and Amazon's cloud services, there are no limitations on who can be a part of either cloud service.

Public clouds have two major benefits – cost savings and business agility. The cost savings include the elimination of capex (capital expenditures), the considerable reduction of opex (operating expenditures), and cost efficiency. The reduction of capex and opex occurs because those costs are turned over to a third-party provider. The cost efficiency exists due to the pay-per-use model of public cloud providers. The pay-per-use model makes it possible for the client organization to plan their expenses when seasonal or other situations increase or decrease the need for cloud storage. Business agility refers to scalability, or the ability to increase and decrease the amount of cloud space needed quickly and efficiently.

While public clouds may be the most cost efficient of the clouds, they have one glaring weakness – security. When an organization places its information on a public cloud, it cedes a significant measure of control to the third-party provider. This situation can lead to a serious lack of transparency that may not be understood by the client organization. In addition, there is always a concern about how good the encryption is that the cloud provider is using. While these concerns seem daunting, in reality, public clouds are used more often than any of the other types of clouds.

The second type of cloud is the hybrid cloud. It is designed as a combination of the two other forms of clouds (public and private). In this structure, each of the two cloud systems remain as unique entities, but they are joined together by standardized or proprietary technology that makes possible data and application portability.[6]

Most often, the hybrid cloud is a combination of public and private cloud. The public/private partnership eliminates or reduces many of the weaknesses of each cloud type, while enhancing the benefits. The hybrid cloud is more cost effective, flexible, and scalable than a private cloud, while providing a much stronger level of security for cloud clients than the public cloud because the more sensitive aspects of the client company can still remain on the private cloud, which is the safest overall of the different cloud types.

Finally, the private cloud is a cloud designed and implemented for exclusive use by a single organization consisting of multiple users within the organization. The private cloud is the most restrictive of the clouds, being available only for those connected with the organization that implemented the cloud. The private cloud can be owned, managed, and operated by the organization itself if it chooses, but can also be owned, managed, and operated by a third-party provider, or by a combination of the organization and the third-party provider jointly. The private cloud can exist within the premises of the organization but does not have to be located there.[7]

Private clouds are by far the most expensive of the different cloud types because all the expenses have to be covered by the organization that owns the cloud. As well as startup hardware and software costs, there are also continuous operating costs – including employees to maintain and operate the cloud on a daily or, at least, regular basis. Due to the expense, private clouds are most often not particularly agile, nor are they easily scalable because the organization generally cannot act swiftly to add additional cloud space if there is a spike in business, and, once purchased, the additional cloud storage can be difficult to reduce should business lessen. However, for that additional expense, the organization gets the most secure cloud type because it controls 100% of the hardware and software and can determine the level of encryption and can tightly control who has access to the cloud.

Cloud Advantages

Using the cloud for storage of data in all forms has a number of advantages over storing data on a local computer or on alternative devices such as CDs, flash drives, or external hard drives.

1 Safety

Storing data on a local computer or on local servers (for an organization) puts that data at risk of being lost due to a hard drive or server crash. Today, there is a whole cloud industry designed specifically to back up data from local sources so that vital, personal, and/or memorable information, photographs, videos, etc., will not be lost in the event of a crash. Companies in this industry charge their customers for continually backing up their hard drives or local servers. Cloud storage units are generally safe from viruses and crashes due to redundancies upon redundancies when it comes to storing data. Should one unit fail, the data are also backed up on additional units for protection against data loss. While organizations can develop redundancies using local servers, the cost of purchasing and maintaining redundancy is extremely high, despite the fact that the cost of servers continues to decline. Costs will be discussed further shortly.

Today, many people choose to store their data not only on their local hard drives, but also on some form of alternative device. Flash drives, external hard drives, and other such devices offer protection to users as backups for data that is stored on a local computer. However, these devices have their issues as well. External hard drives can crash and flash drives can be broken, lost, or stolen. When storing information on these alternative devices, it is generally a good idea to back up the information on several of these devices in case something goes wrong with one or more of them.

When a person's or an organization's information is stored in a cloud, those data are not subject to the types of damages that can occur with external hard drives, flash drives, local servers, and the like. While it can be an annoyance and an extra cost if a notebook computer gets dropped or a car runs over a flash drive, when a businessperson's work is stored on the cloud, it can easily be retrieved from anywhere, unlike a destroyed computer, external hard drive, or flash drive.

Further, clouds are safer because companies offering cloud services design their clouds with layer-upon-layer of security protection, in addition to the redundancies mentioned earlier. While it is always possible for a system to be "hacked" no matter how sophisticated its computer architecture is, cloud-based storage provides the best opportunities for the protection of vital content of all types.

2 Flexibility (Mobility)[8]

As long as a person has a computer and Internet capability, (s)he can access whatever file or information is needed quickly and easily. As long as there is Internet access, businesspersons can access information from home, on the road, from client's offices, or even from a smartphone or tablet. In addition, there is the added flexibility of collaboration among employees on a particular project who could be working together on files and documents even when not physically in the same place. Employees collaborating on a project can view and edit their work from multiple locations, both in the U.S. and abroad.[9] For transnational companies, or companies with partners in other countries, the flexibility of the cloud can be a huge advantage to the success of the business. This same type of flexibility for television today and in the future will become apparent later in the chapter.

3 Portability

In the early days of cloud computing (say, ten years ago or so), portability was considered to be an important advantage because, at that time, the cloud was considered a place for storing content only. Portability was an advantage because the thinking was that while a person or an organization could store content in the cloud – or simply "on the Web" as it was designated then – the usefulness of the content would only be available when that content was downloaded to a local device, whether a computer, a flash drive, external hard drive, etc. The idea of accessing and using that content directly from the cloud was a later consideration.

While the possibility of downloading content from the cloud still exists, in reality, the need for downloading the desired content becomes necessary only when no Internet access will be available at the location where it will be used. As long as Internet access is available, the need for downloading content does not exist. Further, downloading the content to a local device brings into play all the safety concerns mentioned earlier in this section.

4 Cost

The cost of cloud computing can be significantly less than the cost of attempting to operate from a series of local computers or even local servers. Generally speaking, third-party cloud services are designed to provide extensive storage capacity for a monthly fee, which also includes the maintenance of the system. Software can also be stored on the cloud for use by the employees. For small and medium size businesses, a third-party cloud option can be the best choice.

For larger operations, the ability to develop one of the other cloud models (hybrid or private) may be a better option. Start-up costs can be substantial, but long term, the cloud may still be the better choice, given the continual reduction in price of server capacity. Additionally, as mentioned earlier, the cloud provides the most flexibility, especially when employees travel extensively or are located in a variety of places across the U.S. or around the world.

5 Scalability

Scalability is the ability to quickly and efficiently add or remove cloud storage and computing in reaction to the changing conditions of the company. As a company grows, more cloud storage and cloud computing power is needed to keep the company on an upward trajectory. The inability to add additional storage and computing power easily and quickly can limit a company's growth or cause them to miss a window of opportunity when it is available. At the same time, as a company stagnates or begins to decline, or as economic factors worsen, a lack of scalability leaves a company having to pay for storage and computing power it no longer needs. This unused and unneeded storage and computing power can be a further drain on a company's dwindling resources at a time when the company needs to conserve those same resources. Looking at the various cloud types, the public cloud is the most easily scalable, while, on the other end, the private cloud is the least scalable.

6 Green Computing

The use of the cloud is being touted as an environmentally friendly option as it can reduce an organization's carbon emissions significantly.[10] Notably today, they are designed both to reduce the consumption of electricity as well as to reduce the output of emissions that can damage the environment.[11] Many international companies are choosing cloud options today because of the green credentials cloud computing makes available.[12]

The Cloud and Television[13]

Of all the different technologies – both linear and streaming – cloud technology may be the most important technology to the future of television. Cloud technology gives content providers a way of storing their inventory of programming that makes it possible for that inventory to be accessed anywhere, anytime, on any device. Cloud technology gives the content deliverers a way to access these inventories and brings them together in one location so that viewers can easily retrieve and enjoy them. Cloud technology gives viewers a way to enjoy the content providers' inventories using the providers' web sites or television apps on their connected television (CTV) sets, as well as their TV Everywhere devices. Cloud technology is what makes "cloud television" – television today and in the future – possible.

Visualize for a moment television as cloud television. In this scenario, Internet Protocol television (IPTV) is the backbone connecting the viewer with a myriad of television choices in the cloud, or more properly, in a host of clouds, whether by wired connection, Wi-Fi, cellular, or some other types of connections yet to be developed. Through the use of IPTV and cloud television, content providers can reach their audiences with any program or content they desire, anywhere, anytime, and on any platform, whether they are the traditional broadcast and cable/satellite providers; today's alternative providers delivered through set-top boxes (STBs) and over CTV sets using software from Roku, Amazon Fire TV, or others; subscription services such as Netflix, Amazon, and Hulu, among others; advertising-driven video on demand (AVOD) and free ad-supported streaming television (FAST) services like Tubi and Roku and others; or user generated/professional content sites such as YouTube, Facebook, Instagram, and TikTok.

Because the content providers will have their entire inventories of programs and content in the cloud, they will be able to make any episode of any program in that inventory available to the viewer in a perpetual video-on-demand (VOD) format. Gone will be the need for determining which few programs will stay on the air and available for the viewers to watch. Cloud television is a safe, secure, inexpensive, environmentally-friendly way of providing programming to viewers – and providing the viewers with the programs they want to see, when they want to see them, instead of forcing them to watch (or not watch) programs they may not care about, find ridiculous or offensive, or are not in their frames of interest.

Using cloud television, a group of viewers wanting to watch the same *I Love Lucy* episode would simply search for the program on their connected television sets to get the listing of the entire inventory of *Lucy* programs. They would then scroll to the correct episode. Cloud television makes it much easier to watch an episode of a classic television program because the inventory is available on any device connected to the Internet.

The same opportunity to watch a current program holds true as well. Cloud television allows the viewer to watch a current release at a scheduled time – should the content provider schedule the program at a particular time – or to watch the program at some later time. If the program is a live event, the viewer may (or may not) choose to watch the program when it is scheduled. If the program is a scripted one, the viewer can choose when to watch.

For the content deliverer, cloud television makes connecting the content provider with the viewer quick and easy. When all television is in the cloud, programs can be accessed at anytime, anywhere, and on any platform. Whether viewers choose to watch their favorite programs on their big-screen ultra-high definition (UHD) or super-high definition (SHD),[14] 3D holographic[15] television sets, their computers, their tablets, or their smartphones, cloud television makes it easy and simple to watch. Further, viewers can choose to watch their favorite programs anywhere in the world that there is an Internet connection, not just in the country of the program's origin, or a country where the program is telecast.[16]

For viewers, cloud television is the basis for true TV Everywhere. As mentioned in the previous paragraphs, cloud television makes ubiquitous viewing available to anyone as long as there is Internet capability available, whether it is through a wire, through Wi-Fi, through a cellular connection, or through some other form of delivery. Further, combining refined search and promotion[17] with IPTV delivery of programming through apps, makes cloud television the basis for television today and in the future.

Summary

Cloud technology is in a state of rapid development and improvement – it is a technology for both the present and the future. Cloud television, even more than overall cloud computing, is in the relatively early stages of its development. To be sure, cloud technology is increasingly being deployed today by the linear content providers and is in use by the streaming content providers.

Television is made for the cloud and the cloud is made for television. Without the continuing expansion of the use of cloud technology, television will stagnate. Fortunately, that is not happening. Whether it is the networks using cloud technology for archival and retrieval of programming, the local television industry's work with ATSC 3.0,[18] or any of the myriad streaming services available to the consumer at this time, the cloud will be the driving force for television in the future.

However, much more can and will be done with television in the cloud in the future. As the rampant changes in television technology continue to develop and grow, cloud television will play an ever-increasing role in the implementation of 21st century television.

Artificial Intelligence

Today, artificial intelligence (A.I) is impacting every aspect of life and will continue to in the future. IBM defines the term artificial intelligence as "technology that enables computers and machines to simulate human intelligence and problem-solving capabilities."[19] Coursera says A.I. "refers to computer systems capable of performing complex tasks that historically only a human could do, such as reasoning, making decisions, or solving problems."[20] A.I. simulates the intelligence processes of humans using computers. A.I. requires specialized hardware and software for it to work. A.I. works by, first, taking in extremely large amounts of data – specifically, data necessary to produce the output desired – then analyzing the data for the necessary patterns, then using those patterns to produce the requested outcomes. It can serve to automate tasks traditionally done by people more efficiently and accurately, especially those that are repetitive and detail oriented.[21]

A.I. is changing the face of television today and will be a major part of television in the future. The television industry is in the earliest days of using A.I. and, as such, there is both excitement and consternation within the industry. One of the major concerns that was dealt with during the 148-day writers' strike in 2023 was the effect that A.I. would have on writers' livelihoods. The writers got concessions from studios and production houses that require those organizations to disclose to the writers if any material given to the writers has been generated by A.I. Other concessions include that A.I. cannot be credited as a writer, it cannot write or re-write "literary material," nor can A.I. be source material. The 2023 strike is likely to be the first of many such labor battles to come as more and more areas where A.I. can be useful are discovered.[22]

Looking specifically at television, and especially television in the future, A.I. will transform every aspect of the television industries, from production and writing to television journalism and live broadcasts of news, sports, and live events to the highly personalized advertising provided to viewers to increasingly improved content search and promotion to even the equipment (not just sets) that viewers enjoy using for both viewing and experiencing their television programming.[23]

In the area of television production, A.I. is transforming the entire production process – both for good and for not-so-good, depending on where a person is based in the production industry. A.I. has the ability to streamline the production process all the way from writing the scripts to post-production. Using natural language processing algorithms to analyze huge mountains of data, A.I. can develop and produce important insights into current preferences and trends in viewing, making it easier for production houses to develop programs that will appeal either to broad audiences or to specialized niche audiences who hunger for programming on specific topics.[24] In this respect, A.I. will be a major benefit and a crucial component for the development of FAST channels and their success in reaching their desired audiences.

A.I. can also serve as a way to automate repetitive tasks in production. Tasks such as video editing can now, and in the future, be done using A.I.-driven tools that make the task easier and reduce production costs and production time while still maintaining high-quality standards for current and future television programming.[25]

A.I. can also play a major role in content creation, including the ability to develop story ideas and even produce scripts for those ideas. While the idea of content creation using A.I. is still in its infancy, it is a source of great consternation and concern in Hollywood and the major studios and production houses around the country. The writers' strike mentioned earlier shows just how much pressure movie and television scriptwriters are feeling in response to the use of A.I. For instance, Banijay, a French multinational television production and distribution company, and the parent company of Endemol, the Dutch production house responsible for shows such as *Deal or No Deal*, *Big Brother*, and *Peaky Blinders*, among many others, has already developed a fund to back A.I.-created content.[26] When it started the fund in 2023, it said, "While human creativity will always prevail, it's important to work alongside the tools which are available to contribute to the future of ground-breaking entertainment."[27] Eline van Der Velden, the founder and chief executive of Particle 6, a London-based TV production house, is even more bullish on the use of A.I. in television production. To experiment with A.I., she says she gave two versions of a script to a client – one edited by her staff and one edited by Chat GPT. She reported that the client actually preferred the Chap GPT-edited script. Ms. Van Der Velden believes that it will not be long before an A.I.-developed television program will get produced. But she believes that A.I. is a tool and that people will always be needed. She says, "You will still need a creative director, but this is a tool that programme makers should use. It will enable us to reach the next level of our full potential."[28]

In addition to the aforementioned, Fable Studio has launched Showrunner, the world's first A.I. generated streaming service, a service that lets the viewer write, voice, and animate her/his own episodes of a television program.[29] Imagine a future where after the latest episode of a program ends, instead of the viewer waiting for the next episode to air in the coming days or weeks, the viewer simply creates the next episode him/herself – no waiting and it is what the viewer imagines the next episode to be. Or those who were completely dissatisfied with the ending of *Game of Thrones* could use Showrunner or a similar service to write their own ending to the program. Maybe Jon Snow marries Daenerys Targaryen or Jaime Lannister stays with Brienne of Tarth and does not die– it would be possible for every viewer to be satisfied with her/his own final outcome of the show.

In the area of television journalism, trust is the important aspect for acceptance. Will the audience trust a news anchor or news reporters who are A.I. derived? While the news anchors of the major news outlets score high on the trust scale (high, in this case being above 50%[30]), would the same hold true for A.I. generated anchors? Los Angeles-based Channel 1 could be providing some answers to that question. In early 2024 they introduced a streaming TV channel using A.I.-generated news, complete with A.I. anchors and reporters/correspondents. They are not the only ones. Kuwait, Greece, India, Taiwan, and South Korea have all been experimenting with A.I. generated news presenters.[31]

A.I. is also revolutionizing sports broadcasting. A.I. driven camera systems track player movements and provide personalized content about the event for viewers to enjoy. It is improving in-game commentary by providing sports broadcasters with real-time data to use to make their presentations more interesting and authoritative for the viewer. A.I. will also improve the fan's immersion into the sporting event through the use, first, of virtual reality (VR) and augmented reality (AR), and, later, through the development of holographic television. The viewer of the sporting event will have the feel of being part of the action, whether as a fan, or even, in the total immersion situation that holographic television of the future can provide, being a participant in the sport event itself.[32]

A.I. is also having a profound impact on personalized television advertising and search and promotion. In the area of personalized advertising, A.I. is a vital part of aggregated targeted microadvertising, the first step in the three-step process that is the future of television advertising (the process is discussed in the next chapter). A.I. can be used for data gathering and analysis of television viewers, far beyond the demographics information ratings provide, to create a complete understanding of the viewer based on their interests, lifestyle, viewing habits, purchasing history, etc. A.I. can then assist and enhance ad placement through programmatic media-buying and ad delivery through dynamic ad insertion (both also discussed in the next chapter). By including A.I. in the three-step process that is the future of television advertising, content providers can ensure the placement of advertisements in the proper programs, for the appropriate audiences, at optimal times during the day or week. As such, A.I. improves advertising relevance, heightens audience engagement, and significantly enhances overall advertising effectiveness. Users, then, can enjoy a highly personalized advertising experience, making them more likely to engage with advertising specifically designed for them. For advertisers and content providers, A.I. virtually guarantees that advertisers will reach their target audiences more effectively. This effectiveness will lead to higher returns on investment (ROI) and advertising revenue for the content provider.[33]

For search and promotion, A.I. allows the content distributors/over-the-top (OTT) platforms (for example, Netflix, Disney+, Amazon Prime Video, etc.) to analyze their subscribers' preferences, likes, and dislikes to better provide them with recommendations for programs they most likely will be willing and excited to watch. Using A.I., the platforms can use the viewer's preferences and viewing history – including program, genre, time of day, day of week, viewing habits, etc. – to align the platforms' recommendations with each individual viewer to achieve the most effective outcomes. These A.I. recommendation engines empower the platforms to devise a highly captivating and – in the future – highly immersive viewing journey that entices the viewer to look beyond the program being viewed to a broader range of programming that will keep him/her engaged for much longer periods of time.[34]

Future of Artificial Intelligence in Television

As mentioned at the beginning of this section, A.I. is changing the face of television today and will be a major part of television in the future. In the future, A.I. programs, platforms, and even machines (robots) will play major roles in every aspect of television. The continued expansion of A.I. will change the entire industry as more and more programs, advertisements, and promotions will be, in large part, or entirely, designed, scripted, and produced by A.I., and will even star A.I. generated actors that will become widely accepted and enjoyed. Viewers will learn to accept these major changes as normal and commonplace. However, there will still be the need for the human behind the A.I. as the ability to become truly sentient is still in the distant future – though maybe not as distant as believed even in the recent past. It is more likely, for the foreseeable future, that A.I. and humans will work together to bring about the very best television ever seen, viewed, or experienced.

Notes

1. "Cloud Computing," *Oxford Dictionaries*, http://oxforddictionaries.com/definition/cloud+computing.
2. "Cloud Computing," *Dictionary.com*, http://dictionary.reference.com/browse/cloud+computing.
3. "Cloud Computing," *Reference.com*, http://www.reference.com/browse/cloud+computing.
4. Mell, Peter and Timothy Grance, *The NIST Definition of Cloud Computing*, Special Publication 800–145, September 2011, http://csrc.nist.gov/publications/nistpubs/800-145/SP800-145.pdf.
5. Mell, Peter and Timothy Grance, *The NIST Definition of Cloud Computing*.
6. Mell, Peter and Timothy Grance, *The NIST Definition of Cloud Computing*.
7. Mell, Peter and Timothy Grance, *The NIST Definition of Cloud Computing*.
8. These two terms are often used interchangeably. For the purposes of this book, they are used that way. However, for a full explanation of each term and to understand the differences, see Chapter 4: Advantages of the Cloud, in Aycock and Powers (2014), *Television in the Cloud*, Create Space.
9. Arno, Christian, "The Advantages of Using Cloud Computing," *Cloud Computing Journal*, (April 14, 2012), http://cloudcomputing.sys-con.com/node/1792026.
10. Arno, Christian, "The Advantages of Using Cloud Computing."
11. Kumar, Arun, "The Advantages of Cloud Computing," *Bright Hub!*, (May 19, 2011), http://www.brighthub.com/environment/green-computing/articles/10026.aspx.
12. Arno, Christian, "The Advantages of Using Cloud Computing."
13. This chapter provides a general overview of the relationship between television and cloud technology. There is, obviously, much more to say. For a much more in-depth discussion of television and the cloud, see Part II (Chapters 5–10) in Aycock and Powers (2014), *Television in the Cloud*.
14. Ultra-high definition television, also called "4K" television is today's de facto television set. Additionally, there are early generations of 8K super-high definition television sets available for consumer purchase.
15. Holographic television sets are currently in the very early development stage. See the section on Connected TVs in Chapter 5: The Future of Television Viewing.
16. For instance, an American television viewer who is on a business trip to Moscow who wants to watch the latest episode of the *Tonight Show* on NBC, using an app on his

or her tablet, smartphone, or computer, could enjoy the program right in the hotel room, even though the *Tonight Show* may not be available anywhere in Russia.
17 See Chapter 7: The Future of Television Advertising and Chapter 9: The Future of Television Content Search & Promotion.
18 See Chapter 5: The Future of Television Viewing.
19 "What is AI?" *IBM*, (n.d.), https://www.ibm.com/topics/artificial-intelligence.
20 "What Is Artificial Intelligence? Definitions, Uses, and Types," *Coursera*, (updated April 3, 2024), https://www.coursera.org/articles/what-is-artificial-intelligence.
21 Craig, Lev, Nicole Laskowski, and Linda Tucci, "What is Artificial Intelligence (AI)?" *TechTarget*, (n.d.), https://www.techtarget.com/searchenterpriseai/definition/AI-Artificial-Intelligence.
22 Coyle, Jake, "In Hollywood Writers' Battle Against AI, Humans Win (for Now)," *Associated Press*, (September 27, 2023), https://apnews.com/article/hollywood-ai-strike-wga-artificial-intelligence-39ab72582c3a15f77510c9c30a45ffc8.
23 While the topic of A.I. and television is discussed here, the topics in this sentence are all discussed in the various chapters of this book. For instance, advertising is discussed in Chapter 7: The Future of Television Advertising; television sets (and other ways of viewing/experiencing television) were discussed in Chapter 5: The Future of Television Viewing; and search and promotion are discussed in Chapter 9: The Future of Television Content Search & Promotion.
24 Mbatia, David, "Transforming Television: The Impact of AI in TV Content Production," *LinkedIn*, (February 21, 2024), https://www.linkedin.com/pulse/transforming-television-impact-ai-tv-content-david-mbatia-eylkf/.
25 Mbatia, David, "Transforming Television: The Impact of AI in TV Content Production," *LinkedIn*.
26 Power, Stephanie, "Will AI Dream Up the Hit TV Shows of the Future?", *BBC.com*, (May 8, 2024), https://www.bbc.com/news/business-68897555.
27 Power, Stephanie, "Will AI Dream Up the Hit TV Shows of the Future?".
28 Power, Stephanie, "Will AI Dream Up the Hit TV Shows of the Future?".
29 Heritage, Stuart, "A New AI Service Allows Viewers to Create TV Shows. Are We Doomed?", *The Guardian*, (May 31, 2024), https://www.theguardian.com/tv-and-radio/article/2024/may/31/fable-showrunner-ai-tv.
30 Hayden, Erik, "America's Most Trusted News Anchors Are…" *The Hollywood Reporter*, (May 23, 2024), https://www.hollywoodreporter.com/business/business-news/america-most-trusted-news-anchors-1235906257/.
31 Stokel-Walker, Chris, "TV Channels Are Using AI-generated Presenters to Read the News. The Question is, Will We Trust Them?" *BBC.com*, (January 26, 2024), https://www.bbc.com/future/article/20240126-ai-news-anchors-why-audiences-might-find-digitally-generated-tv-presenters-hard-to-trust.
32 Caprari, Ecaterina, "AI in Sports Broadcasting," *Cuez by TinkerList*, (January 4, 2024), https://cuez.app/ai-in-sports-broadcasting/.
33 Team DigitalDefynd, "Use of AI in OTT [10 Examples] [2024]," *DigitalDefynd*, (n.d.), https://digitaldefynd.com/IQ/ai-in-ott/?wsiqAIinSmartTVs.
34 Team DigitalDefynd, "Use of AI in OTT [10 Examples] [2024]."

Part III
The Future of Television Monetization

7 The Future of Television Advertising

Television in the future will be significantly different from today's television. Today's television is – for the most part – little changed from television in the 20th century. In fact, in terms of television advertising, almost nothing has changed since television was first introduced in the 1950s (when television became a household product) except the length of the commercials and the sophistication of the creative aspects of the production (with notable exceptions).[1]

However, as television progresses through the 21st century, from the linear media delivery systems to Internet protocol television (IPTV), video-on-demand (VOD) (and all its subcategories), cloud storage and delivery, the numerous platforms on which television will be available, and even the alternative delivery systems that are on the near horizon (such as ATSC 3.0), television advertising itself must change. No longer can television professionals hope to use the techniques of today to reach the vast and fragmented audiences of television in the future. The antiquated ways and methods of linear media advertising must change, or those media will be replaced, to the detriment of the viewers.

Fortunately, though, ideas about how to advertise to the future television viewer are changing and evolving as new companies develop and make available new tools for monetizing television. While the broadcast media – especially the local stations – are most likely to cling to the traditional, though archaic, forms of advertising delivery, the cable and satellite industries, and even the broadcast networks are looking for ways to monetize their products. Whether it be ATSC 3.0, expansive retransmission consent agreements (which will ultimately disappear), or new structures of television advertising, the linear media continue to look for ways to improve their bottom lines.

As a reminder, since the late 1940s, American viewers have been continually conditioned to accept that television will have commercial breaks. The first official, paid television advertisement (commercial) was run in the United States on July 1, 1941, by the Bulova Watch Company. It was a very simple, understated, and popular advertisement running all of 10 seconds. The advertisement showed the face of a Bulova clock superimposed over a map of the U.S. with a voice-over saying, "America runs on Bulova time." The commercial was run on the New York station WNBT (later WNBC), and was run just before a major league baseball game between the Brooklyn Dodgers and the Philadelphia Phillies.[2]

DOI: 10.4324/9781003625384-11

After World War II, all aspects of the television industry began to grow rapidly as the U.S. moved from a wartime economy to a peacetime economy. Television advertising grew rapidly, as did the number of TV sets and the size of TV audiences. As an example, in 1948 less than one percent of U.S. homes had television sets; by 1952, one out of every three homes had a television. Likewise, in 1949, spending on television advertising was $12.3 million; two years later in 1951, TV ad spend had grown to $128 million, and by 1954, television had become the leading medium for advertising.[3]

Initially, commercials generally ran for one minute at a time. As television advertising progressed and viewer sophistication with television advertising grew, the one-minute spot gave way to the classic 30-second spot, which has dominated the television advertising landscape for most of the industry's history. Even now, the 30-second spot lives on, although – once again, because of increasing viewer sophistication with television advertising – more 20-second and even 15-second spots are airing on programs. It is now possible to tell the advertising story in as little as one-fourth of the time that it took to tell the story when television was young, thanks to the ever-increasing sophistication of both the advertising creative professionals and the viewing public.

Why, then, are television executives, especially broadcasters, so certain that the public will not watch, or watch only a minimum amount of commercials, on television programs viewed over the Internet? After all, the broadcasters and advertising professionals have worked hard and diligently for more than half a century to make sure the viewing public is conditioned to watching numerous commercials every hour. Certainly, viewers conditioned to watching television in the traditional ways will watch television in the same way over the television delivery systems using the Internet.

Fortunately, advertising-driven video-on-demand (AVOD) is beginning to take hold, with Amazon being one of the more recent entrants into the AVOD business with its launch of FreeVee and then its move to making the basic tier of its Instant Video service advertising driven. Amazon joins, among others, Disney+, Tubi, Crackle, Pluto TV, Philo, Xumo, and The Roku Channel.[4] Additionally, the subscription video-on-demand (SVOD) giant, Netflix, has also entered the AVOD space, and in the 18 months its AVOD service has been available, the service has grown to 40 million monthly users.[5]

One advantage AVOD has today is the ability to decide just how long commercials will run during the breaks. While linear television is still wedded to the 15-, 20-, and 30-second commercial, AVOD is loyal to no such tradition. The key is the difference in how linear television and AVOD television are programmed. Linear television, because of its nature, has, since its founding, programmed its offerings according to a schedule throughout its programming day – around 18 hours in the early days and, of course, now 24 hours each day. Each individual program is bracketed by other programs on either side of it. Therefore, each individual program must "fit" into its programming window and end in such a way that the following program can begin at its appointed time – either at the top of the hour or the bottom of the hour (at least in the U.S. – other countries' start and end times differ).

Commercials, then, must fit neatly into the various ad blocks, so traditional-length advertisements work well in this scenario.

AVOD, on the other hand, has no concern for program scheduling, and therefore, no real need for standard ad lengths. While programs may have a number of episodes making up each season, each individual episode is – in a real sense – a standalone. It has no other programs bracketing it, and, being VOD, can be watched at any time. It can be binge-watched with other episodes in one sitting, or it can be watched alone. How long the episode lasts simply does not matter because there is no schedule to have to fit the program into. Therefore, AVOD services are running odd-timed episodes instead of the 30- and 60-minute ones that make up linear media daily schedules. Episodes can run for 46 minutes, or 32 minutes, or an hour and 12 minutes – it just does not matter.

Likewise, AVOD services are running odd-timed commercial spots and are even bringing back the venerable 60-second spot, which, in reality, has not truly been seen since the 1950s and early 1960s when television was young and commercials were still developing. I personally have witnessed advertisements of unusual lengths in AVOD programs, including advertisements that ran for 13 seconds, 26 seconds, 31 seconds, 40 seconds, 45 seconds, and even 60 seconds, including in shows running on mainstream services like Disney+ and Peacock, to say nothing of the other AVOD services. Not needing to fit commercials into neat little time packages gives both the content providers and the advertisers the freedom to develop commercials and the desired creatives that can speak to and connect with their audiences. It also allows advertisers to provide those audiences with all the necessary information they need to make purchasing decisions.

However, even though these services are experimenting with a variety of lengths for their streaming advertisements, unfortunately, they are still using a mass appeal approach to delivering ads, just like linear television has been doing since the beginning of television. They still have not embraced the tremendous value afforded them by the full use of addressable advertising. While a variety of advertisement lengths is a move toward the future of television, there is still much left to do – first, most likely by the AVOD and free ad-supported streaming television (FAST) services, and, then, ultimately by all of television.

So how will advertising work on the television of the future? In reality, it will be more efficient and more effective than on television today. Traditional television advertising has been a shotgun approach – you advertised to the largest number of people and hoped that a reasonable number of viewers responded to the advertisement. If they did, the advertisement was effective. If not, well, you tried something else. While there is always talk about the target audience, the target market, and advertising to specific demographic and psychographic groups, in reality, advertising on television still remains a shotgun approach because it is simply not possible to target more narrowly on traditional over-the-air (OTA), broadcast television.

For cable and direct-to-home (DTH) satellite services, it is easier to target specific groups because so many of the channels are niche-audience focused. However, even on those most niche-oriented channels, targeted advertising is not nearly as specific as it could be. Most cable- and satellite-delivered channels see their viewers as aggregate audiences even if they are more tightly defined, at least on their traditional cable delivery systems. While, say, the History Channel may target history buffs, or ESPN might target football fans in the fall, basketball fans in the winter and early spring, and baseball fans in the summer, those groups are still lumped into single aggregate groups and only rudimentarily broken down any further. Nevertheless, the examples of the niche audiences on cable and satellite TV today begin to demonstrate the possibilities for television in the future. Because the programming is already niche, the advertising can also be niche – but not to the degree television in the future will offer.

Then there is the question of interactivity. Traditional television is simply one-way television. Television advertisements are delivered to the audience with almost no way for the audience to respond directly to the message. The communication is one-way, not two-way. Cable has the ability to deliver interactive, two-way advertising, but, for the most part, it has not done so. Traditionally, cable television channels have taken the same approach that the broadcast television channels have taken – delivering their advertisements in a one-way manner. Whether it is the broadcast channels or the cable-specific channels, one-way advertising – as well as one-way programming to their audiences – is the time-honored tradition. The two-way programming that has occurred on television and more often on cable is in the form of home shopping networks, infomercials, and hard-sell advertisements that request immediate 1-800 telephone call orders, or in the form of certain reality programs where the audience is urged to call, text, or log on to the channel's website to vote for a favorite participant. While these are all – in a sense – interactive, they are poor examples of what is possible with true, interactive television advertising.

Television delivered as Internet protocol television (IPTV) provides a whole new level of advertising possibilities that are either not available, or exceed what is available, currently on linear television. In fact, some have suggested that we could eventually see not only completely interactive television commercials, but also true microadvertisements, or advertisements literally targeted to an individual. The first is certainly possible; the second is, most likely, not economically feasible, because it is not possible to make millions of different commercials to deliver to millions of different viewers on a true one-to-one basis. However, the technology for microadvertising does exist and is available today.[6]

There is, however, an alternate form of advertising using certain aspects of microadvertising, that will be economically feasible as well as extremely desirable. This alternate form of microadvertising will require a three-step process (each step is explained in the coming pages).

In the future, total interactivity will be a mainstay of IPTV. With a click of a remote control or a mouse – or even a voice command, using Amazon's Alexa or Google's Google Home (the two best-known of such systems), or a wave of the hand – viewers will be able to change views of the product, change colors, open windows to provide additional product information, find locations to purchase the product, etc. Additionally, depending on the specific product, interactivity will include the ability to make an immediate purchase, upgrade an existing product, extend warranties, etc. With the connected televisions (CTVs) of today (and even more so in the future where it will be possible to have separate windows on the screen for widgets, chat rooms, websites, etc.) the ability to have total interactivity is available to advertisers. They just have to deliver commercials that have interactive elements in them so that the viewer can make decisions immediately.[7] Such interactivity will provide not only a much richer purchasing environment over the television, resulting in more impulse sales of products and services, but will also provide the advertising agencies and their clients with continuous feedback on the success or failure of their advertising campaign creatives.

What is most important to advertising agencies and their clients, however, is the ability to target much more narrowly their chosen audiences and markets. This ability allows advertising professionals and their clients to have maximum impact with their commercials and maximum success with their campaigns. The idea of narrowly targeting the audience is often referred to as "addressable advertising." Gartner Research defines addressable advertising as:

> technologies [that] enable advertisers to selectively segment TV audiences and serve different ads or ad pods (groups of ads) within a common program or navigation screen. Segmentation can occur at geographic, demographic, behavioral and (in some cases) self-selected individual household levels, through cable, satellite and IPTV delivery systems and set-top boxes (STBs).[8]

Addressable advertising is the way in which television advertising in the future will be delivered and how viewers will receive their advertising. It will be targeted to them, delivered to them with exactly the advertising they want, in the manner in which they want, at the time they want, through the platform they want – anytime, anywhere, anyway.

To accomplish the goals and abilities of addressable advertising, the process will occur in three steps. The first step in the process is *Aggregated Targeted Microadvertising*, or ATMA. This is a term created by myself because at this time there is no descriptive label for this step. Aggregated Targeted Microadvertising provides the mechanism by which audiences are segmented so that each segment can be delivered advertising that is right for them – the proper products and services, the proper creatives, the proper messages, designed for that specific audience segment and delivered in the way most likely to produce a winning response.

The second step in the process is *Programmatic Advertising* (PA), or, more properly, *Programmatic Media Buying*. Programmatic Media Buying takes the audience segmentation results produced using ATMA and first matches the segments with the current programs those segments regularly enjoy. Next, Programmatic Media Buying matches the audience segments with programs that are similar to those current programs both in the past inventory of programs the content provider has available as well as new programs the provider is planning to introduce in the near future. The final step is the purchase of advertising time during those specific programs for each audience segment.

The third step in the process is *Dynamic Ad Insertion* (DAI). According to the Interactive Advertising Bureau, DAI is:

> The process by which an ad is inserted into a page in response to a user's request.... At its simplest, Dynamic Ad Placement allows for multiple ads to be rotated through one or more spaces. In more sophisticated examples, the ad placement could be affected by demographic data or usage history for the current user.[9]

The Interactive Television Institute's *itv dictionary* says about DAI, "With dynamic ad insertion, network operators can provide targeted ads that can be swapped in and out of that television program as it's delivered to the enduser."[10] In terms of use, development, and understanding, DAI is currently the best known and understood, while ATMA is the least understood and in its most nascent development, with PA being somewhere in between. Each of these three steps in a successful addressable advertising process is discussed in much more detail later in this chapter.

Aggregated Targeted Microadvertising

ATMA is the first step in producing advertising for television in the future. In ATMA, the key word is "aggregated." ATMA can be defined as "the process of determining large subset groups of an audience for any particular television program, based on numerous specific characteristics that are inherent in every member of the subset, then developing an ad or a series of ads tailored to meet the needs and desires of each particular subset."[11] Given that, during each television program more than one subset is likely to be identified, an advertisement for any particular subset would be specific to that subset, with a different advertisement being delivered to each subset. The result is that the total number of advertisements running in each commercial time period will equal the total number of viewer subsets watching the program.

I chose the phrase ATMA because at this time there is no one term generally accepted by the television or advertising industries for this first step in the addressable advertising process.[12] Today, television professionals use (or, rather, misuse) the term DAI to describe what DAI actually covers as well as ATMA. I, however, more correctly separate the two terms and add Programmatic Advertising/Media Buying as its own term, using each of the three terms to identify the correct function for each step in the whole addressable advertising process.

How Aggregated Targeted Microadvertising Works

As mentioned earlier, the key word in ATMA is "aggregated." For any program there are multiple subsets of viewers in the audience who are different from each other in certain aspects and alike in others, but who intersect at the program. To begin the ATMA process, the various subsets of the audience watching the program who are interested in a particular product are segmented from each other by their demographic and psychographic details, along with all the additional information gleaned from their purchasing patterns, their geographic locations, their social media use and habits – in essence, any information that allows the advertiser to understand as fully as possible what is needed to reach each subset successfully. Each of these subsets is studied carefully to determine those aspects of the product and commercial creatives that are successful at connecting with the subset members and are the most likely to be persuasive for that subset.

Once the agency has developed those creative aspects that will make each subset highly likely to identify with, and be persuaded by, a particular type of commercial, the advertising agency then produces a variety of different commercials, with the number of commercials that must be made being dependent on the makeup of the subset. Each commercial need not be completely new and different from all the others. Quite possibly, the differences will be as slight as the person selected as the spokesperson for the product. In one advertisement, a young woman might be featured; in another, a young man. A third advertisement might have an older woman; and a fourth, an older man. A fifth might have a couple; the sixth, a family. Other slight changes could be the race, the ethnicity, or the lifestyle preference of the spokesperson(s). Depending on the specific subset, the setting might also change. One commercial might be set at a sporting event; another might be at a picnic; a third might be set at a concert. Additionally, because products almost always have at least one secondary target audience, the selection of the individual might appeal to the primary target audience subset, while the setting could appeal to a secondary audience subset, or, possibly, the other way around, depending on which aspect would be the most powerful for reaching the primary target audience subset. The research (discussed later in the chapter) would be designed to let the advertiser know what choice(s) would be most likely to be successful.

Even though the costs of production would likely be higher than for today's advertisements, the ability to reach the target audience with advertisements that will have a very high degree of acceptance and response by the members of each particular audience subset will more than make up for the extra costs associated with the creation of multiple advertisements. Even the youngest of viewers choose to watch advertisements that appeal to them – ones that have their favorite products; their favorite stars and spokespersons (from the worlds of sports, music, film, etc.,). In addition, in each case, there will likely be one or more scenarios that appeal to each of the particular groups of that target audience subset. Combining these two elements with others learned about through the research makes each commercial a powerful delivery mechanism for a product.

Additional subsets of viewers watching the same program at the same time, but who are not interested in the product, will be receiving advertisements for their preferred products, with the creatives that will be most successful. In that way, content providers will be able to sell the same timeslot multiple times to different advertisers, each reaching the audience subset they desire. The resulting revenue from the numerous simultaneously sold commercials for each timeslot will more than equal the amount of today's one-ad-for-one-timeslot commercial delivery for television.

Reaching the Future Television Viewer

An important consideration is how the advertiser will know what type of advertisement each viewer will like. One of the advantages of television in the future will be the ability to track the audience in detail. Much as today, and even more so in the future, the viewer will go to the connected TV content provider site of the program (s)he wishes to watch. Every time the viewer watches a particular program on the content provider's site, that information will be stored automatically by the content provider for future use. The first time the viewer goes to that particular site, a computerized profile will be set up for the viewer. That profile can be kept both on the connected TV's platform as well as on the content provider's site. As the viewer continues to watch programs on the site, additional information will be added both to the platform's and to the provider's profiles of the viewer. When the viewer changes content providers to select a different program, the connected TV platform will add that information to the viewer's profile. This information can be passed along (or sold) among the various content providers to further provide a more complete picture of the programming the viewer enjoys. As the profile of the viewer becomes more and more detailed, the content provider would be able to deliver suggestions to the viewer for new or different programs that fit with the viewer's profile.

Because the content providers have a number of programs that are similar, even from the initial selection of a program from the inventory of programs, the content provider will be able to begin the recommendation process. Just as Amazon provides recommendations for virtually any product that a shopper might show an interest in, the content provider will be able to do the same for programs. This form of "push" programming will drive viewers to watch more programs that appeal to them, exposing them to more and more commercials that have been selected for them based on their ever-growing profiles.

A second way the profile of the viewer will be built is through social networking.[13] As an example, already, content providers have Facebook fan pages. These Facebook fan pages encourage their fans to post about the programs they are watching and to get their Facebook friends to "like" the content provider's Facebook page. Further, because Facebook friends can observe the profiles of their friends, the content provider is able to learn much about the fan by checking the fan's profile page. Such additional information allows the network to further refine the profile of the fan and to be able to better target the fan with both programs and advertisements that (s)he would be interested in watching. For fans who were already viewers of the content provider, the profile pages would be additional information used to better develop a more complete and thorough profile of the viewer.

As viewers engage with Facebook fan pages, the content provider collects more data about each individual fan, giving the content provider more information with which to build the profile of the fan and deepening and enriching the fan's profile,. Ultimately, the content provider will have such an in-depth understanding of the fan that it will be able to drive programming and advertising to her/him that the content provider can be virtually certain the fan will watch. The fan then becomes a viewer and a consumer of the advertising on those programs.

While all this is occurring on Facebook, the same is being done on X, Instagram, Snapchat, and all the other social networking websites available to the consumer. Every X tweet provides information about the viewer. Every status change on any of the social network sites provides additional information about the person who posted the information. Social media is one of the most powerful forces available to the television content provider in understanding the viewer as well as the potential viewer, and in developing a rich enough profile of each viewer to allow the content provider to deliver the exact programming and advertisements that will be effective in capturing and holding the attention of the viewer.

An additional way that content providers and platforms, for that matter, can enrich the depth and complexity of the viewer's profile is through the purchase of affinity card data. Grocers, retailers, restaurants – pretty much any retail company today – has some type of affinity card program that records when a purchase is made and what that purchase is, and how often and when that viewer users that affinity program. By purchasing the data (or even bartering for the data sets), the content provider, the advertiser or its agency, and even the connected TV platform can build a rich and complex profile of the viewer.

So where does this leave advertising going forward? By developing such a rich and in-depth profile of each viewer, the content provider can then offer those viewers to advertisers with a virtual certainty that they can match advertiser and viewer together. With such rich metadata, the ability to provide advertisements that elicit positive responses from the viewer can be virtually assured. It is important to remember that John Wanamaker, the great Philadelphia retailer of the turn of the 20th Century, said, "Half the money I spend on advertising is wasted; the trouble is I don't know which half."[14] That has been the traditional thinking of advertising.

In the future, Wanamaker's phrase will never again hold meaning, except as a whimsical historical comment from the ancients. With the ability to target advertising so carefully, and to understand the viewer so completely, a better phrase from the viewer's perspective will be "I don't like to watch advertisements, but I do like to watch advertisements that I like." By providing the viewer with advertisements that (s)he likes to watch, and only those advertisements, the likelihood of the advertisement being watched and watched with interest is almost virtually assured. Because an advertisement watched with interest is an advertisement that builds desire and calls for the viewer to take some action, television advertising in the future will be delivered to an audience that is ready, willing, and eager to receive it, making the advertising extremely likely to be effective. From the advertiser's point of view, television of the future will allow them the opportunity to alter Wanamaker's famous phrase to "Half of my advertising may be wasted, but I know for certain it isn't my television advertising."

At this point, a question might be who would be willing to part with the amount of information it would seem to take to produce a viable ATMA system of advertising. According to the Pew Research Center report on "The Future of the Internet – 2010," the title of one portion of the larger research study says it all: "Millennials will make online sharing in networks a lifelong habit."[15] In the report, researchers surveyed 895 experts in a non-random survey designed to gather the thoughts of those who were most likely to have informed opinions. In response to the question about how the willingness of Generation Y/Millennials[16] to share information might change as they age, 69% of the 895 expert responders agreed with the following statement.

> By 2020, members of Generation Y (today's "digital natives") [Generation Y has been renamed the Millennial Generation – the term Generation Y is an older term] will continue to be ambient broadcasters who disclose a great deal of personal information in order to stay connected and take advantage of social, economic, and political opportunities. Even as they mature, have families, and take on more significant responsibilities, their enthusiasm for widespread information sharing will carry forward.[17]

By contrast, only 28% disagreed with the statement, with 3% not responding to the question.[18]

More recent research studies and other experts agree with the Pew study. Elaine B. Coleman, the managing director in 2012 and 2013 of Media & Emerging Technologies for Bovitz, Inc., says:

> Millennials think differently when it comes to online privacy. It's not that they don't care about it – rather they perceive social media as an exchange or economy of ideas, where sharing involves participating in smart ways. Millennials say, 'I'll give up some personal information if I get something in return.'[19]

Jeffrey I. Cole, director of the Annenberg Center for the Digital Future at the University of Southern California, is more straightforward about the subject:

> Online privacy is dead – Millennials understand that, while older users have not adapted. Millennials recognize that giving up some of their privacy online can provide benefits for them. This demonstrates a major shift in online behavior – there's no going back.[20]

Further, in more recent Deloitte studies on television, young viewers consistently show a willingness to surrender some or all of their privacy in exchange for information and opportunities. You really have to look no further than your own children's and their friends' social media pages to realize instinctively that, for young people, being social is most important, with other considerations coming in second, third, fourth, etc.

If the results of the Pew Research and other studies are correct (and given the work of the Pew Research Center and USC Annenberg over the years, it is reasonable to assume they are likely to be close), then the information necessary for ATMA will easily be within the grasp of content providers and advertisers through the various means described earlier in this chapter.

Programmatic Advertising

PA (or Programmatic Media Buying) is the ability to use computer programs to determine what people watch, when they watch, where they watch, what content providers they watch, etc., and then establish "buy" opportunities on programs specifically aimed at the audiences most likely to be interested in the products of specific advertisers. PA, in general, can be defined as "the use of software to purchase digital advertising, as opposed to the traditional process that involves requests for proposals (RFPs), human negotiations, and manual insertion orders."[21] As such, PA is the second step in the process that will be television advertising of the future. It takes the information and profiles developed by ATMA and matches the profiles to programs that those people watch.

PA is computer driven. It uses highly specialized computer software to determine trends in audience viewing that make it possible for agencies and buyers to purchase advertising more successfully. PA software is used in much the same way that computer software is used in brokerage houses to spot trends and allow traders to make stock trades more successfully. The advantage of PA and its software is that it makes it possible to match advertisers directly to their most likely consumers and the programs they watch. No longer is there a need to focus on ratings and the overall popularity of a program to determine where to place advertising. PA is and will be used to match the advertiser with the specific programs that her/his consumers watch, regardless of the overall popularity of the program. In this way, PA makes it possible for an advertiser to expect every advertisement that (s)he runs to be highly successful in driving the consumers most likely to purchase the product to find out more about it and to make purchases, either through an impulse buy right on the screen or a purchase in-store or online. For the content provider, every advertising time slot becomes a "premium" slot, with the possibility (or more likely, virtual guarantee) of selling each spot for a higher price than a traditional ad buy would cost.

Traditionally, and still today, ratings and shares drive the advertising world. Ratings, gathered at various times, provide the starting point for determining where to place ads to reach viewers. Ratings data only include information about the program watched, the number of males who watch the program, the number of females who watch the program, and a specific set of age categories of viewers (for example: males 18–49, females 25–54, children 2–10). The numbers are then compared to the population of the market as a whole. For the share, the same numbers can also be compared to the number of people in the market who actually had their TV sets turned on to any program at that time.

Based on the rating and the share of a program, the content provider will set a price for an advertisement, depending on the time length. The larger the rating and the share, the more the content provider can charge for the advertisement. Notice, the only information the ratings data provide are the overall number of the viewers watching the program, and how the numbers data break down among males and females and a handful of age categories. On that information alone, advertisers have been taking a "shotgun approach" to placing ads on content providers' programming, hoping to successfully reach 15–20% of the program's audience. The traditional mantra has been that you "sell on your quantity or on your quality." That means that if the ratings are large, boast about your overall rating and share. If the ratings are small, then find your largest audience and sell that group to advertisers.

Throughout the history of television (and radio before it) the following have taken place.

- Programs have stayed on the air or been cancelled, depending on how the ratings were for that program over time. Today, that time frame can be as short as just a few weeks, given that weekly ratings of all programs aired each week are available to the content providers.
- Program schedules have been changed, including moving successful programs to other days and time slots to bolster or serve as an anchor program for a weak ratings night (almost always to the detriment of that successful program).
- Advertisers have paid billions to purchase airtime on television programs, with little chance for large rewards given the shotgun approach to television advertising. However, when the shotgun approach is the only option, advertisers learn to live with the results and find ways to justify their actions.

In the future this will seem silly. That is why PA is so important. More specifically, programmatic television advertising is "the data-driven automation of audience-based advertising transactions. It inverts the industry standard, in which marketers rely on show ratings to determine desirable audiences for their ads. Instead, with programmatic tech, marketers use audience data to pipe advertising to optimal places."[22] Eric Blattburg writes that PA provides more specificity. He says, "Rather than relying on ratings for specific shows or channels, marketers can use programmatic tech to reach a more specific subset of consumers, like men with a $50,000 income who own an Android device."[23] Blattburg goes on to say, "They [marketers] don't care if that ad shows up on *X Factor* or *X Games*, as long as the target audience is watching."[24] Sound familiar?

Let us look more closely at the definition of PA (which says that it is "data-driven automation of audience-based advertising transactions" that "inverts the industry standard") and break it down into its individual parts.

- Data-driven: With PA there is so much more information to consider than just the ratings data. All the data gathered through ATMA can be used to make

decisions in PA. ATMA provides the data profiles of viewers and PA uses that data to determine the best matches in terms of programs.
- Automation: The decisions are automated; all the data are loaded into the software package, and it does the matching.
- Audience-based advertising transactions: Just like with ATMA, note that the unit of focus is the viewer, not the program. Traditionally, the focus has been on the program and matching the advertisement to the viewer through the program. PA changes the dynamic.
- Inverts the industry standard: This is what is so hard for traditionalists. PA changes the whole way advertisers and content providers have been doing business. Instead of relying on "show ratings to determine desirable audiences for their ads," the determination is made through ATMA data, of which show ratings are a miniscule part.

Artificial Intelligence and Programmatic Advertising[25]

Programmatic ad buying is the process of using software to buy digital advertisements. Instead of going through human negotiations and manually inserting orders for advertisements on digital platforms like Google and Facebook, media buyers use software to go through an auction-based process to have their advertisements served in a network of their choice.

Buyers use big data to target their most valuable customers by segmenting their audience through characteristics like age, gender, and region, among others. They go, then, through an auction process and decide whether they will pay the price an ad slot is worth at the moment to have their ad seen by this specific audience.

Programmatic ad buying reduces costs and improves brand performance in the advertising industry. This technology is now getting an upgrade and advertising software is becoming smarter due to artificial intelligence (A.I).

A.I. is the concept of replicating human intelligence in machines so they can perform activities that would require the human brain to be involved, such as making data-based decisions. This is accomplished by the use of machine learning, which is a type of A.I. that provides computers with the ability to learn things by being programmed specifically to certain tasks, improving its knowledge over time the same way the human brain does. As such, it focuses on mimicking our own decision-making methods by training a machine to use data to learn more about how to perform a task. In terms of advertising, machine learning algorithms can analyze data and draw conclusions from it, so that it operates similarly to an experienced buyer and becomes capable of diagnosing, predicting and planning. Additionally, for advertising purposes, you can use a form of machine learning called "deep learning" to combine different factors to draw conclusions from them and learn, for example, how people who live in a particular region, are of a specific age, and like folk music are more likely to buy sports clothing.

A.I.-powered systems help companies save money by working at a faster speed than humans beings and with less potential errors. If you apply this technology to the advertising industry, you bring efficiency to the media buying process, freeing media buyers from tedious work and allowing them to focus on strategic and creative tasks.

How Does Artificial Intelligence Tie to Programmatic Advertising?[26]

PA is the automated process of buying and selling ad inventory through an exchange, connecting advertisers to publishers. This process uses A.I. and real-time bidding for inventory across all channels. A.I. can analyze the complexity of media buying via programmatic in a way that is not humanly possible or not possible by human media buyers and planners.

A.I. gives marketers the ability to take control of their data to achieve the results they are looking for. It gives them the power to optimize their digital marketing campaigns pre-bid. They can determine exactly where they should place their bid, how much they should bid, and when they should bid – all before they even place the bid. The goal is to help them monetize their campaigns and deliver the best possible return on investment.

The purpose of A.I. is to take the massive amount of consumer data that is collected, and analyze the information it contains about consumer demographics, interests, and purchasing preferences. Marketers then use this analysis to determine the right audience for an advertisement so they can create more focused and targeted ads, which leads to better campaign results. This is especially helpful in video ad campaigns, where the proper placement and timing of the advertisement is a critical aspect of a campaign's success.

A.I. and predictive modeling techniques boost campaign effectiveness by accelerating the decision-making process in terms of determining which advertisement should be delivered to which user, what type of format should be used, and the best time to deliver it.

Benefits and Challenges

In terms of benefits, A.I. can increase marketers' knowledge and understanding of consumer behavior in ways that were never possible before, making for more relevant, cost-effective, and optimal advertising. A.I. can process and analyze the quantity and complexity of big data in a way that has not been possible before. The result is marketing on a scale that has never been imagined, let alone achieved.

A.I. delivers better advertising campaign control because it employs more quantified and automated strategies. These strategies can be used to improve the customer's shopping experience, to test advertising campaigns, and to make campaign bidding decisions more cost-efficient. The main challenge with A.I. is having the technology predict the right action, in context. Algorithms need to work seamlessly to make decisions in real time. Not every organization has the resources to build these capabilities. Getting from the theoretical to reality is a challenge that not all companies are prepared for. It is also an issue of personnel. The motivation for a company to become fully automated is often questioned by workers who fear what that might mean for their job security.

Dynamic Ad Insertion

DAI is the third step in the process for delivering television advertising now and into the future. DAI can be defined as the ability to simultaneously insert different ads into different video streams, for different viewers. It is the end result of addressable advertising.

History of Dynamic Ad Insertion

Of the three steps in the process, DAI is the oldest. The forerunner of DAI goes back to the 1930s when magazines would use "split-run" advertising for research. A magazine would choose a few test markets and run an advertisement for a product to half the subscribers, and a different advertisement to the other half. The more popular of the two would then be used nationwide.

Post-1975, when cable had begun to flourish as an alternative to OTA television, cable companies also began using split-run advertising on a limited basis, again for research purposes.

The process would be the same – half the subscribers got one advertisement; the other half got a different one. The more popular one would then be used nationwide. In both cases, the use of the split-run was for research purposes, not for directing advertising toward different audiences.

The first real discussions and attempts to use DAI came in the mid-to-late 1990s, when radio stations first began streaming their signals over the World Wide Web. Numerous small start-up companies specializing in various forms of DAI – some simple and others more complex – began to make DAI available to the terrestrial radio stations and the Internet-only stations that were also beginning. For those start-ups, the world came crashing down when, in the U.S., the Federal Communications Commission (FCC), responding to the pressure of the music industry, ruled that each stream was a separate program and could be charged copyright royalties. So, if a station had 50,000 listeners to its streaming program, according to the FCC, the music industry could demand payment as if the station was broadcasting 50,000 different programs simultaneously.

The costs were more than stations could afford, so stations shut down their streaming services, making DAI advertising useless. Virtually every early DAI company went out of business.

Dynamic Ad Insertion Today

Today, the DAI industry has recovered from the situation of the 1990s but has not yet reached its full potential. Only in the past decade or so have content providers started streaming their programming to audiences, and, initially, only on a delayed basis. Further, the linear media companies continue to be reticent toward moving significant portions of their programming to their streaming platforms (using only the streaming channels to reach audiences who are cord-cutters or cord-nevers and who choose not to have OTA antennas), fearing that to do so might reduce the viewership of traditional television. Additionally, in the U.S., the content providers receive billions of dollars each year from the cable and satellite companies for the right to carry their programming – money which would go away with the move to all streaming. Also, there is still the belief – at least among some of the most traditional of linear broadcast professionals – that people will not watch commercials if they watch programming on the Internet, or at least not enough advertisements to make it worthwhile to give up their traditional methods. As such, the DAI industry is still in its relatively early stages, waiting for the time when the content providers finally move to all-IPTV and their industry begins to flourish.

Where DAI is and will be most effective is in CTV and video-on-demand (VOD), which, of course, are the ways television will be delivered in the future. That fact suggests a dynamic future for DAI.

There are two ways in which ads can be inserted into television streams – from the server side and from the client side. Server-side ad insertion (SSAI) is a technology that allows ads to be inserted into a video stream before that stream goes to the viewer's television set (or other device such as the smartphone, computer, etc.) It is generally the more popular way of placing ads in a connected or over-the-top (OTT) STB environment and is generally more efficient than client-side ad insertion.[27]

Client-side ad insertion (CSAI) is a technology that, unlike SSAI, moves the insertion-process to the client side, which means that it takes place on the viewer's device (TV, smartphone, etc.) instead of originating on the server that delivers the content. CSAI makes it possible for more flexibility in ad formats and enriched personalization.[28]

Future of Television Advertising Using the Three-Step Process

VOD has become a popular platform not only for consumers but also among television networks, advertisers, and cable service providers for its ability to be measured and therefore monetized. It has created the right atmosphere for new advertising opportunities in the non-traditional television world to take off. As such, VOD has created the ability for television advertising to expand beyond the traditional approaches of yesterday and today and embrace the new future of television advertising described in this chapter. It is now up to the content providers to make that change or suffer the consequences of continual shrinkage of their revenues. The future of television is change, not stasis. Television content providers must begin to embrace that change. Addressable television advertising that reaches the viewers where they are on whatever streaming platforms they may be using at any given time is the direction television advertising must move toward. That simply cannot be accomplished without embracing the three-step process of ATMA-PA-DAI.

Let us look at the various benefits that can be reaped through using this ATMA-PA-DAI process.

1   **Each individual advertisement reaches a smaller, more narrowly focused group of people than traditional advertisements.**

    Addressable advertising is used to segment the audience. Once the first two steps – ATMA and PA – have been completed and the audience for a given show and its accompanying ad time have been segmented, DAI places the appropriate advertising messages to reach every segment of the audience. As such, each segment is smaller, but more directly reachable with specific advertisements than if the whole audience were watching the same commercials during any given commercial time slot.

2. **By targeting the viewer with an advertisement for the desired product in the desired way, the advertisement can have a much higher success rate of both attention and engagement.**

    Today's television markets' ad time is designed to reach the entire audience during each commercial time slot. That is not cost-effective. In a recent study at the University of Chicago, researchers found that traditional television advertising is no longer worth the costs. The researchers found that, with traditional television advertising, companies had to double their number of television advertisements to increase sales by only 1%. Further, the results showed that return on investment (ROI) was negative for more than 80% of the 288 products studied in the research.[29]

    By segmenting audiences through the in-depth analytics of ATMA, matching those segments with the programs and advertisements that will most appeal to them using PA, and inserting those ads into the streams of those programs for those audience segments using DAI, each member of the audience only sees advertisements specifically designed and chosen for her/him. By providing each viewer with advertisements for products and services that are of most interest to that viewer, the likelihood of a successful ad increases dramatically. Additionally, because advertisements can be embedded with a QR code or even a direct link, the viewer has the opportunity to immediately click on the product during the advertisement and make an impulse buy, thus adding to the success of the commercial.

3. **Because the product is something the viewer is interested in, (s)he will almost always watch the complete commercial, leading to a high success rate.**

    As has been pointed out, viewers hate commercials except for the commercials they like. If, through the three-step process of ATMA, PA, and DAI, the viewer is being exposed to those things that (s)he likes, the viewer is virtually guaranteed both to watch the commercial and to engage with the commercial in a positive way. In fact, when DAI first begins providing the commercials for viewers that ATMA and PA have planned, the viewers will most likely be so happy and amazed that it appears someone is actually listening to them that the success rates of those advertisements will be close to 100%.

4. **Because of the high success rate, content providers can charge a "premium" on each advertisement (each one is more expensive).**

    Granted, each advertisement for each of the various segments of the viewing audience for a program will be delivered to a smaller – possibly significantly smaller – audience compared to today's "shotgun blast" commercials. However, for the advertiser, that will mean the advertisement is no longer falling on "deaf ears," those people for whom it has no relevance or cannot influence for whatever reason. Instead, the advertiser will be reaching only those viewers who are her/his most likely customers or potential customers. To be able to reach those customers and not have to waste money on all the non-customers, the advertiser will happily pay a premium for the advertisement. While any one commercial for any one advertiser will not equal the full price of today's "shotgun" commercial, the ability for the content provider to stream multiple commercials to multiple segments of the audience simultaneously during each commercial slot will far exceed the value of one of the "shotgun" advertisements that airs today.

5   **Advertisements in streams cannot be skipped by the viewer.**

Today's advertising on television allows the viewer numerous ways to ignore the commercials. Using the ATMA-PA-DAI process, the fact that the advertisement cannot be skipped requires the viewer to watch the ad (or ignore it) at real-time speed. The viewer can still leave the room or multitask while the advertisement is playing, but using the three-step process of addressable advertising will make the advertising so enticing that the desire to ignore or skip the advertisement will be eliminated, or, at worst, reduced significantly. When the viewer is offered an advertisement that is for a preferred product or service, delivered with the right creatives, in the way the viewer prefers, on the platform of the viewer's choosing, the viewer is going to watch and enjoy it. Further, by making it possible for the viewer to click on and immediately go to the website of the product virtually assures the advertiser numerous impulse buys.

6   **The ads can be used throughout all the viewers' choices. Remember, it doesn't matter the program; it's the individual that is important.**

For television in the future, the viewer is in charge – (s)he selects the program, the time of watching, the location for watching, and the platform for watching. By being in charge, the viewer makes it clear which programs (s)he prefers and chooses to watch, and the content provider as well as the advertiser knows this information. Most likely, as people do today, the viewer will compile a list of the programs (s)he wants to watch during a certain time period (day, week, etc.) on his/her connected, smart television sets. Further, the viewer may also set aside time to watch programs according to her/his schedule or fall into a regular viewing pattern, reflecting when (s)he prefers to watch. That information will also be on their television sets and will be known to the content producer and the advertiser. (I use the television set as an example, but the schedule could just as easily be on a computer, tablet, or smartphone. The information will have to be shared with the content provider and the platform connected to the provider when watching the chosen show.) Regardless of what the program is or when, where, and what platform it is watched on, the advertising will be available because the ad inventory will be keyed to the individual viewer through the repeated choices made by the viewer. No matter what program the viewer chooses to watch, the correct ads will be sent to her/him for viewing and enjoyment.

7   **Advertisements can be completely interactive.**

Because IPTV is interactive, advertisements also can be interactive. While the interactive nature is discussed more fully in the following chapter, which is on product placement, it does deserve mention here as well. Advertisements on television in the future (as well as programs for that matter) will be fully interactive. The viewer is also in charge when it comes to responding to the advertisement and to the product or service. When an ad is presented to the viewer, (s)he can choose to click on it at any time and be taken directly to the home page of the website, or even to the "buy" page. If the viewer goes to the home page, then (s)he will have the opportunity to see what choices there are for the product, including such things as size, color, levels of choice (for example, basic, deluxe, premium), warranty information, and price(s). Remember, as discussed earlier, television sets will continue to increase in size, smartphone screens will likewise, and all platforms will have the ability to display multiple pages across a single screen. The viewer can continue watching the advertisement (or the program if the advertisement has finished) on one portion of the screen while making his/her decision about the product on a separate portion of the screen.

8   **Ads can be delivered to their targeted audiences wherever they are worldwide.**

As will be discussed in Chapter 10: The Future of U.S. Television in the Global Television Market, television of the future will be a complete global commodity. It will be able to reach audiences no matter where they are in the world. As such, content providers and advertisers will reach new audiences and potential customers in other countries with their programming and their advertisements. For many companies, television in the future will be a way of allowing those companies opportunities to establish new markets in countries where previously they had not been able to or could not afford the cost to establish the market. The global nature of television in the future will also make it possible for the viewer to watch their favorite programs and advertisements whenever they go abroad. Regardless of the time zone, the time of day, or the country (s)he is in, through VOD, viewers will be able to watch his/her favorite programs and advertisements in his/her own languages when (s)he wants, where (s)he wants, how (s)he wants, and on whatever platform (s)he wants or is available. Further, the viewer will be able to order whatever product (s)he wants or needs immediately and have it shipped directly to her/his location wherever (s)he may be. All that will be needed is an Internet connection, which is available virtually everywhere throughout the world.

9   **Different ads can be delivered to different audiences at the same time.**

The great thing about this process is that the ability to insert advertisements into a program delivered by IPTV is limited only by the number of streams. Because there will likely be more than one subset of an audience for a program, each commercial time slot can be sold numerous times to reach each of the different subsets. As discussed earlier, the ability to reach these subsets with the advertisements they want for the products and services they want, in the way that they want, means that each advertisement will have an extremely high rate of success. Content providers, then, will be able to sell those audience subsets to the appropriate advertisers for a premium, and therefore make even more money than they can make using today's advertising strategies and techniques.

10 **Ads can be placed in every program in the content provider's library of programs. This ability makes every program valuable to the content provider and the advertiser.**

Because every program now has value no matter how new or how old it is, there will be an audience (and likely more than one audience subset) that can be reached by television advertising of the future for every program. Now, every viewer has value too, because even small audiences can produce revenues for both the content provider and the advertiser that have not been available before, given the nature of today's television. No longer will shows have to be removed from a content provider's inventory of programs. A loyal viewer will continue to watch her/his favorite programs (even ones that would normally be cancelled in today's television environment and removed from the inventory), potentially again and again and again, receiving and appreciating commercials from advertisers (s)he prefers, who remain dedicated to the program and the small, but extremely loyal, audience. That appreciation will produce small but continuing revenues from those audiences, which will likely be an important revenue supplement for both the advertiser and the content provider.

11 **Everyone gets what (s)he wants.**

The advertiser knows the advertisement will be successful because (s)he can potentially expect a very high success rate. The content provider makes a lot more money because (s)he can sell each advertising spot at a premium and sell multiple spots for each commercial time slot, with the number of different advertisements being dependent on the number of different segments of viewers there are for the program. Finally, the viewer is happy with the advertisement (s)he is watching because it is for a product or service (s)he wants or uses, with the creatives that (s)he likes, on the platforms that (s)he likes, in the programs (s)he likes, and at the time (s)he likes. The result of the three-step process of ATMA-PA-DAI is truly a "win-win-win" situation.

Summary

The three-step process of ATMA-PA-DAI is designed to provide the best opportunity possible to reach the viewer no matter where or what program (s)he is watching.

ATMA first determines the specific audience for a product or brand and makes it possible for the advertising creative department to design the advertising campaign to reach that specific audience, as has been described in the previous section. Programmatic technology, then, uses the data provided by ATMA to determine where those audiences are – the program(s), the time(s) of day, the location(s),[30] content provider(s),[31] etc. – and establishes "buy" opportunities to reach those ATMA audiences. In other words, PA matches the audience information and the advertising creatives with the programs that are best suited to those audiences and purchases advertising time in those programs. This matching of the programs with the audiences and creatives ensures a high probability of success for those advertising vehicles with those audiences.

Once ATMA and PA have done their jobs, the DAI technology takes over, inserting the specific ads determined by the previous two steps of the process into those locations where the audiences for that brand are located, and reaching the audiences that give the advertisements for the brand or product the highest possibility of success. DAI is a concept that has been discussed in the industry since the earliest days of streaming, first with radio and then with television/video. The reason is simple: DAI, along with ATMA and PA, has the potential to create the largest single revenue opportunity for content providers and advertisers in the history of the electronic media, and, when fully implemented, will provide the monetization for a coming "diamond age of television," the likes of which the world has never seen.

The three-step process of ATM-PA-DAI will be the financial engine for television in the future, as it makes it possible for advertisers to present fresh, relevant, highly targeted advertisements to viewers/customers anywhere, anytime, anyway, and on any platform, and to reach audiences around the world, opening new markets to advertisers and exposing viewers/consumers to new products and services. In this way, content providers can add billions (potentially even trillions) of dollars to their bottom lines.

To conclude – the three-step process of ATMA-PA-DAI is the future of television advertising. As television moves more and more to the Internet through IPTV and VOD delivery to all platforms everywhere, the three-step process will become the de facto advertising strategy of choice. No other advertising strategy can deliver the revenues and the viewers better. It is truly a win-win-win situation for all concerned and the key to television's future diamond age.

Case Study – Anypoint Media

It is not often that you find someone who is enacting the ideas you have come up with when looking to the future of television. So, it was a thrill when I came across such a company: Anypoint Media.

Anypoint Media is a company that "gets it," when it comes to the future of advertising. The company is in the process of revolutionizing the television landscape by being a pioneer in addressable television advertising, both for Pay-TV and OTT and FAST channels. Their partners include television companies throughout Asia, the Pacific Islands, and India.

While Anypoint Media is primarily a DAI company, it is the first to combine elements of ATMA and PA, along with the earliest development and use of ubiquitous product placement (discussed in the next chapter). As such, the company provides a cutting-edge solution for reaching highly specific, targeted audiences and making it easy for those audiences to receive the information they are looking for that will lead them to make successful purchases of the products they desire. As such, they are able to bring together the advertisers and the audiences that specifically desire those advertisers' products in a seamless manner that allows for virtually guaranteed attention and extremely high engagement from those audiences.

Anypoint Media's program – called "Flower" – is designed for both Pay-TV and OTT/FAST companies. For both providers, Anypoint Media makes it possible to determine the right advertisement, down to the individual household that has the greatest chance of successfully completing the advertisement. It also makes it possible for the viewer to simply "click" anywhere on the advertisement to view additional material and make purchases while the advertisement is still running (without having to deal with an intrusive and distracting QR code that forces the viewer to have a mobile phone camera ready to focus on the QR code and to then follow a link to view the product). The success of this process, of course, assumes the QR code is of sufficient quality for the mobile phone's camera to read the code, that the viewer has the phone at the ready, and that the link stays on the screen long enough for the viewer to complete the process of successfully scanning it. Instead, when the viewer simply clicks anywhere on the advertisement itself, Anypoint Media's system sends a notification with the product link directly to the viewer's mobile phone, which the viewer can then open and use to consider and purchase the product.

Additionally, the Flower system can store data about the household's decision-making regarding response to advertisements and can use that information to further refine the types of advertisements that will be most successful for that household in the future. Subsequent selections by members of the household can further refine the data to determine the likely makeup of the household in terms of males and females, the likely age groups in the household, and their personal preferences for products – for instance, whether there is one parent or two, and whether there are children/teens, whether they are females or males, and what are their favorite products. As more data is collected, stored, and retrieved, the more successful subsequent advertisements will be for the advertisers. This process allows Anypoint Media to accurately determine ATMA groupings, to know their product and creative preferences as well as their preferred television programs, and to successfully connect those advertisers with the viewers who will attend to, engage with, and successfully complete the advertisements by responding or even purchasing the product or service.

For Pay-TV providers, Flower offers frame-accurate ad insertion and seamless playback using Flower's proprietary Ad Pre-Decisioning System which proactively determines which advertisements need to go to each viewer's STB to pre-cache, independently of the ad breaks. The system then prevents ad traffic congestion, which is especially effective during those times when there are large numbers of viewers watching the same program. Pre-decisioning allows Pay-TV operators to deliver ads more efficiently and get the right advertisements to the homes where they can be the most effective.

Additionally, the Flower system makes ad podding more efficient and exact. As discussed earlier in the section on DAI, ad podding can be used both for OTT and FAST channels (for which it was initially developed) as well as for Pay-TV operators. Flower's ad podding is a two-step process – Super Ad Podding and Exact Ad Podding. The Super Ad Podding step first creates a list of potential advertisements to be played on an STB, regardless of the television channel. This list is called the Super Ad Pod. These advertisements would be ones that the viewer connected to the STB would most likely attend to and engage with. Once the Super Ad Pod has been created, as many of the ads from the Super Ad Pod as the STB will hold are downloaded to the STB.

The second step is Exact Ad Podding. When the STB receives a cue for an ad break, the STB, using Flower's software development kit (SDK), determines the final ad list to play, depending on the current channel, time of day, and other factors. Because the advertisements are already loaded onto the STB, there is no need to rely on a back-end ad decisioning system (from the server). If an advertisement is not pre-loaded, but is part of the Exact Ad Podding, it can be downloaded by the STB "on-the-fly" from the content delivery network (CDN). Using the Flower system is more efficient and offers the Pay-TV operator substantial savings. Additionally, for longer ad breaks, the Flower system pulls numerous advertisements from the Super Ad Pod as needed to fill the break.

Anypoint Media also partners with many of the major PA companies to expand its coverage for clients worldwide. By partnering with these companies, Anypoint Media can provide clients with the ability to reach potential consumers anywhere they are in the world. As such, the company can offer clients opportunities to expand their revenue potential by enabling clients to move into new markets that they were not able to penetrate before.

Finally, by identifying all the devices belonging to a particular household, Flower makes possible cross-device targeting, conversion, and attribution. For cross-device targeting, the company's clients can, if they choose, select a particular audience segment using mobile data and target only those STBs that are paired with mobile devices belonging to that audience segment. For cross-device conversion, Flower can turn television ad viewers into active users by driving them to take action on their PCs or mobile devices, such as visiting the client's website, downloading the client's app, or even making a purchase directly. For cross-device attribution, Flower can track and report on conversions that happen on those PCs and mobile devices after the viewer has been exposed to a particular advertisement, thus allowing the client to see if and/or how successful that advertisement was in reaching that viewer. This process allows for TV and digital advertising to be fully integrated, bringing in a variety of different – and often new – advertisers.

For OTT/FAST channels, Anypoint Media provides a complete end-to-end advertising solution. Because of their innovative product, Anypoint Media has the ability to fill every ad inventory with the highest possible revenue. Just like for linear channels, for OTT/FAST channels, Anypoint Media's Flower software operates on the client side, rather than from the server-side. Operating from the client side, the software can manipulate the playlist on the client's (the viewer's) side. This makes possible interactive capabilities, eliminates scalability issues and the additional costs associated with server-side ad insertion, and can maintain ad playback capabilities that are seamless. Additionally, with the Flower product, OTT/FAST linear service providers have the ability to accommodate both performance video advertisements as well as brand video advertisements, even on television sets

Flower also provides an Ad Decisioning System (ADS) that can create a personalized linear ad pod for viewers. Flower has the ability to obtain advertisements from a variety of sources such as Direct IOs, Google Ad Manager (GAM), Supply-Side Platform (SSPs), and Exchanges, with the goal of maximizing the ad fill rate. This makes it possible to create a linear ad pod that completely fills an entire ad break – no more, no less.

Additionally, the playlist module in Flower makes it possible to accurately determine which advertisements are currently playing on the device (primarily the viewer's TV set). This allows Flower to easily overlay advertisements with components such as banners and clickable buttons that show more information or trigger impulse buys. As such, OTT/FAST service providers can use advertisements with overlay components, which can attract more advertisers for increased revenue.

Flower also provides a conversion manager that links a click anywhere on a video advertisement to a conversion request on other apps or devices. The viewer simply has to press the OK/Select button on her/his remote anytime during the advertisement to trigger a pop-up screen on a mobile device (smartphone, tablet, laptop computer, etc.). This, then, allows the viewer to buy the product featured in the advertisement, or, if the viewer is actually watching on a mobile device, to go to a landing page for the product. As such, Flower makes it possible for OTT/FAST service providers to make additional cost-per-click revenue in addition to cost-per-thousand (CPM) revenue.

Because it is client-side based, Flower can provide detailed information on accurate ad exposure, which can be categorized in a variety of ways, including by region, time, channel, viewer demographics, and other criteria. These reports can also be accessed anytime, anywhere, from any devices with an Internet connection. This ability allows OTT/FAST service providers to improve the quality of their services for advertisers by providing accurate and reliable reports.

Further, Flower provides its own mediation function, handling multiple demand sources and a variety of deal types. Flower has a multi-win bidding feature that is specially designed for long ad breaks of two minutes or more. When an advertisement request is received, Flower's ADS will usually prioritize the highest bidding price at a time. However, for a lengthy ad break, Flower may also select multiple advertisements with higher prices at once, leading to increased fill rates. In addition, Flower can make multiple and interspersed advertisement requests during long ad breaks, especially when they are coming from programmatic ecosystems, which can maximize the fill rate and efficiently fill the ad break. Combining Flower's mediation function and incremental ad podding abilities allows OTT/FAST service providers to enhance their revenue by maximizing the fill rate using Flower's mediation function.

Finally, Flower is integrated with the major global demand partners in the programmatic buying ecosystem. As such Flower helps to expand the demand base by connecting it to this ecosystem.

Compared to a typical server-side ad insertion solution, Flower is a comprehensive solution that offers all the essential features for advertising services, including campaign management, publisher management, mediation, inventory management, filler management, etc.

As a reminder, this case study is included here to show what can be done to provide personalized, targeted advertising to the viewer using the tools described in the future of advertising chapter and those that will be discussed in the next chapter on product placement. This is a company on the cutting edge of personalized advertising, and therefore deserves inclusion as a case study on the beginnings of the future of television.[32]

Notes

1 Zucker, Jeff, "Keynote Address," 2008 National Association of Television Program Executives Convention, January 28–31, 2008, Las Vegas, NV.
2 Ruether, Traci, "The History of Commercials and TV Advertising," *Strategus*, (May 24, 2023), https://www.strategus.com/blog/the-history-of-commercials-and-tv-advertising.
3 "History of Television," *Weebly*, (n.d.), https://melisashen.weebly.com/uploads/2/5/4/7/25478745/the_history_of_television.pdf.
4 "Now It's Digital Quarters for Analogue Dollars," *Videonet*, (March 3, 2011), http://www.v-net.tv/now-it%E2%80%99s-digital-quarters-for-analogue-dollars/.
5 Whitten, Sarah and Alex Sherman, "Netflix Ad-supported Tier Has 40 Million Monthly Users, Nearly Double Previous Count," *NBC News*, (May 15, 2024), https://www.nbcnews.com/business/business-news/netflix-ad-supported-tier-40-million-monthly-users-rcna152463.
6 See the section on Connected TVs in Chapter 5: The Future of Television Viewing and Chapter 3: The Future of Television Delivery Systems.
7 "Dynamic Ad Insertion," *IAB Wiki*, http://www.iab.net/wiki/index.php/Dynamic_ad_insertion.
8 "Addressable TV Advertising," *Gartner*, https://www.gartner.com/en/information-technology/glossary/addressable-tv-advertising.
9 See Chapter 9: The Future of Television Content Search & Promotion.
10 "Targeted Advertising," *ITV Dictionary*, www.itvdictionary.com/targeted_advertising.html.
11 This is my term and definition.
12 See "Chapter 17 – Retransmission Consent Fees" in Aycock, Frank A. (2015), *21st Century Television: The Players, The Viewers, The Money*, 2nd ed., (Charleston, SC: CreateSpace).
13 See Chapter 9: The Future of Television Content Search & Promotion.
14 "John Wanamaker," *Advertising Age*, (March 29, 1999), http://adage.com/article/special-report-the-advertising-century/john-wanamaker/140185/.
15 Anderson, Janna and Lee Rainie, "Future of the Internet IV," *Pew Internet & American Life Project*, (February 19, 2010), http://www.pewinternet.org/Reports/2010/Future-of-the-Internet-IV.aspx.
16 Anderson and Rainie, "Future of the Internet IV."
17 Anderson and Rainie, "Future of the Internet IV."
18 Anderson and Rainie, "Future of the Internet IV."
19 Boris, Cynthia, "'Online Privacy is Dead' Says Study and Millennials Are Okay with That," *Marketing Pilgrim*, (April 22, 2013), http://www.marketingpilgrim.com/2013/04/online-privacy-is-dead-says-study-and-Millennials-are-okay-with-that.html.
20 "Is Online Privacy Over? Findings From the USC Annenberg Center for the Digital Future Show Millennials Embrace a New Online Reality," *USC Annenberg – News*, (April 22, 2013), http://annenberg.usc.edu/news/around-usc-annenberg/online-privacy-over-findings-usc-annenberg-center-digital-future-show.
21 Marshall, Jack, "WTF is Programmatic TV Advertising?" *Digiday*, WTF Series (February 20, 2014), https://digiday.com/media/what-is-programmatic-advertising/.
22 Blattberg, Eric, "WTF is Programmatic TV Advertising?" *Digiday*, WTF Series (October 13, 2014), http://digiday.com/platforms/wtf-programmatic-tv-advertising/.
23 Blattberg, Eric, "WTF is Programmatic TV Advertising?".
24 Blattberg, Eric, "WTF is Programmatic TV Advertising?".
25 All the information in this section is quoted, with thanks, from Aguilhar, Ligia, "The Differences Between AI, Machine Learning, Programmatic Buying and Deep Learning," *strikesocial*, (n.d.) https://strikesocial.com/blog/the-difference-between-ai-machine-learning-programmatic-advertising-deep-learning/.
26 All the information in this section is quoted, with thanks, from Elkin, Tobi, "How Artificial Intelligence Ties Into Programmatic Media," *MediaPost*, (December 29, 2016),

https://www.mediapost.com/publications/article/291939/how-artificial-intelligence-ties-into-programmatic.html.
27 Boyle, Alyssa, "AdExplainer: What Is Server-Side Ad Insertion (SSAI)," *ad explainer*, (July 11, 2022), https://www.adexchanger.com/adexplainer/adexplainer-what-is-server-side-ad-insertion-ssai/.
28 Trichkov, Filip, "What is Client-Side Ad Insertion (CSAI)?" *JW Player*, (Dec. 11, 2023), https://jwplayer.com/blog/what-is-csai/.
29 Tuchman, Anna, Bradley Shapiro, and Gunter Hitsch, "TV Advertising Is Usually Not Worth It," *Kellogg Insight*, (March 1, 2021), https://insight.kellogg.northwestern.edu/article/tv-advertising-is-usually-not-worth-it.
30 Locations in this case can refer not only to a city or state, but also a region, or even any country around the world where the viewer(s) can be reached.
31 Content providers can be networks and cable channels from the legacy media, as well as all the new media channels (OTT, subscription, YouTube-style, etc.).
32 I learned about the company Anypoint Media at the 2024 National Association of Broadcasters' (NAB) convention when I saw a presentation on their product. I have no association with the company, nor is this case study presented for any reason other than to show a company that is on the cutting edge of personalized advertising, and to provide an example of future of television advertising.

8 The Future of Product Placement

Product placement is "an advertising technique used by companies to subtly promote their products through a non-traditional advertising technique, usually through appearances in film, television, or other media."[1] While you might question the "subtlety" of product placement these days, it is an ever-growing way of advertising on television and will be an even more integral part of television in the future. A simpler way to define product placement is when you see a product displayed or being used in a production and you can read the name or recognize the logo or product. As an example: you are watching a television program and see a Samsung computer in a scene and you can recognize it or see the Samsung name or logo – that is product placement.

While product placement has traditionally been considered a part of the movie industry, product placement on U.S. television will generate $18.48 billion by the end of 2024, according to Statista, and $23.56 billion by 2026.[2] Globally, product placement spending is expected to reach close to $41.5 billion by 2026.[3] While linear television still accounts for the majority of all product placement dollars, over-the-top (OTT) television (in its broadest form) is the fastest growing service in terms of product placement spending. This includes original programs that are on both Netflix and Amazon Prime Instant Video, neither of which accepted traditional advertising commercials until just recently. Additionally, in a 2023 research study, three quarters of U.S. consumers stated that they had searched for a product/brand online after seeing it in a program they were watching.[4]

History of Product Placement

While the history of product placement on television is a relatively short one, product placement has been used extensively in movies from their earliest days. One of the earliest examples of product placement came in the 1919 movie *The Garage,* directed by and co-starring Fatty Arbuckle, when Red Crown gasoline was displayed during the movie.[5] The use of product placement in silent films established the ability of movie production companies to finance in part or in whole their movies by allowing companies to place their brands prominently in a movie so they could be easily seen. Product placement in movies is still common to this day.[6]

DOI: 10.4324/9781003625384-12

Product placement in television has also existed since the industry's early days, often overtly in children's television. Though the practice is not called product placement, children's programming has always had a product placement aspect to it, in that the associated toys, clothing, cereals, etc., have always been tied to the programs starring the cartoon figures or children's shows actors and actresses. Going back to the earliest television days (of the author's own youth), children could buy – or have their parents buy for them – Woody Woodpecker stuffed toys, Superman clothing, Roadrunner wind-up toys – pretty much some kind of merchandise for just about any television show that children watched on a Saturday morning or after school. The characters themselves became, in a real sense, the embodiment of product placement. In fact, Saturday morning cartoons got so close to being thirty-minute- or hour-long product placement advertisements (the *Smurfs* is generally cited as a prime example of such programming during this time) that the Federal Communications Commission (FCC) finally acted to limit the connections between the programs and the adjacent commercials that could be shown.[7] Other countries around the world also limit such forms of advertising.[8]

Adult television programs have also had their share of product placement, although there was more subtlety to them in the earlier days. Automobiles, because of the ease of integrating them into stories, figured heavily in product placement on television. Crockett and Tubbs chased criminals in their Ferrari Testarossa in *Miami Vice*; *Magnum P.I.'s* Tom Selleck drove a Ferrari 308i; for the Duke boys in *Dukes of Hazzard*, it was a Dodge Charger named "General Lee." Even early television programs such as *The Prisoner*, made good use of automobiles. In the case of *The Prisoner*, the automobile was a Lotus 8.[9]

Game shows such as *The Price Is Right*, *Let's Make a Deal*, and today's *Wheel of Fortune* all make use of extensive product placement. *The Price Is Right* was virtually an hour-long product placement as the viewers looked forward to hearing the call "It's a new car!". Game shows are adept at product placement, providing extensive publicity of and focus on the product in exchange for a free prize.

Today, of course, product placement is used extensively in television programs. Whether it is the top seven competitors in 2025's *American Idol* visiting all the different Disneyland attractions in California or *The Biggest Loser* contestants making a visit to Planet Fitness (or Anytime Fitness, or the gym of choice for the season) or filling their water bottles from a Brita pitcher, television programs today find that product placement is an exceptional form of additional advertising revenue to help fund the production and distribution of the program. Reality shows, especially in the U.S., are just one product placement after another. Often, the product placement is very obvious. Everywhere a reality show contestant goes, everything (s)he does, everything (s)he wears is a product placement. If the contestant goes to a luxurious spa for a weekend – it is a product placement. If the contestant rides in a limousine or flies in a private jet – that is product placement.

Live sporting events are also not exempt from product placement. Professional golfers are walking product placement billboards – in addition to getting paid for using various companies' products, they are also paid every time they appear on camera – a real additional incentive to play well each week. Professional race car drivers are also walking billboards, as are their cars; they have similar arrangements with the companies regarding their appearances on television. Think about football teams, especially European football teams (soccer in the U.S.). Each team player has the name of the team's sponsor – some corporation – sewn in large, bold letters across the front of her/his shirt. The team name and crest is a small (often unrecognizable to anyone but ardent fans) patch over the left breast of the player. The importance of product placement to the sport is obvious. In Korea, major league baseball teams are not named after the city in which they are located (like they are in the U.S). Rather, they are sponsored by major corporations, so every player is a continuous example of product placement and even mentioning the team name (for example, Kia Tigers located in Gwangju or LG Twins located in Seoul) is product placement. When teams are on television, the entire game – from pre-game through to post-game – is product placement for the two teams and the corporations that sponsor them.[10]

Advertisers are happy to associate their products directly with a popular program – or even a less popular one, if the program has the right demographic makeup – because viewers cannot skip over product placement in the same way that they can skip commercials or leave the room when the commercial break is airing. Further, seeing contestants or stars using a product makes the product more credible to the viewer, especially when the viewer identifies with a contestant or has an affinity for the star in the first place.

How Product Placement Works

When a television program is being developed, often the content producer will look for ways to include products that are relevant to the program in scenes during each episode. It may be as subtle as a brand name showing on a computer that is being used or a product billboard that is recognizable. It may also be as obvious as the vacation the contestant wins on *Wheel of Fortune*, the luxurious getaway that figures into the *Batchelor* and *Batchelorette,* or the weekly Ford music video on earlier *American Idol* seasons, where the contestants were seen enjoying and frolicking around a Ford automobile.[11] Regardless of the subtleness or lack of subtleness, product placement can be a significant source of continuing revenue for the content producer as the program unfolds.

While the aforementioned examples are from over-the-air (OTA) network television, streaming services can also use product placement successfully. Products used in movies and original series on Netflix, Amazon Instant Video, Hulu/Hulu+, YouTube, and other streaming services are examples of product placement. These days it is hard, if not impossible, to find a program on television – broadly defined – that does not have some form of product placement at some point during the program.

Product placement opportunities are generally set up through an agreement between the product maker and the content producer or the content deliverer in such a way that the product maker pays a set amount for the exclusive right to have its product displayed during the program. By exclusive right, I mean that Apple, for example, would not agree to have a MacBook featured in a program alongside a Dell Windows-based computer, because they would be competing against each other.

Having two products competing directly against each other would negate the purpose of the product placement of both products, unless the product that has the contract is being shown to be far superior or preferred in comparison to the competitor.

There are four main ways product placement agreements are reached. First, sometimes product placement is used as a barter opportunity. A television content producer may need products to offer to contestants or the public (for example, on game shows), or may need a product for the company, staff, or actors. If so, the content producer may choose to swap the placement of the product in the program for the product itself rather than have to buy the product outright. No money changes hands and the content producer receives the product for use or distribution while the company producing the product gets built-in advertising opportunity(ies) that viewers will not be able to avoid by fast-forwarding or leaving the room during commercial breaks.

Second, product placement can combine barter with a promotional fee. In this scenario, the television content producer will swap product placement opportunities for the products themselves but will also charge a fee for the promotional announcement. Often, these types of product placement are seen in programs with stable, and most likely, large followings, either in the total aggregate audience or in the audiences most desired by the company considering the product placement opportunity. The promotional fee charged by the content provider will be less than the cost of purchasing advertising time in the program.

A third option is a sponsored deal – what, today, is called branded entertainment. The product maker pays a fee to sponsor the telecast of a program. Depending on the agreement, the product maker will have its name associated with the program as well as product placement opportunities during the telecast of the program. Usually with this type of agreement, the product maker will also have a number of commercial spots during the telecast in order to keep the product maker's name in front of the audience during the commercial breaks. Additionally, depending on the agreement, the product maker may also have significant input into creative aspects of the program. This type of agreement was used extensively in 1950s television programs and is often used today in college football bowl games, golf tournaments, and specials such as the live versions of *The Sound of Music* and *Grease* that aired on NBC.

A fourth option for product placement is a straight payment deal. In this option, the product maker simply pays for the right to have the product placement opportunities during the program. No form of barter, where the content producer keeps the product in exchange for the placement, occurs. Usually the product is placed within a scene during the program. For example, a billboard with the product's name and image prominently displayed, or a laptop sitting on a counter with the top open so that the logo can easily be seen by the viewer. The product maker has paid for the opportunity to have that product placement in the program.

Why Product Placement Works

There are a number of arguments that one can make to explain why product placement works, some going back to academic research of the 1900s. Without turning this section into a thesis on theory, nevertheless, the following are two theories that can serve as arguments for why product placement works.

In his 1922 book, *Public Opinion*, journalist and author Walter Lippman wrote that the public does not respond to events in the actual world in any direct way, but they live in a sort of "pseudo-environment" made up of "the pictures in our heads," and the media play important roles in shaping those pictures and designing the pseudo-environment.[12] Following on from Lippman's ideas in their study of the 1968 presidential election (and in later studies), two researchers, Dr. Maxwell McCombs and Dr. Donald Shaw – both of the University of North Carolina-Chapel Hill – described the media as "agenda-setters," writing "that the media were not very good at telling the public what to think, but were extremely good at telling the public what to think about."[13] In other words, the media's real influence with the public is in setting the public's agenda for what is important to them in their daily lives. While the original studies focused on news media, it is easy to see how agenda-setting can explain why product placement is so successful.

From an advertising point of view, if the media in general – and television, specifically – are, in the words of McCombs and Shaw, "stunningly successful" at setting the public's agenda for what is important to them, then product placement, by its sheer ability to keep a product before the viewer in a program would potentially have a tremendous impact on the viewer's buying habits. Advertisers are extremely concerned with both brand awareness and brand recognition. Commercials on television can be skipped by the viewer using TiVo or a DVR or can be ignored by changing the channel or leaving the room during commercial breaks. Product placement negates the ability to do either. Whether overt or more subtle, product placement can drive both brand awareness and brand recognition, and, by sheer weight of continued exposure, can influence buying decisions. Product placement is excellent for helping to set 21st century television viewers' agendas for what they choose to purchase and will choose to purchase in the future.

Additionally, product placement can have farther-reaching effects than just the ability to set the agenda for television viewers' buying decisions. In 1940,[14] and again in 1948,[15] Paul F. Lazarsfeld led teams of researchers studying how people made decisions, first in a presidential election (1940) and then with regard to buying decisions for a number of everyday items (1948). From these studies came the idea for what the researchers called the "two-step flow" theory of communication. The two-step flow theory says that the mass media have only an indirect influence on the public at large, and that the media influence opinion leaders of peer groups and those opinion leaders then influence their groups.

Peer groups are everywhere. Except for those people who are truly perpetual loners, anyone can think of groups of peers they are associated with. Peer groups can be formed at a job, a church, a sports team, a school or university – anywhere and any way groups of people get together to share things they have in common. According to the two-step flow, every peer group has at least one opinion leader to whom the other members of the peer group look to make decisions on what to wear, how to style their hair, what type of automobile to drive, where to go out to eat – all aspects of life. Applying the two-step flow to television can explain how television has a direct influence on the opinion leaders of peer groups who then exert influence on the other members of their peer groups who make up the rest of the public.

Product placement, then, has a crucial role to play in the decision-making of the members of the peer groups that make up the public. With its ability to keep the product name and image before the television viewer, product placement is an excellent way to influence the opinion leaders who will then influence the other members of their peer groups. Further, because the other members of the peer groups will be watching many, if not most or all, of the same programs that their opinion leaders are watching, the other members of the peer groups will also be aware of and recognize the brands when the opinion leaders decide to use the brands and influence the other members to do the same. Product placement also has the ability to strongly influence the opinion leaders because, as mentioned in regard to agenda-setting, product placement cannot be ignored or skipped in the same way that commercials can. The products are integrated into the program and are seen throughout the show.

Taken together, agenda-setting and the two-step flow make a powerful argument for the success of product placement as a powerful influencer of people's buying decisions. Agenda-setting suggests that product placement, by virtue of its continuous integration into television's programming, can be "stunningly successful"[16] at influencing viewers to seriously consider making buying decisions based on the products they see. The two-step flow, then, says that opinion leaders in the public will take those buying decisions to their peer groups, which then extends the influence of the product placement to the public at large.

On a more practical matter, product placement makes brand awareness and recognition more accessible in the viewer's memory. When people are required to:

> reach into their memory for a product, just as when they reach for a word, those that come to mind quickly, the ones that are at the top of the mental agenda, have a distinct advantage over those that only emerge after extensive dredging.[17]

When a product maker uses extensive product placement on a television program, by seeing that product on screen in a television program time and again, the viewer is that much more likely to notice, recognize, and select the product when (s)he is shopping, and is more likely to make it a point to look for that product because, through product placement, that product is most accessible in the viewer's memory.

As mentioned earlier in the chapter, reality shows are the television programs most heavily packed with product placement. As far back as 2011, researchers Emma Ashton and Julie Houston surveyed 400 viewers nationwide for their Reality TV Insights Survey. The two researchers found that 94% of the viewers' purchasing behavior had "been influenced by what they have seen on a reality show. 60% of viewers have purchased something after they saw it on a reality television show."[18] Notice that the researchers were specifically looking at product placement on television. The study suggests the power of product placement to influence viewers' brand recognition and active consideration to purchase a product, and, even better, the actual buying decisions of those viewers. Ashton says,

"It appears product placement is a win-win situation for both the shows, and the advertisers. Television networks need the sponsorship to ensure production values of the shows are high to attract viewers and therefore make a profit."[19] She goes on to say, "Advertisers are definitely getting a bang for their buck aligning with reality shows and there is probably much greater potential than is in play right now, if advertisers can think outside the box."[20] The 2023 study mentioned at the beginning of this chapter provides further support for Ashton's earlier findings. Product placement works.

Future of Product Placement

Product placement will continue to be an ever-growing part of television in the future. The possibilities for additional revenues through the use of product placement are too numerous to ignore. Content providers will continue to use product placement as a source of revenue for their programs, and advertisers will find product placement an ever-more important way of reaching the television viewer because the viewer simply cannot avoid a product placement like (s)he can a commercial. Additionally, the ability to target viewers with specific advertising through the use of Aggregated Targeted Microadvertising (ATMA), Programmatic Media Buying, and Dynamic Ad Insertion (DAI), discussed in the previous chapter, combined with what the author calls *Ubiquitous Product Placement*, or UPP, gives the content provider an extremely effective one-two punch that will allow television revenues to grow ever larger and to flourish.

Product placement on television of the future will be significantly different from the product placement of today. Today's product placement is in its infancy compared to the future possibilities of the advertising strategy. Television in the future will provide a continuous stream of product placement opportunities for advertisers to reach their intended audiences. In the near future, product placement will move from the Diet Coca-Cola glasses that were on the desk of the *American Idol* judges to UPP, a situation where everything in every frame of the television program will be a product placement. However, lest you imagine a television world that looks like a NASCAR driver and his automobile, the product placement of television in the future will be much more subtle, and therefore much more effective, than the NASCAR driver with his/her sponsors plastered all over the car and uniform. (However, the NASCAR automobile and driver will also be subject to UPP, thus enhancing those product placements as well.)

UPP on television in the future will be designed in the following manner. Everything in the program will be an opportunity for a product placement. Every item in every frame will be linked to the product's website where the viewer can go to find out more about the product and to make a purchase. Given the ability of the connected television (CTV) set to allow multiple windows to be open on the television screen, and the Internet's ability to deliver multiple simultaneous operations such as allowing the viewer to watch television, chat with friends, and look up background information on his/her favorite actor, director, musician – all at the same time – the delivery of numerous simultaneous product placement web links to the viewer is not only a distinct possibility, but an almost guaranteed reality on television in the future.

For instance, imagine you, the television viewer, are watching the current season of *American Idol* (to stay with the example from earlier). One of the judges, Lionel Richie, has on a jacket that you like very much. With a quick wave of your hand to the lapel of the jacket and a squeeze of your fingers (no longer a mouse, but you could use one if you are old-fashioned), a second window appears on the screen giving you information on the jacket – who the maker is, what colors you can get the jacket in, what material it is made from, etc. Further exploration of the website tells you the location of outlets – both online and brick-and-mortar – that sell the jacket, the cost, shipping information, and provides you with an opportunity to order the jacket immediately. Additionally, you think that Carrie Underwood's bracelet would look good on your spouse's wrist. With the same wave of the hand and squeeze of the fingers or a spoken word you are taken to a website in a third screen giving you information on the bracelet – who the designer is, whether is it gold, silver, or some other metal, what stones (if any) are on the bracelet along with their cuts and weights – and what outlets sell the bracelet, along with costs, shipping, etc.

Thinking about one of the most prolific product placement programs, imagine you have gone back in time and are watching *The Biggest Loser*. As you watch, you notice the treadmill the contestants are using. Selecting the treadmill sends you to a second window where you find the same type of product and purchase information that was described in the previous example. However, on this particular *The Biggest Loser* episode, the contestants are enjoying 'Makeover Week,' so every outfit, every hairstyle, every piece of makeup used, becomes a clickable link. In addition, each contestant is taken to a special location where (s)he reveals her makeover to the people (spouses, children, family members) closest to her/him. That special location will also be a clickable link, which, if you select it, will open a window to provide you with information about the location and how to book your own trip there.

Several weeks later, the contestants participate in *The Biggest Loser* marathon, where they show off their new-found abilities to run, walk, or limp to the finish line of a 26.2 mile race. In television of the future, every location the contestants pass, everything you see in the scenery behind them, will be a clickable link that takes her/him to an additional window(s) for more information and to potentially make purchases.

Summary

Much like addressable advertising on television in the future, UPP will be another way for advertisers to reach their preferred audiences. Initially, the ability to target subsets of the audience in the way that ATMA is able to will likely not be available. However, as the sophistication of the content providers and the advertisers improves, the likelihood that some form of ATMA could be combined with UPP to place a Coca-Cola bottle in the streams of a subset that prefers Coke and a

Pepsi-Cola bottle in the streams of a different subset that prefers Pepsi is almost assured. The opportunity to sell different product placements to different advertisers in the same program will further increase revenues for the content providers.

Further, as audiences become ever more comfortable and familiar with UPP in all their favorite programs, the expectation is that they will use this ability to find out more about products and services that interest them. The audiences' desires for instant gratification will lead to more and more impulse buying and increased revenues for advertisers. In addition, as UPP opportunities increase in number and sophistication, content providers will once again, like with addressable advertising, be able to increase the price of UPP insertions by charging a premium for each insertion, because the advertiser will be assured that its product will reach the desired target audience.

When everything in every shot becomes a clickable link, UPP becomes a continuous gold mine for everyone involved in the television program of the future – the content producer, the content provider, the product maker, and the advertiser. Even the viewer benefits by having instant access to anything (s)he sees on the television screen that draws his/her attention or interests her/him. In the future of television, product placement is not just a "win-win" situation; it is a win for everyone.

Notes

1 *BusinessDictionary.com*, http://www.businessdictionary.com/definition/product-placement.html.
2 Navarro, J. G., "Product Placement Revenue in the United States From 2021 to 2026," *statista*, (August 30, 2023), https://www.statista.com/statistics/915182/product-placement-revenue-us/.
3 Navarro, J.G., "Product Placement Revenue Worldwide From 2021 to 2026."
4 Sutton, Kelsey, "Product Placements Can Drive Searches and Purchases, Research Finds," *Marketing Brew*, (August 17, 2023), https://www.marketingbrew.com/stories/2023/08/17/product-placements-can-drive-searches-and-purchases-research-finds.
5 *Harrison's Reports*, (January 17, 1920), pg. 9.
6 For a good list of movies that have made use of product placement throughout movie history, see http://en.wikipedia.org/wiki/Product_placement#cite_note-12.
7 "Children's Educational Television," *FCC Guide*, http://www.fcc.gov/guides/childrens-educational-television.
8 Mueller, Barbara (2004), *Dynamics of International Advertising*, (New York: Peter Lang), 284–285.
9 Neer, Katherine, "How Product Placement Works," *howstuffworks*, http://money.howstuffworks.com/product-placement.htm.
10 I spent two summers in Gwangju, South Korea. As a baseball fan, I went to a number of Kia Tigers baseball games and had the opportunity to watch all the teams in the Korean major league baseball.
11 The two programs are known for their extensive use of product placement. Generally, they are the two programs on television that have the largest number of product placement mentions each season.
12 "Agenda Setting Theory," *International Agenda Setting Conference*, http://www.agendasetting.com/index.php/agenda-setting-theory.
13 "Agenda Setting Theory," *International Agenda Setting Conference*.

14 Lazarsfeld, Paul F., Bernard Berelson, and Hazel Gaudet, "The People's Choice: How the Voter Makes Up His Mind in a Presendential Election," in Shearon Lowery and Melvin L. DeFleur, *Milestones in Mass Communication Research*, (New York: Longman, 1983), 85–112.
15 Katz, Elihu and Paul F. Lazarsfeld, "Personal Influence: The Part Played by People in the Flow of Mass Communication," in Shearon Lowery and Melvin L. DeFleur, *Milestones in Mass Communication Research*, (New York: Longman, 1983), 177–203.
16 "Agenda Setting Theory," *International Agenda Setting Conference*.
17 Sutherland, Max, "Why Product Placement works," http://www.sutherlandsurvey.com/Columns_Papers/Why%20Product%20Placement%20Works_Feb05.pdf.
18 "Product Placement Works on Reality TV, Says Report," *Public Citizen's Commercial Alert*, (August 22, 2011), http://www.commercialalert.org/news/archive/2011/08/product-placement-works-on-reality-tv-says-report.
19 "Product Placement Works on Reality TV, Says Report," *Public Citizen's Commercial Alert*.
20 "Product Placement Works on Reality TV, Says Report," *Public Citizen's Commercial Alert*.

9 The Future of Television Content Search and Promotion

One of the most important aspects of television in the future will be the need for content providers to continuously promote their programs and services. With the demise of scheduling brought about by the growth of video-on-demand (VOD), and the requirement for 24-hour-a-day television everywhere and on all platforms, making sure that audiences can find the programs they want to watch will be critical to the success of both linear and streaming content providers.

As has been discussed in previous chapters, all content providers will need to have huge libraries of programming available to their audiences. The networks, especially, will be expected to make sure that more than seventy years of programming is available to anyone and everyone, anytime, anywhere, and optimized for every platform – including virtual reality (VR) and even windshield displays for autonomous automobiles. Ensuring audiences know about and find these programs will be a daunting task for all content providers.

The traditional cable channels, with their niche programming structure, will still have backlogs of programs that their specialized audiences will want to view whenever and wherever they wish to view them. No longer will programs show up one week on, say, The History Channel, and several weeks or months later, on The Smithsonian Channel or The Discovery Channel. Instead, The History Channel will have its own library of programming that will be unique to that content provider and will be viewed only on that provider. The other traditional cable channels will have the same.

Instead of using traditional methods for letting audiences know what programs are available for viewing, in the television universe of the future, filters will become the promotional tool of choice for the content providers. Filters will make it possible for the viewer to sort through the programs that are offered by each content provider and find the ones that (s)he wants to watch. But the filters of the future will be much more comprehensive than the filters of today – they will work in the following manner.

The connected television's (CTV's) search function will be the most important link to the audience. The search function will be cross-referenced in a variety of ways – alphabetically by program name, by character, by genre, by lead actor, by setting or locale, by time of day the program traditionally aired, or by any number of other factors. The number of potential ways to categorize programs is vast. The

DOI: 10.4324/9781003625384-13

more ways a program can be cross-referenced for the audience, the better. The viewer would need only to know one thing about the program to be able to find it with just a few clicks of the remote, a wave of the hand, or a verbal command.

The television viewer of the future will be able to easily, quickly, and smoothly navigate to his/her desired program without a second thought. For example, if the viewer wanted to watch, say, the third episode of the second season of the program *The Big Bang Theory,* a CBS Network situation comedy, the viewer could simply go to her/his TV's search function, enter "*The Big Bang Theory*," select the season, and then the episode. Another way would be simply to go to the search function and enter the character name "Sheldon Cooper," which would then bring up "*The Big Bang Theory*," then select the year, then the episode. The viewer could also enter the name of the actor who plays Sheldon, "Jim Parsons," then "*The Big Bang Theory*," and then select the season and the episode. The search function would not only allow every character or actor name as an entry point, but also the name of any guest star or even a setting. Any aspect of the program then becomes a potential entry point in the search function of the CTV set.

Once all television sets of the future are fully motion controlled, mouse clicks will be replaced by a wave of the hand. When television sets are fully voice activated, the only voice commands needed to watch the *The Big Bang Theory* episode in the example above would be "*The Big Bang Theory*, Year Two, Episode Three." Using voice commands or motion control for selection will be much easier and will eliminate the need for extra hardware.

Some of what has just been described is already occurring on CTV sets. However, in the future, the search function will become more extensive, but also easier to navigate. While inputting the various links will be a very large task at the outset, once the cross-reference scheme has been devised and implemented, it will only have to be updated as new programs are added. After the initial setup, all the procedures will occur seamlessly through the cloud service controlled by the CTV set platform.

Additionally, for television of the future, interactivity is key, so while the viewer is watching his/her program, there will be recommendations for other programs that the viewer might enjoy, based upon the viewer's program choice or profile. Today, those recommendations are on the search page of the program or on the episode home page. In the future, those recommendations will be located in a different portion of the television screen and will have embedded links to each of the suggested programs. Further, as the viewer watches a particular episode of a program, (s)he will be asked whether (s)he would like to include that program or even that episode in a "Favorites" category, which will make it easier for the viewer to return to it in the future. On the home search page, the viewer will then be able to access his/her "Favorites" category and go straight to those programs (s)he has included.

A second way the viewer can find the program (s)he wants, will be to work through new search engines devoted exclusively or primarily to television programming, and available online and on social media sites. The search engines will be used when the viewer knows the name of a program or some information about the program but does not know the content provider that has the program in its inventory. When using one of the search engines, the viewer will insert any portion of the name of the program, lead character, lead actor, etc., and with only a click or two, a wave of the hand, or a voice command, be on the content provider's website or in its library, at or near the program s(he) wants to see. The process will occur in a manner similar to the *The Big Bang Theory* example given previously, but with the search engine as the starting point. The more information regarding the program or episode that is provided by the viewer at the beginning, the fewer clicks, hand-waves, or voice commands will be needed.

Additionally, the specialized search engines designed for television specifically will make it possible for the viewer simply to input a particular aspect of the program into the search engine. The search engine will then take the viewer directly to the program or near the program, with little to no intermediary steps to navigate.

But what about new programs? Production houses will be running at full capacity to keep up with the demand for new programs from the ever-proliferating universe of future television content providers. These new programs must be promoted and promoted heavily if they are going to succeed with the viewer and with the advertiser. The most obvious place for promoting new programs will be on the content provider's social media sites. Because scheduling no longer exists, nor the need for "seasons," new programs can be introduced continuously. Further, like the suggestions for alternative programs mentioned earlier, on a portion of the screen will be blurbs about new programs that are available for the viewer to watch, with clickable links embedded in the blurbs to "jump" the viewer straight to the new program. There could even be a section on the television screen where the titles of the provider's new programs (as clickable links) scroll so the viewer can see the listings and choose to "jump" to a new program right away. Alternatively, there could be a section of the screen where, instead of a list of the provider's new programs, there could be a list of programs of the same genre or with the same lead actor or with the same or a similar setting, etc., regardless of content provider, that would scroll for the viewer to consider and possibly select. The choice of how the scrolling list is compiled could even be left up to the viewer's preference.

With television in the future, there is no problem with the viewer jumping to a new program episode from the one (s)he is watching. If every program is available all the time, the viewer can jump to the new program, watch it in full or in part, then jump back to the program (s)he was originally watching. Viewers will also be able to enjoy the same opportunities on their tablets, computers, and smartphones, although most likely a more basic version, depending on the device. While, at this time, it may seem as though there will be numerous distractions on the screen as a person watches a program, television viewers of the future will consider this type of viewing normal, especially the younger age groups for whom multitasking is just a way of life. In fact, Deloitte studies on TV viewers consistently show that Millennials and Gen Z already multitask using as many as three or four different devices simultaneously.[1]

A second way of promoting new programs to the viewer is directly as (s)he is watching television. Here is where knowing the viewer is extremely valuable.

Once the viewer has logged in to his/her account on the CTV platform, all of his/her preferences, likes and dislikes, demographic and lifestyle information, as well as television habits and previous choices, become available to the content provider to help determine which of the new programs being introduced the viewer is most likely going to want to watch. As soon as the logged-in viewer makes his/her first selection for the program (s)he wishes to watch at that particular time, blurbs for new programs of the same or similar type will begin appearing on the screen to entice the viewer to try the new programs out. A simple click, wave, or verbal command will take the viewer directly to that new program or save it to a "New For Viewing" category if the viewer wishes to watch it at a later time.

It is important to remember that the *viewer* is choosing what (s)he wishes to watch, when (s)he wishes to watch; therefore, because all programming is on-demand, it does not matter whether the viewer jumps to the new program or not. If (s)he does jump to the new program, after the viewer finishes watching the new program, (s)he can simply return to the program (s)he was originally watching. If the viewer saves the program for later viewing, then (s)he can watch the new program at his/her leisure. Regardless, the program, with its included commercials, gets watched.

Further, if two or more people are watching television together, and both are logged in, then blurbs for new programs designed for each viewer will be displayed on the screen, and those programs can be saved to each viewer's "New For Viewing" folder. The viewers can finish the program they are watching together before going to one of the saved programs, or they can jump to a new program that one of the viewers wishes to watch. It will even be possible, if the television screen is large enough, to split the screen into multiple smaller ones at the same time. This will be especially important when dealing with children and the desire of each child to watch his/her own program. Now there will be one smaller screen for each child. Such a showing of multiple programs would require a separate headset or earbuds for each child, providing the correct audio for each child's program to the child.

The use of split screen or multiple split screens would also be available for adults, when the need arose. For instance, as described earlier, two or more viewers are watching a program together and they are all logged in. Because they are all watching the same program together, each time a blurb for a new program appears on the screen, any or all of the viewers will have the opportunity to save the program into their own "New For Viewing" folder, regardless of who the program blurb was designed for. Multiple savings of the blurb for the new program makes it possible for the content provider to reach more viewers in addition to the intended viewer, allowing the content provider to increase the potential audience for the new program. Further, if one or more of the viewers (but not all) decide to watch the new program immediately, by selecting the new program, additional windows would open on the television screen for each viewer who wants to watch the new program. Headphones/earbuds, then, would be needed for each viewer to receive the audio from either the new or the original program.

New program offerings can be shown on the various pages of the specialized search engines. In the future, there will be more search engines than the current ones. Search engines devoted specifically to television programming will become the *TV Guide* of the future, providing the television viewer of the future with the ability to filter programs in the ways described previously. Television search engines will function much as a regular search engine, but with the convenience of providing links to television programs. Advertisements, promotional materials, news blurbs (if desired), and other informational content could be included on the search engine pages, and logged-in viewers could be prompted to watch her/his favorite types of programs up front by reminders with links to those programs. Additionally, international search engines – specific to television – will provide opportunities for content providers to reach audiences around the globe. Having their libraries of programs listed on international search engines would make those programs even more readily available to new viewers and new audiences in general. Providers being able to reach global audiences would lead to huge numbers of new viewers for the programs, and would open up numerous opportunities for advertisers to reach massive numbers of new consumers.

In addition to the use of search engines and filters to promote both new programs and programs already in the library of the content provider, social media will become increasingly important for promoting a content provider's programming. Facebook, Linkedin, X, SnapChat, Instagram, Pinterest, and other social media sites will offer television content providers numerous opportunities to promote their programs directly to their "friends" and "fans" via pages, likes, tweets, etc. As users of social media sites provide more and more personal information about themselves, programmers will be able to target their friends and potential friends with information and content designed to drive viewers to programs, especially new programs. When a new program or a new season of a current program is about to "hit the air" (is it even relevant to use that term any longer?), the distribution company's promotion departments will begin firing out messages and videos to those with connections on X, Instagram, Facebook, and all the other social media sites, letting them read promotional blurbs and watch short videos from the producer, director, the stars, and the distributor talking about the new program or season that will be premiering. Additionally, the production house and the distribution company will post similar promotional blurbs on their social media sites for their friends and fans to comment on. Those friends and fans can then pass along information and comments about the new program to their friends in a continuous web of promotion. Further, on social media sites, the production house and the distribution company will post short promotional videos about the program designed to build the interest of their friends and fans who will ultimately become their viewers, much as movie trailers today can be posted on such social media sites.

Once the program has been purchased by a content provider, the provider's promotion department will begin its work. Much as described earlier for the production house and the distribution company, the content provider will use the same variety of social media sites to promote its programs to viewers and potential viewers. The provider will begin with a series of tweets on X, status updates on Facebook, SnapChat, and WhatsApp, short, streamed teasers on Instagram, and other such promotional announcements on additional social network sites. Messages to friends and fans will get the process going as those supporters begin to tweet and "statusfy" about the new program or programs being offered.

Viewers will update their status on Facebook or other social media sites, stating their feelings (hopefully, positive feelings) and reposting the short promotional videos. Others will see their friends or friends-of-friends' positive reactions to and interest in the new program and will begin talking about and sharing content about the program themselves. Each Facebook status update, video post, tweet, or other addition to social media sites by the viewer has the opportunity to reach even more potential viewers of the program. These promotional tools will begin to generate "buzz" (the word-of-social-media, an alternative to, and, increasingly, a replacement for, word-of-mouth) that will yield significant numbers of viewers for every program in the content provider's inventory, not just the new program that got the discussion started. The same thing will occur simultaneously on all the other social media sites, increasing exponentially the number of opportunities for the content provider to drive viewers to the program.

Further, because the program will be telecast over the content provider's CTV app, the likelihood to draw viewers to the new program in international locations would be virtually certain, increasing the total number of viewers of the program. At the same time, the promotion work will encourage viewers in international locations to explore further down the "long tail" of the content provider's inventory of programs. These programs will often find favor with international viewers in different locations, especially if they have not seen the programs due to the lack of international distribution efforts. The "word-of-social-media" promotional efforts by the production house, the distribution company, and the content provider will open numerous new opportunities for classic programs to find new life internationally, with new viewers and new opportunities for advertisers to reach existing markets, or to develop new markets around the world. Those opportunities, then, become new sources of revenue that will enhance, and, potentially, could eclipse the revenues generated domestically.

Additionally, the social media pages of the content producer, content distributor, and content provider will be involved in even more forms of promotional engagement with viewers. Friends, fans, etc., could have the opportunity to watch program clips and rate the program even before its first episode has aired. In addition to promoting the program, such responses could provide feedback on the potential popularity of the program, although, once a program is in the inventory of a content provider, it will cost virtually nothing to continue to provide opportunities for the program to be seen. Even a program that does not start out with a strong following, could, over time, develop a large or at least loyal following. In other words, the days of allowing a good program to grow into its audience (if no longer its time slot) would return. Further, by using social media as one of the major promotional platforms, the content providers could develop contests for their friends, fans, and potential friends and fans to participate in, thus building interest in the program and in the content provider while providing additional ways for viewers to become engaged with the provider.

Social media pages would be used as a way to introduce friends, fans, etc., to the actors starring in a new program. The stars will Tweet, update their status, etc., on all the various social media sites, share information about their backgrounds (especially if they are not well known), become "friends" with the viewers and potential viewers of the program, and direct the viewers and potential viewers to their personal websites. In this way, viewers and potential viewers could develop a relationship with, and an affinity for, the actors. By building viewer interest in the actors, the content provider will be enhancing its own closeness with the viewer. All this "closeness" will encourage potential viewers to "check out" the program and give the viewer even more reason to return again and again to watch the content provider's other programs that will be suggested to her/him with his/her profile in mind.

By sharing profile information on their various actors to their social media fans, the content provider will also be giving fans a way to access those actors' own social media fan pages. There the fans could learn even more about the actor, gaining background information about the star, his/her likes and dislikes, what other programs (s)he has been a part of (thus building interest in other programs the content provider might have in its library), what the star thinks about the current program (s)he is in – anything that might heighten the interest of the fan in the star and thus in the program.

Social media is one of the most powerful forces available to the content provider in reaching the viewer in a meaningful way, and, in developing such a rich relationship with the viewer and the potential viewer, the provider can make available the exact programming that will be effective in capturing and holding the attention of the viewer. While much of what is described here is already being done at least to some degree, promotional work using social media sites still has a long way to go compared to the possibilities of what will be able to be accomplished in the future.

Last, but certainly not least, there is YouTube and other user-generated video sites, along with X, Facebook, Instagram, and other social media sites that include videos. Already, content providers are putting clips from their programming onto YouTube and other such sites in an effort to drive viewers to their programs. As program delivery grows ever more complex, such sites will be primary tools for promotion that the content providers will use to get the word out about the programming they have available.

One of the best uses of YouTube and other such sites is to promote new programs as they come online. In addition to the other promotional opportunities mentioned above, user-generated sites will serve as excellent tools for promotional campaigns for the content providers' new programs. Further, because YouTube has branded channels, those channels can be used by the content providers and content producers to "test out" new programs, new talent, new plots, etc.[2] Additionally, YouTube itself has begun to deliver its own original content through its channels, so that becomes an additional channel for previewing programs before they move to more mainstream content providers.[3]

Weeks before a new program is to debut, short promotional videos designed to entice viewers to watch the new program will air on the user-generated sites, and audiences will be directed to video samples through the content provider's social media pages. But these videos will not only be designed to pique the viewer's interest. User-generated sites will offer the content provider the opportunity to run videos that have added features. These features will include interviews with the stars of the program, the director, the producer, and possibly testimonials from viewers who have had a chance to participate in viewings and screenings prior to the promotional campaign.

In conjunction with the user-generated site campaign of video material, the content provider will begin a "kick-off" promotional campaign for the new program on its social media pages and its website. The campaign will tout the new program, its stars, its debut date and time, and share opportunities for viewers to get a first-hand look at the new program, along with behind-the-scenes information about the new program, by visiting the user-generated sites where the campaign is taking place. The content provider will then begin a social media campaign, delivering news of the new program to friends and contacts, urging them to check out the user-generated sites for the new program and the extra material they can find there, and passing along their thoughts on the new program. Additionally, given the extensive knowledge that the content provider will have about its viewers, the promotional campaign can be targeted to those viewers who will most likely be the program's primary and secondary audiences.

As the date of a new program's debut grows close, more enticing videos will be placed on the user-generated video sites, either in addition to, or as a replacement for the earlier videos. The content provider's website will begin touting the new program and promotional spots will be placed on the search engine results page, especially for programs expected to be blockbuster-type hits (but not necessarily for extreme niche programs unless the spots are on niche search engines dedicated to that type of program). The program's stars will begin serious and extensive use of their social media sites, engaging with their friends and encouraging them to watch the program. What will be produced is a highly organized, extensive, multi-faceted promotional campaign that will be extremely effective in driving preferred audiences to a new program, and not only cost-effective, but virtually cost-free. The cost savings compared to the extremely expensive promotional campaigns of today's television will be enormous, while the results will be significantly more positive.

In addition, advertisers can assist in promoting the content provider's new program. Advertisers expecting to run commercials in the new program could begin adding promos for the new program to the home pages of their websites and social media pages, with encouraging comments about the program and links to the different video sites where promotional videos are occurring and to the content provider's website as well. Given the potential for huge revenues from television in the future, it will be in the advertiser' best interests to work closely with the content providers to promote programs the advertiser plans to place commercials in.

The promotion of new content will not be the only use for such sites. Content providers will find that they can promote their entire inventories of programming via these sites. By promoting whole libraries on such sites, content providers will be able to reach new viewers who have never experienced such classic shows as *I Love Lucy*, *The Jeffersons*, *The Ed Sullivan Show*, and *Rowan and Martin's Laugh-In*. By promoting those older (ancient in the minds of the new viewers!) programs to new audiences, content providers will have the potential to pick up additional new viewers for whom these programs are a fascinating new treat.

Likewise, the promotion of programming over user-generated sites would also reach those older viewers for whom such classic shows as those mentioned above would hold fond memories. Often, in the bombardment of ever-new and ever-changing programming, classic shows are forgotten until something stirs an idea in the mind. YouTube and other user-generated sites would serve as the catalyst needed to stir those memories and drive viewers to those programs.

The use of YouTube and other such sites as promotional devices to drive new audiences to classic programs, as well to drive familiar audiences to those same classic programs, yields an additional benefit – the ability to deliver advertising not only to a whole new generation of viewers but also to familiar audiences, thereby developing additional sources of revenue. While the audiences may be small compared to those of new programming and current programming at any one time, classic programs and those that will become classic programs as time progresses will still have their audiences and will still be able to deliver revenues. With virtually no associated costs, these programs could provide comparably substantial revenues.

YouTube and others offer additional opportunities for content providers to promote and even air special programs – possibly on a trial basis, but not necessarily so – on a YouTube branded channel belonging to the content provider. Alternatively, given the percentage of programs the networks, especially, own and telecast today, the content providers of television in the future could choose to air original programs they have produced and/or own on YouTube as original content. Content providers would have the opportunity to reach millions of viewers in a short period of time on the best-known of the user-generated channels, which would be an excellent way to test new program concepts and ideas, introduce and test new genres (or reinvigorate otherwise "dead" genres), and give new writers, producers, directors, and actors the chance to develop loyal audiences before moving to the content provider's website and inventory of programs.

Summary

Promotion will become even more important to television in the future, when there will be no scheduling and content will be on-demand, anytime, and anywhere. Websites, search engines devoted strictly to television programming, social media sites, and user-generated sites will be the sources of information for future television audiences. Those audiences will not only find out about the newest programming being offered on all of the different content providers' channels, but also about current, slightly older, and even classic programs that are available to them.

Promotional strategies and techniques will make viewers aware of what is available and what is soon to be available. They will inform and entertain the television viewer of the future, while also leading the viewer to the programming (and, by extension, the advertising and product placement) that is right for each her/him. In short, promotion will be critical to the success of every future television content provider and every viewer.

Notes

1 Deloitte Corporation, *Digital Democracy Survey: A Multi-generational View of Consumer Technology, Media and Telecom Trends,* 9th ed., (2014), www.deloitte.com/us/tmttrends.
2 For examples of top YouTube branded channels, see Santora, Jacinda, "Top 20 YouTube Brand Account Examples (And How They Got There)," *Influencer Marketing Hub*, https://influencermarketinghub.com/youtube-brand-account/,
3 Barr, Merrill, "Is YouTube Preparing for a Netflix-Style Original Content Push?", *Forbes,* (November 20, 2014), http://www.forbes.com/sites/merrillbarr/2014/11/20/is-youtube-preparing-for-a-netflix-style-original-content-push/.

10 The Future of U.S. Television in the Global Television Market

So far, this book has looked at the major players in television of the future and the revenue streams and promotional developments available for participants in that future. The final piece of the puzzle is to consider the idea of future television as global television. While other chapters have mentioned the global nature of television in the future, this chapter explores the possibilities in full. While addressable advertising and Ubiquitous Product Placement (UPP) will produce revenues that can compete with the money brought in by traditional advertising, it is the global nature of television in the future combined with addressable advertising, UPP, and continuous promotion that will usher in a new "diamond age of television," the likes of which will surpass even the wildest dreams of today's television industry. It is the development of a global television industry that will become the future of television.

We live in a global society. Since the end of the Second World War, the world has continuously seen a move away from isolationism and a move toward globalization. No longer can a country – regardless of the size or the abundance of its natural resources – successfully choose an isolationist stance. Those countries that have chosen isolationism have seen themselves relegated to irrelevancy and often pariah-nation status. The question these days is not whether to go global, but how to make it happen.

Interestingly, U.S. television has traditionally been a nation-specific set of industries. U.S. television, whether over the air (OTA) or cable, has, for the most part, been limited to the fifty states, plus the incidental spillover that occurs along the U.S.'s borders with Canada and Mexico. For subscribers to DirecTV and Dish Network, their international reach has been ancillary to their U.S. subscribership. Their international reach is limited to the Western Hemisphere, and has, for the most part, been aimed at the immigrant population in the U.S. who wish to still connect with their home countries in their native languages. While television programming from the U.S. travels the globe very well – showing up on local stations in many, if not most countries of the world – the networks themselves have focused only on delivering their programming to the U.S. television audience. That, however, is changing.

Using satellite delivery, the networks – especially Fox and NBC, along with a number of cable channels such as CNN, Discovery, and ESPN – have been

DOI: 10.4324/9781003625384-14

moving to open up the rest of the world to their programs, either in English or in the local language in some form. CNN, of course, in many ways started the globalization of the U.S. television industry when it launched CNN International in 1984, an English-language news channel provided to upscale hotels in countries around the world, and aimed primarily at American and other English-speaking-or-understanding businesspersons and tourists.[1]

Today, viewers around the world can see a number of different programs on specialized American television channels if they have a home satellite system or cable. These specialized channels generally are not available in the U.S.; they are designed for the international audience, although they often telecast programs that are also shown to the U.S. audience. Depending on how the television channel chooses to telecast the programming, audiences might hear the English language version, an overdubbed version (in a language that is dominant in the region or country), a local language version, or an English language version with subtitling. Advertising is often country-specific or regional in scope and can be considered in the same category as local advertising.

Please allow me to share a few personal examples. I have had the opportunity throughout my career as an author and a university faculty member to travel extensively. As such, I have had the chance to watch a variety of television channels in countries in Europe, Central and South America, Asia, and Oceania. I have been able to watch one of the CNN channels regardless of what country I was visiting at the time. I have had the opportunity to watch the NBC SuperChannel, CNBC, Fox Sports, live college football bowl games, tape-delayed NBA basketball games, the occasional MLB game of the day, and even on rare occasions, NFL games. I have had the chance to watch Discovery Channel programs around the globe. Further, I have had the opportunity to watch my favorite scripted television programs on a delayed basis in virtually every country I have visited.

To turn the situation around, I can also watch BBC America on my YouTube TV app on my connected television (CTV) set, BBC programming on PBS stations, and, at one time, I could have watched news programming from Canada. Further, depending on where I am in the U.S., I have had the opportunity to watch programming from Japan, the Middle East, Mexico, and even China Central Television on the television set in my hotel room.

One more turn of the situation – in my travels around the world I have had the opportunity to watch television channels from countries other than the one I am visiting. Satellite television has made it possible for pan-European and pan-Asian delivery of channels, both country-specific and those that are truly pan-continental.[2]

The point is that television – both the programs as well as individual channels – is becoming more and more global. Television is no longer a local, regional, or even national entity. Television has transcended national boundaries, and has made itself into a global commodity, taking with it programming genres, sports leagues, and niche channels. Developing television technologies will take television into a future where all television is global television. The possibilities are virtually limitless.

The Future of Television Is TV Everywhere

The future of television is truly global television. It makes it possible for every content provider to reach every Internet user on the planet directly with programming, advertising, product placement, and promotion. That is a potential audience of almost 5.56 billion people around the globe as of April 2025. That's 67.9% of the total world population, and a growth of more than 1500% since the turn of the 21st century.[3] Northern Europe has the highest penetration rate at 97.9% and Europe as a whole has four of the top five penetration rates, with North America the only intruder (third at 93.3%). The only regions below the worldwide average of 67.9% are the countries of southern (53.8%), western (42.5%), middle (33.6%), and eastern (28.5%) Africa – those countries generally described as sub-Saharan Africa.[4] Each one of those almost 5.56 billion Internet users worldwide becomes a potential viewer of television in the future and a consumer to be reached.

The National Association of Broadcasters (NAB) is the largest organization of its kind in the world. Before COVID-19, every year, more than 100,000 participants converged on Las Vegas, Nevada, to take part in this convention (today the NAB is still recovering with participant numbers in the 50-to-60,000s). One-fourth or more of those participants come to the convention from outside the U.S. Yet, time and again, convention-opening addresses mention the global participants only in passing if at all. Participants from around the world still enjoy the convention because they realize that the future of television is a global television universe, and they have a part to play in that universe. Indeed, many countries around the world already play major roles in the development of the future of television, even taking the lead and showing the U.S. the possibilities that are available. For instance, South Korea is leading the world in the development and implementation of ATSC 3.0, rolling it out to the entire country and promising to deliver its television entirely through ATSC 3.0 by 2027.[5] ATSC 3.0 in the U.S., as mentioned earlier, is still in the development stage and it remains to be seen if it will even become a reality and a serious competitor to the other Internet-protocol-television-based (IPTV) distributors.

The future of television is not country-specific, nor is it country-specific with bleed-over on the borders. Rather, television in the future is a global enterprise with ownership of content providers crossing national boundaries to become global enterprises. In some ways, television is already a global industry. Satellites beam television signals from and to anywhere in the world. Syndicators sell programs across the globe. Comcast, Charter/Spectrum, and others, through the development of TV Everywhere, are making their programming available to their subscribers any time, on any platform, and – literally – everywhere a compatible cellular or a Wi-Fi signal is available, anywhere in the world.

In the future, the television audience will demand even more – and television of the future will provide. With television's move to the Internet, through the use of IPTV, content providers will no longer be limited by channels, local affiliates, or even national borders. Netflix is today demonstrating what can be accomplished as it is currently in more than 190 different countries around the world (virtually every country in the world, and it is currently negotiating with China for access there).[6] The television universe of the future will provide the viewer not only the possibility of television anytime, anywhere, and on any platform, but also any program regardless of its country of origin.

With the development of global television as the standard fare for the television viewer of the future comes new opportunities for revenues for the content providers. Combining Aggregated Targeted Microadvertising (ATMA), Programmatic Advertising (PA), and Dynamic Ad Insertion (DAI) conducted worldwide, with expanded UPP, gives the content provider the opportunity to develop numerous revenue streams by delivering different advertisements during the same commercial break and different product placements to viewers around the world. By having the entire inventory of a content provider on its home website or available through its app, a television content provider in the future will be able to reach its worldwide viewers with advertisements and product placements no matter who they are or where they are. The opportunity to provide programming seamlessly to viewers around the world opens up television to an entirely new universe of opportunities for ever-increasing worldwide revenues that makes the future exceedingly bright.

21st century television viewers want their television anywhere, anytime, and on any platform – that point has been made again and again. A possible subtitle of this chapter, "TV Everywhere Fulfilled," makes the point that everywhere means exactly that – the viewer is not limited by geography or national boundaries or even oceans. It does not mean that viewers can watch their favorite programs anywhere, with the exception of the broadcasters whose online signals must stay in their own markets. For the networks and their local affiliates, that is a suicide plan.

Ultimately, though, the networks will not sign on to a plan that guarantees their ultimate demise. As discussed in Chapter 1: The Future of the Broadcast Industry, the networks will not go down with their affiliates, choosing instead to compete with all other content providers by delivering their programming directly to their viewers. This decision, which will occur almost certainly by 2040 (and possibly earlier), will be driven by the networks' continuously expanding use of cloud technology for storage of their program inventories, along with the ability to deliver their programming through IPTV, be it wired, Wi-Fi, cellular, ATSC 3.0, or some other form yet to be developed. The decision to drop their affiliates also removes the networks from the burden of non-overlapping geographical markets as well as national borders with their spillover concerns, and allows them to reach their audiences anywhere, including any location outside the U.S.

The networks are already making moves in this direction, and, in a sense, are already global broadcasters. Currently, they make it possible for viewers everywhere to watch archived episodes of programs on their websites and by providing apps for smartphones, tablets, and computers that allow viewers to watch streamed programs directly on their devices.[7] For the networks, taking the final step of airing their programming online at the same time as their affiliates broadcast them OTA makes the affiliates redundant and removes the last hurdle to turning the networks themselves into complete global broadcasters with the ability to draw viewers from around the world. One example of one of the networks simulcasting at least some of its programming online is CBS Television/Skydance with its CBS All Access (now Paramount+) streaming service.[8] However, the service is not designed to take the place of its local affiliates, but to operate in conjunction with them. Nevertheless, it is easy to imagine a time very near in the future when CBS Television/Skydance would decide that charging $5.99 a month per subscriber, plus the opportunity to keep all its advertising fees, might just be tempting enough to drop its affiliates and go à la carte as a standalone app, in addition to being available on virtual Multichannel Video Programming Distributor (vMVPDs).

The major direct-to-home (DTH) satellite companies, DirecTV and Dish Network, have both gone international, but in a different way. While both can be received in the western hemisphere, making it possible for viewers in all the Americas to become subscribers, both companies have launched international packages. These international packages allow viewers whose first language is not English to watch programming in their own language. In addition, both companies deliver programming from around the world as part of the international packages, thus making both companies global players, but in the opposite way to the cable channels and the networks.[9]

Others have been even more aggressive in making international moves. Google's YouTube has been and continues to be a global sensation, with videos from around the world available to worldwide audiences. Netflix has become an international distributor, providing its programming in 190 different countries, and worldwide, has slightly less than 270 million subscribers as of the first quarter of 2024, 70% of which are international.[10,11] Amazon Prime Video/Instant Video – perhaps the major competitor to Netflix – has itself gone global and now reaches audiences in more than 200 countries, surpassing Netflix in total countries reached.[12] Online channels that are international and global abound on over-the-top (OTT) set-top boxes (STBs) such as Roku, Amazon, and Apple TV.

Going Global and Audiences

Television is global, no doubt about it. Trade shows such as *Marché International des Programmes de Télévision* (MIP-TV), *Marché International des Programmes de Communication* (MIPCOM), the American Film Market, and National Association of Television Program Executives' (NATPE) convention are all examples of opportunities for countries around the world to sell programming to each other.[13] Syndicators can turn programs that never even make it to U.S. television into revenue-makers by selling those programs in countries across the world where audiences enjoy them. Additionally, successful U.S. television programs are sold worldwide, with episodes sometimes airing within a week or less of when they aired on U.S. television. The worldwide syndication market has been and continues, at this time, to be a critical part of the financial success of U.S. television.

So why change? While global syndication has been a boon for U.S. television overall, going global opens the content providers up to vast new audiences around the world directly, without having to work through syndication channels. Television content providers of the future, through their ability to deliver programming worldwide using the cloud for storage and delivering programming from their websites through IPTV, will have the potential to reach almost 5.44 billion people around the world and that number will continue to grow in the years to come.[14] Further, because U.S. television programs sell well today around the world, there is a ready-made worldwide audience for U.S. programming. Because of that ready-made audience, the delivery of television in the future will likely help to spur the pace of the increase of Internet deployment across the globe.

Because U.S. programming is well-known worldwide through the practice of U.S. companies syndicating programs, going global gives U.S. content providers the opportunity to control the delivery of their programs to countries around the world. Going global gives the content provider the ability to bypass the scheduling decisions of the various content distributors in other countries and deliver the programming directly to their worldwide audiences, in the way that Netflix does today. Because television in the future is not delivered over the airwaves but reaches viewers through the Internet via the various delivery methods, the rules that govern television programming delivered over the airwaves in other countries can be eliminated or at least minimized. Content providers will be able to deliver programs so that audiences worldwide can enjoy them directly, without having to watch their favorite programs when their television stations carry them, and without whatever changes might have been made to the programs to allow them to meet each government's television codes regarding ethics and decency. Audiences worldwide will be able to enjoy the same television programs and learn of new programs that have not been available to them before through the full implementation of global television.

In that way, U.S. content providers can build worldwide brand images, grow the size and diversity of their audience, compete directly with global content providers from other countries, and, in general, become significantly more profitable. World audiences love to watch U. S. television programming – going global gives U.S. content providers the ability to reach those worldwide audiences at the same time they are reaching their home audiences. Television in the future, then, makes TV Everywhere, truly TV everywhere.

By going global, television in the future allows U.S. viewers to enjoy their programs at any time no matter where they might be traveling in the world. Regardless of the country, U.S. viewers will have the chance to keep up with their favorite programs as new episodes become available and they will able to watch programs live. As long as television viewers have the opportunity to connect to the Internet in some manner, their favorite programs will be available for them directly, without the need for additional intermediary hardware, software, or subscriptions.

Further, because television in the future will be delivered as VOD, viewers will be able to view any and all of their favorite programs as they become available, either at the time of initial airing – especially important for live events and for those who are avid fans of a particular scripted program – or at a later time, but still while outside of the U.S. Going global also makes it possible for viewers in international locations to watch their favorite programs on their tablets and smartphones in addition to their computers, as long as they have Internet access.

The Future of U.S. Television in the Global Television Market 169

As has been described in previous chapters, television in the future makes a content provider's entire inventory available to viewers. Going global, then, makes it possible for a content provider's entire inventory of programs to be available worldwide all the time, for the entire world to enjoy again and again, on the widest range of devices. The possibility of massive worldwide audiences enjoying the inventory of a content provider makes going global a requirement for television in the future.

Going Global and Revenues

Chapters 7 and 8 featured in-depth discussions about the enormous potential of television in the future to produce tremendous revenue streams through advertising[15] and UPP.[16] Going global magnifies the possibilities of those revenue streams by delivering worldwide audiences who want to watch advertisements that are relevant to them (delivered using ATMA, PA, and DAI[17]) and enjoy UPP as they watch their favorite programs.

The content providers of U.S. television today – more specifically, the networks and the cable/DTH satellite channels – fill their advertising slots with commercials from companies that have nationwide appeal. When you examine those advertisers, virtually all of them are transnational corporations with products and services that reach around the globe.[18] A further example – in the *2024 BrandZ Top 100 Most Valuable Global Brands*, published by Kantar, nine of the top ten and 14 of the top 20 most valuable global brands were U.S. brands, led by Apple, Google, Microsoft, and Amazon. Coming in at number ten was Tencent. The five international brands in the top 20 were Louis Vuitton (#12), Aramco (#14), Hermes (#17), Moutai (#18) and Accenture (#20). Of the full Top 100, at least 87 of the brands were either U.S. brands or brands that have a significant presence in the U.S. (for example, Toyota, RBC, Accenture).[19] Every one of those 87 brands advertises on U.S. television. In reality, then, the 79 most valuable global advertisers for 2024 were both U.S. national advertisers and worldwide advertisers (the other eight were U.S. only advertisers).

The tremendous advantage of television in the future is its ability to reach audiences around the globe directly and to deliver them to advertisers. Consider for a moment how much more cost effective, and therefore, how much more valuable it would be for global advertisers to place their advertisements on content providers' programs that reach audiences in countries throughout the world. Further, given the targeted nature of Programmatic Media Buying and DAI, both driven by ATMA, advertisers could expect to successfully reach upwards of 90% of a program's audience worldwide. While each advertisement would be playing potentially to a smaller audience overall due to the extremely targeted nature of ATMA, the opportunity to sell an individual ad insertion numerous times to a variety of advertisers, along with the ability to sell each advertisement at a premium due to a high success rate, more than offsets the smaller audience for each advertisement. The result, then, would be a larger total revenue for each ad insertion location, especially if each specific ad insertion was reaching a highly targeted audience in each of 200 or more different countries. Such an opportunity for success would be extremely profitable for both the advertisers and the content providers.

The ability of television of the future to deliver global audiences also brings into play the opportunity for content providers to connect with international advertisers that might not otherwise advertise on U.S. television. Remember, 13 out of the top 100 most valuable global brands of 2024 do not have a presence or do not have a significant presence on U.S. television because their target markets do not include the U.S. at this time. Given the nature of television in the future, every one of those 13 top 100 brands would likely find it extremely profitable to advertise with television content providers. They would be able to reach their audiences around the world via the powerhouse programs of the U.S. content providers, as well as introduce their products and brands to U.S. television audiences. Further, because eleven of those 13 top 100 brands without a significant presence in the U.S. are based in China, bringing those companies onto global television in the future would open up China's markets and its 1.09 billion Internet users[20] to viewers around the world, and advertisers from around the world to those Chinese Internet users. The reciprocal nature would offer exceptional opportunities for all concerned.

Today, for a U.S. program airing in, say, 20 different countries around the world, advertisers – both U.S. as well as international ones – must negotiate (or more likely the advertising agency representing the advertiser must negotiate) with each of the different television stations carrying that program in those 20 countries or even with their respective governments. To place advertising in that program in all 20 countries requires, first, that the advertiser or the agency have a presence in each country in some form. Second, there are likely to be different requirements for placing advertising in that program, depending on the country. Third, payment likely must be made in several different currencies (unless the 20 countries are all in the Euro zone), requiring conversion of each currency at a fluctuating exchange rate. Fourth, depending on the country, there may be a lack of protection for the advertiser in certain areas – for example, to prevent rate increases during a contract period or the advertisement running directly against its competitors during the same break, or to ensure make-good opportunities should an advertisement not run as scheduled. While there are numerous other considerations that would need to be negotiated, these four are representative of the potential problems that might occur when attempting to advertise on a given program when it airs in a variety of different countries. These problems and others make such advertising complex, time-consuming, and expensive.

Television of the future's global reach eliminates or minimizes all these concerns. With television of the future, the advertiser contacts the content provider originating the program and negotiates the placing of advertising into the program for each country, thus eliminating the need for a presence in each one. Because the television program is delivered over IPTV, there will be only one set of requirements for placing the advertisement on the content provider. (Note: There may still be requirements when it comes to *airing* the advertisement in one or more of the countries, but any such requirements of that nature would be handled at the outset of negotiations and would still be discussed between the advertiser and the content provider.) Payment is made one time, in one currency, eliminating the need for multiple currencies and multiple currency exchanges.

Protections for the advertiser would be negotiated only with the content provider because the content provider would be the only one delivering the program to the 20 countries. Other concerns and problems would also be negotiated between the content provider and the advertiser, so instead of a complex, time-consuming, and expensive multi-country process, television in the future requires only one set of negotiations, making the process simple, much less time-consuming, and far less expensive. (The process at least; the cost of the advertising could be more expensive, but the total cost of both the advertisement plus the process would be less expensive, especially when time and complexity are figured into the costs.)

Further, television in the future allows advertisers from other countries the ability to advertise on a given content provider's program only in the countries where they have markets. Using the previous example, today, if an advertiser wanted to reach only ten of the 20 countries airing a particular program, the advertiser would still have the same concerns as before for each of the 10 countries. In the future of television, the advertiser would negotiate with the content provider to air targeted ads using Programmatic Media Buying and DAI, both driven by ATMA, for those ten countries only, leaving space for one or more advertisers to reach one, a few, or all of the other ten countries where the availability still exists. In addition to being simpler, less time-consuming, and less expensive overall, television in the future also provides flexibility that is simpler, less time-consuming, less expensive for the advertiser(s), and likely much more profitable for the content provider.

Going global also allows the coming television universe to expand its opportunities for UPP within the programs of the content providers. Globalization has brought and will continue to bring the world's products and services to audiences across the globe. As television programs in the future evolve and develop, new locations, new peoples, and new cultures will continue to be introduced.[21] With that evolving program diversity will come opportunities for new and additional product placements for content providers to sell to advertisers.

Much as with advertising, the future of television will make UPP a reality and an enormous potential revenue stream, one that is already currently developing in both online and linear media programming. UPP opportunities for companies all over the world will help to create new markets for companies' products. Through UPP, companies will be able to reach consumers anywhere in the world with their products. Those consumers, then, have the chance to learn about products they likely have never seen before. They can explore those products in depth, get excited about them, and make purchases. Suddenly, new markets have opened to companies making use of UPP.

In the same manner, enterprising entrepreneurs will see a product they find interesting, new, and enticing in a scene from a television program. When they click on the product, they will be taken to the product's website where they will find out that the product is not currently available in their locations. Making the decision to contact the company that makes the product, those entrepreneurs will begin the process of bringing the product to their markets. This scenario can and will happen again and again as the global aspect of television in the future is realized. Going global makes product placement an ever-growing revenue stream for content providers and has the potential to open new markets and produce tremendous new revenues for their advertisers. It's a "win-win" scenario for all concerned.

Potential Impediments to Global Television

Going global, at this time, has its challenges, mostly from governments and their regulatory requirements. As mentioned earlier, although Netflix is in 190 countries worldwide and Amazon is in over 200 countries and territories, they – along with YouTube – are not currently in China or North Korea.[22,23,24] Each of these countries, along with others that block one or two of the services, do so for political and cultural reasons. Additionally, other countries have blocked services for a short period or insisted that a program or video be removed because of the topic or current cultural or political situation in that country at that specific time.

Global television, at this time, is usually blocked for two different sets of reasons: (1) content-based reasons or (2) access-based reasons. In addition to the political and cultural sensitivities, content-based reasons can also include religious or moral objections to programming. This is what has occurred most often when countries have objected to a program or series of programs on a service, leading to that service being blocked or threatened with blockage until the offending program is removed.[25,26,27,28]

Access-based reasons can include licensing and distribution rights, protecting local industries, cost and revenue considerations, and technical limitations.[29,30,31,32] While these reasons can be a concern, most, if not all, of them will likely disappear in the coming years as the economics of the future of television will make these concerns obsolete. The one area of concern that will be most likely to linger beyond the others is that of protecting local industries. We have seen this problem for a number of years in countries like New Zealand, where, 20 years ago, I witnessed first-hand the concern for its local television industry. At that time 85% of programming on New Zealand television was produced outside of New Zealand – most of which came from the U.S.[33] One answer to this problem could be for countries to require global content distributors to include a certain number or percentage of country specific programs (a quota) on their distribution platforms.[34] Given that we are in the earliest days of viewers around the world – and more specifically, in the U.S. – enjoying programs from other countries (for example, South Korea's *Squid Game* on Netflix), the need for any sort of quota or percentage requirement may be short-term only.

Summary

The ease and profitability of going global provides another powerful reason why global television is the television of the future. Netflix is the current leader in reaching out to almost 270 million subscribers worldwide with its programming. The other major online content providers – subscription video on demand (SVOD), advertising-driven video on demand (AVOD), free ad-supported streaming television (FAST), and any future services that will be developed – will not be far behind in moving to a global marketplace for their programming. Content providers in other countries will also take advantage of the abilities of television in the future to deliver global audiences by reaching out across the globe with their programming. Those that do not quickly follow suit will be left to struggle against the inevitable flow of global programming.

Already, cable organizations such as Disney (ESPN, along with Disney programming), NBC Universal, Discovery, Turner channels, and, of course, the major cable news channels, reach out to international audiences around the globe through their global or regional offerings. Some provide the programming with subtitles, others with local language voiceovers. Additionally, television is following sports teams as they work to extend their audiences worldwide, whether it be the NFL, the NBA, MLB, or now, even college football. Having their games televised to audiences in the U.S. or around the world brings those sports new viewers and potentially new sources of revenue, while the content providers of those games reap the benefits of additional eyeballs in new locations to sell to advertisers. Further, the worldwide coverage of sporting events, such as the Olympics, the Super Bowl, World Cup soccer, and the majors in golf and tennis, also makes it possible for television advertisers to reach global audiences The success of these organizations, even given the requirements that they must work under, shows that the potential for even greater opportunities is within reach of each future television content provider.

With the ability to reach global audiences, content providers will be able to increase their audiences and introduce new viewers to their program inventories. Additionally, content providers will be able to build audiences for even classic television programs in those locations that may never have had the chance to watch the programs before. Further, with the ability to accurately target audiences around the world with advertisements they want to watch, revenues from both advertising and product placement will soar. Analog dollars to digital pennies? No, with television of the future combined with its global reach, it will be analog dollars to digital trillions!

Notes

1 "CNN International," *Wikipedia*, http://en.wikipedia.org/wiki/CNN_International#History.
2 For instance, pan-European channels would include the channels of Sky Television, EuroNews, and EuroSports, among others, while a good example of a pan-Asian channel would be Star Television. Additionally, in Europe, viewers can see a mixture of the various countries' television programming, so that, for example, the French can watch British and German TV and vice versa.
3 Petrosyan, Ani, "Number of Internet and Social Media Users Worldwide as of April 2024," *Statista*, (May 22, 2024), https://www.statista.com/statistics/617136/digital-population-worldwide/.
4 Petrosyan, Ani, "Global Internet Penetration Rates as of April 2024, By Region," *Statista*, (May 7, 2024), https://www.statista.com/statistics/269329/penetration-rate-of-the-internet-by-region/.

5. Jessell, Harry A., "FCC Need To give OVDs MPVD Status," *TVNewsCheck*, (May 18, 2012), http://www.tvnewscheck.com/article/59567/fcc-needs-to-give-ovds-mpvd-status?utm_source=Listrak&utm_medium=Email&utm_term=FCC+Needs+To+Give+OVDs+MPVD+Status&utm_campaign=Jessell%3a+FCC+Needs+To+Give+OVDs+MPVD+Status.
6. Jessell, Harry A., "FCC Need To give OVDs MPVD Status."
7. Jessell, Harry A., "FCC Need To give OVDs MPVD Status."
8. Jessell, Harry A., "FCC Need To give OVDs MPVD Status."
9. http://www.syncbak.com/.
10. Stoll, Julia, "Number of Netflix Paid Subscribers Worldwide From 1st Quarter 2013 to 1st Quarter 2024," *Statista*, (May 22, 2024), https://www.statista.com/statistics/250934/quarterly-number-of-netflix-streaming-subscribers-worldwide/.
11. Anderson, Neil, "More Than Half of Netflix's Content Spending Now Outside of North America," *Ampere|Analysis*, (March 11, 2024), https://www.ampereanalysis.com/insight/more-than-half-of-netflixs-content-spending-now-outside-of-north-america.
12. "Prime Video Offerings – Support – Video Central," *Amazon.com*, (n.d.), https://videocentral.amazon.com/home/help?topicId=GWKF2YM3PC5WLAZ8&ref_=avd_sup_GWKF2YM3PC5WLAZ8.
13. Bibel, Sara, "2014–2015 Season: NBC Leads Among Adults 18-49 & CBS tops Total Viewers Through Week 35 Ending May 24, 2015," *TV By the Numbers*, (May 27, 2015).
14. Petrosyan, Ani, "Number of Internet and Social Media Users Worldwide as of April 2024," *Statista*, (May 22, 2024), https://www.statista.com/statistics/617136/digital-population-worldwide/.
15. See Chapter 1: The Future of the Broadcast Industry.
16. For more information on the international packages offered by DirecTV and Dish Network, go to www.directv.com or www.dish.com and search for their international packages.
17. "What We Do For You," *AmericanTV2Go*, http://www.americantv2go.com/Basics/WhatWeDo.aspx?&Hash=eb44a996-6725-49fd-8ee7-20d1e620083a.
18. "Where is Netflix Available?" *Netflix Help Center*, https://help.netflix.com/en/node/14164 and Huddleston, Tom, "Netflix Is Testing Something You May Not Like," *Time*, (June 1, 2015), http://time.com/3903995/netflix-testing-commercials/.
19. "Kantar BrandZ Most Valuable Global Brands 2024," *Kantar*, (n.d.), https://www.kantar.com/nl/campaigns/most-valuable-global-brands-2024.
20. Kemp, Simon, "Digital 2024: China," *Datareportal*, (February 21, 2024), https://datareportal.com/reports/digital-2024-china.
21. See Chapter 7: The Future of Television Advertising.
22. "Countries That Have Blocked YouTube," *Wikitubia*, (n.d.), https://youtube.fandom.com/wiki/Countries_that_have_blocked_YouTube.
23. "How Many Countries Is Netflix Available In," *Netflix Help Center*, https://help.netflix.com/en/node/14164.
24. "Amazon Prime Video," *Wikipedia*, https://en.wikipedia.org/wiki/Amazon_Prime_Video#:~:text=Prime%20Video%20is%20available%20worldwide,Belarus%2C%20Syria%20and%20Vietnam).
25. "Blocking, Filtering, and Monitoring," *Congressional-Executive Commission on China*, (n.d.), https://www.cecc.gov/blocking-filtering-and-monitoring.
26. "Censorship in China," *Wikipedia*, (n.d.), https://en.wikipedia.org/wiki/Censorship_in_China.
27. Pan, Jennifer, Zijie Shao, and Yiqing Xu, "The Effects of Television News Propaganda: Experimental Evidence from China," *SSRN*, (April 17, 2020), https://papers.ssrn.com/sol3/papers.cfm?abstract_id=3579148.
28. "Television Censorship," *Wikipedia*, (n.d.), https://en.wikipedia.org/wiki/Television_censorship.

29 "Blocking, Filtering, and Monitoring," *Congressional-Executive Commission on China*, (n.d.), https://www.cecc.gov/blocking-filtering-and-monitoring.
30 "Why Streaming Platforms Use Geo-Blocking to Restrict Content in Countries," *Close-Up Culture*, (Sept. 3, 2022), https://closeupculture.com/2022/09/03/why-streaming-platforms-use-geo-blocking-to-restrict-content-in-countries/.
31 Henry, Alan, "Why Do Media Companies Block Movies, Music, and TV Based on Location?" *Lifehacker*, (January 27, 2024), https://lifehacker.com/why-do-media-companies-block-movies-music-and-tv-base-1509912540.
32 Burke, Kelly, "Australia Joins International Call for Local Content Quotas on Streaming TV Platforms," *The Guardian*, (January 17, 2024), https://www.theguardian.com/culture/2024/jan/18/australia-joins-international-call-for-local-content-quotas-on-streaming-tv-platforms.
33 I was in New Zealand directing an international internship program at regional TVNZ stations for my university department and had a number of opportunities to discuss the situation facing New Zealand television at that time.
34 Burke, Kelly, "Australia Joins International Call for Local Content Quotas on Streaming TV Platforms."

Part IV

The Future of Television in the Mid-21st Century and Beyond

11 Final Thoughts and Future Visions

As this book approaches its final thoughts and visions, I thought it would be interesting to look back at a vision of the future of television developed in 2011 by the Cisco Corporation through the eyes of its Internet Business Solutions Group (IBSG). The report was delivered at the Over-the-Top (OTT) Set-Top Box (STB) conference in San Jose, California, in March 2011. The text of their report is reprinted here with permission from Cisco Corporation. I would like to thank the Cisco IBSG and its at-that-time head, Scott Puopolo, for the use of this report.

The Future of Television: Sweeping Changes at Breakneck Speed

10 Reasons You Won't Recognize Your Television in the Not-Too-Distant Future

Imagine watching television with no channels, no remote control, perhaps not even a TV set. You might catch the news on the bathroom mirror as you brush your teeth, and then check sports scores after work on the family-room window. If a football game really captures your interest, you could watch the action from any perspective you choose—the end zone, on the 50-yard line, or even in the middle of the huddle. During the commercial break, the irresistible aroma of pizza wafting from the TV might compel you to click on the logo and order a large double cheese right from the screen.

It won't be long before these scenarios become reality. The Cisco Internet Business Solutions Group (IBSG) recently interviewed more than 50 experts—producers, engineers, and scholars—to develop a picture of the future TV landscape.

The experts agree that almost every aspect of TV will be transformed: how we interact with the TV; how we interact with one another while watching TV; our relationship with the content; the nature of the TV screen itself; how content is produced, packaged, and paid for; and who makes money from it.

Cisco IBSG believes the convergence of three key drivers—technology, consumer behavior, and business models—will move us toward this "Jetsons" vision. New technology is rapidly increasing the resolution of display, and social networking technology is making it easy to share and interact with content. Improved Internet connectivity and performance allow delivery of high-definition video without interruption. As a result, consumers' TV usage is changing: they increasingly expect access to content anywhere, anytime. In terms of business models, advertisers are scrambling to adjust as the DVR, Internet video, and other time-shifting options pull the rug out from under traditional, linear TV advertising, causing many to question whether it is still the most effective model for reaching consumers. Already, some content providers are testing the waters by bypassing aggregators and delivering TV content straight to the consumer.

After examining these drivers and holding in-depth discussion with TV experts, Cisco IBSG developed 10 predictions for the future of television. Although we asked the experts for their perspective on the television landscape *20 years from now,* the current, blistering rate of change could cause some of these predictions to become reality in the next five years.

10 Predictions that Will Transform the TV-Viewing Experience

1. Channels Go Away

Most viewers will watch customized, on-demand streams, or they will access unlimited content from available libraries using powerful search-recommendation engines.

As consumers increasingly "time-shift" their TV viewing (watching what they want, when they want), traditional channels have less mindshare and brand awareness. The number of channels and the size of content libraries have grown to the point that channel searching now frustrates consumers.

From a technological standpoint, Internet-connected television (CTV) devices such as the Xbox, Apple TV, and Roku will see an adoption explosion in the next few years. As they do, consumers will start to associate Internet-like search and discovery with the TV. They'll also demand integrated functionality that's part of a single, simplified interface—no more multiple boxes.

One hundred percent of the TV experts agreed with this prediction.

2. Kiss the Remote Goodbye

Consumers will use natural language, gestures, and adjunct devices such as smartphones and iPads to interact with their TVs as easily as they do with another person.

In the past, interactive TV enhancements stalled, due in part to the lack of a good interface device. Even today, experts criticize the recently launched Google TV device for what they call a clunky remote-keyboard interface. However, interface innovation is making its way into the market. Several companies, including Verizon and Comcast are already providing software that enables consumers to control their TVs using their iPads or smartphones. The Nintendo Wii, with its unique gesture-based controller, has had a major impact on the gaming market. Driven by competition, Microsoft has released its own gesture-based interface, Kinect, which is rapidly gaining popularity. Sony has also released its own interface for the PS3. In addition, we are now seeing a third-party applications market develop around gesture interfaces, such as GestureTek's Xbox 360 gesture-control tools, which is likely to further accelerate innovation. Couple this with the hierarchical data-display improvements and advances in speech and facial recognition technologies, and we should expect a user experience beyond the one envisioned in the movie "Minority Report," where the TV can recognize your mood and respond accordingly with appropriate content.

Nearly all the experts—94 percent—agreed with this prediction. They cited voice technologies and the early adoption of the iPhone and iPad as key factors that are advancing the market.

3. Screens Do Anything, Anywhere

Today, Nielsen research estimates that 116 million American homes have a device universally recognized as a TV.[1] In 20 years, that will no longer be true: Americans will invest in screens. Some will be thinner, larger, and have even higher definition than the ones we know today. Some will occupy a whole wall. Many will be contained within the higher-quality descendents [sic] of the portable devices we carry in our pockets today, such as smartphones, tablet PCs, and portable gaming players. Some may be expandable, flexible, or even wearable. Screens will be everywhere and each screen will be multipurpose. These screens could be used to monitor a backyard security system as easily as to watch TV.

Imagine a screen on your bedroom wall that displays a replica of your favorite painting. With a wave of your hand, you transform it into your personalized TV. When your program is over, a few more gestures transform the screen into a video-conferencing suite so you can say goodnight to your children at their grandmother's house. At bedtime, you set your alarm clock on the same screen, which darkens for the night. When it's time to wake, the screen slowly brightens to mimic the sunrise.

In the future, these screens will not be purchased as "TVs"—the TV experience will be detached from a specific device. From the outset, the enabling devices or screens will be valued as multifunctional, multipurpose devices.

All of the survey respondents agreed that the TV itself would change dramatically. While 40 percent thought these changes would occur relatively slowly, 30 percent believed they would happen quickly.

The subsequent wave of change will bring holographic projectors that project life-size 3D images of TV shows right into your living room, though this will take longer to realize. Only 17 percent of the experts thought holograms would be commonplace by 2020.

4. Ads Get Personal

Advertisers increasingly believe that their ad spending is not effective; they are looking to reach target customers in ways that were not previously possible. In the future, advertisers won't rely on separate "commercials" that viewers can easily ignore by skipping over them with their DVRs or by running to the kitchen for a snack. Rather, the majority of ads will be contextual, highly interactive, and laser-targeted to each viewer.

Picture the following scenario: Viewers will simply point at or click on an object in a television program to receive advertising information. Imagine pointing at the BMW in the latest James Bond movie and receiving information on available models, configurations, and even incentives at nearby car dealerships. Intelligent systems could continuously comb through consumers' past viewing and purchasing behaviors (including those pertaining to their social networks), and dynamically pair these within the context of the program being viewed. These systems would then make a selection from an ad inventory customized for each viewer. For example, if the program is about the great outdoors and the viewer likes to camp, then ads for camping gear would be shown.

In the survey, 83 percent of respondents agreed with this prediction. However, of those, 40 percent thought this transition will take longer than some innovations to occur.

5. Don't Just Watch—Get Involved

Consumers are already interacting with some TV content ("Lost," "CSI") across different modalities: games, social media, and other arenas. In the coming years, this trend will gain momentum, and consumers will interact with certain TV content even more seamlessly and often. For example, in an extension of current consumer and industry trends, viewers may "friend" their favorite TV characters or investigate plot twists using resources in their own communities. They could, for instance, collaborate with other fans to aid key characters in solving a crime or mystery.

Although the "fan" mentality has always existed, it will morph from a process of collecting and following to one of interacting and influencing. Technology innovation and adoption have reached levels where this type of interaction is not only possible, but also can be supported without enormous budgets. Social networking and smartphones, key enablers of this experience, have achieved mass-market adoption. In addition, tools to create special-purpose webpages and collaboration sites already exist. Finally, studios have already invested in "transmedia"—storytelling across multiple forms of media—to create more buzz and loyalty so their content doesn't get lost.

Eighty-seven percent of survey respondents agreed with this prediction. Of those, 45 percent felt that the TV experience would change in the near future. These respondents believe that consumers' relationship with television has already expanded beyond the bounds of TV episodes.

6. Watch Together, Virtually

TV will be an enabler of social interaction, encouraging group participation at home with remote friends and family. TV's valuable role as a social-gathering mechanism will grow beyond the living room and water cooler. Technology—from motion capture to video telepresence to holograms—will enable remote friends and family to watch TV together and interact naturally. Much as they do today, families will congregate around a central viewing device to watch their favorite shows. However, with the help of social networking technologies, viewers will also invite friends and remote family members to join them in a virtual setting. Viewers will experience a sense of community for the duration of the program.

The technology to enable this vision is available today—it just needs an integrated solution. Social networking technology such as Facebook could provide an effective platform and user interface, while adjunct devices such as tablet PCs and smartphones could enable interaction off the main viewing screen.

Eighty percent of survey respondents agreed with this prediction, although 43 percent thought it would take longer than some innovations to be fully realized.

7. Is It Real, or Is It Television?

Advances in the TV-viewing experience will introduce new sensory elements and enable consumers to have more choice in how they interact with their content. Olfactory reproduction will enable viewers to perceive smells and taste in real time. Tactile reproduction will let them feel the impact on a driver as he crashes his car, or the waft of a sea breeze at the beach on a warm summer day. Above all, the experience will be natural and nonintrusive. Viewers will not need clumsy helmets or glasses, and will be able to "disengage" from sensory stimuli as simply as turning down the TV's volume. But when viewers do fully engage, the TV experience will be immersive and deeply stimulating.

Last, consumers will have more choice in how they experience content. They may view plots from different characters' viewpoints, or from different camera angles. Producers will cater to these trends by developing specialized content that incorporates these sensory and plot elements.

In the survey, 90 percent of respondents agreed with the prediction; of those, 44 percent thought adoption would take longer than for certain other advances.

8. Your TV Follows You

With superior-quality handheld devices, pervasive screen options, and cloud-based storage, consumers' TV content—all of it—will be instantaneously accessible anywhere. Consumers will no longer be tethered to a particular device or network, and there will be limited ties to time itself. As a result, consumers will choose what they want to watch while they stand in line for groceries, travel on the train, sit in the back seat of a car, or walk down the street. Moreover, they'll be able to transfer content seamlessly across devices (for example, from a smartphone to a friend's TV screen, just by pointing the phone at the TV).

We have already seen a change in the way people consume entertainment content. One notable example is the move from home stereos to iPods. TV is now following the same path: apps for Hulu, Netflix, and Sling already work on smartphones. Beyond consumers' personal preferences, external factors will also begin to drive this vision. For example, as the population grows, overcrowding and high energy costs could force more people to mass transportation—a transition that will allow them to experience the value of mobile TV.

A full 93 percent of survey respondents agreed with the prediction, and 43 percent thought the prediction was too conservative.

9. "Regular Joes" Go Hollywood

Semiprofessional and amateur film and TV-making will flourish, and decentralized methods to create, fund, and deliver content to the mass market will thrive. As professional editing and production tools continue to plummet in price and reach the mass market, user-generated content (UGC) will acquire a high level of quality. Furthermore, experienced but out-of-work Hollywood professionals and other skilled amateurs will produce their own high-quality content on shoestring budgets. The box office success of low-budget films such as "Paranormal Activity" and "Slumdog Millionaire" demonstrates that viral marketing can fuel positive revenue outcomes for the independent film market. Going forward, web-based collaboration tools will give these amateurs alternatives not only for marketing their content, but also for bankrolling their projects and finding affordable, skilled technical and creative people they need to execute their vision.

Further, even-greater percentages of UGC will be ready for prime time. Online (or software) agents or "bots" will mine, cull, and publish these popular stories on future "YouTube" sites. This will result in an extremely long tail of content, with literally billions of titles served side-by-side with traditionally produced studio content.

Ninety percent of survey respondents agreed with this prediction and, of these, more than 40 percent felt the pace of change would happen more quickly than for some other innovations.

10. Creation Goes Viral

Content creators are always looking for ways to stay fresh and in sync with the pulse of the consumer. One of the best ways to do this is to invite consumers directly into the process. Imagine that your favorite show airs on Wednesday night. Until Friday night, you can participate in online collaboration sessions to develop and vote on new ideas for the next week's episode. On Friday night, the discussion is closed, and the producers write and tape the show between Saturday and Tuesday. On Wednesday, we all tune in to see the show's latest episode.

Gaming also will provide a new consumer-created content source. Today's massive multiplayer online games have a look and feel that rivals that of newly released films. Given the visual quality of a game like "Prince of Persia" and the compelling interactions among avid gamers, a portion of that game time can be immensely watchable, even to those not actively participating in the game.

Almost three-quarters of respondents—73 percent—agreed with this prediction. However, of these, 45 percent think it may take longer to fully realize this vision than for other advances.

Business Model in Flux

Television's current business model is delicately constructed, with many players and numerous, interdependent revenue streams. Parts of the experience that we have grown to accept as core—$70-plus monthly subscription packages; programming across hundreds of channels; the 30-second TV commercial; delayed release windows for DVDs; free premium shows on the Internet—are all a result of the business model in place today. That model is under pressure, and while there is a great deal of debate and disagreement among industry experts about exactly how it will evolve, there is no question that it will change dramatically over the next five to 10 years.

The views among the experts were varied:

- Forty-six percent thought the role of carriage fees in the business model would become less important, and the other 54 percent disagreed.
- Thirty-eight percent believed that advertising would play a less important role in the business model; the remaining 62 percent disagreed.
- Thirty-eight percent thought government sponsorship of public channels would play a less important role, while the remaining 62 percent held a different opinion.

However, most experts agreed that in the future, consumers would enjoy more flexibility in how they purchase TV. Eighty percent of respondents felt that consumers would have the flexibility to build their own TV subscription packages by adding only content they want.

Permanently Changed Landscape

Television in the not-too-distant future is sure to provide an immersive, collaborative experience that even the Jetsons might never have imagined, and much of the groundwork for that future is already in place. Technological innovation is accelerating, as evidenced by HD flat-screens, "3D TV," and smartphones entering the mainstream in a matter of months rather than years. Consumer behavior is evolving, illustrated by the move toward time-shifted TV and the increasing role that social networks are playing in consumers' purchasing and viewing decisions. And, the business model is changing as the complex, interdependent business models supporting the TV industry face pressure to adapt to the Internet age. This pressure is increasing as new and old players explore novel ways to monetize online content. One example of this is Netflix, whose streaming audience grew from 41 percent to 61 percent in just one year.[2]

Cisco IBSG believes the current rate of change in technology, consumer behavior, and the business model will accelerate our vision of the future of TV, bringing enormous changes in the next five to 10 years. While any one of these drivers in isolation would not be a catalyst for appreciable change, in combination they are unleashing forces that will permanently and dramatically alter the entertainment landscape.

Final Thoughts and Visions

So, what is the future of television? How do you define something that encompasses such disparate forms as advertising-driven video-on-demand (AVOD), subscription video-on-demand (SVOD), transactional video-on-demand (TVOD), premium video-on-demand (PVOD), free ad-supported streaming television (FAST), UGC, Internet protocol television (IPTV), 4K, CTV, OTT, linear, virtual reality (VR), augmented reality (AR), broadcast, cable, direct-to-home (DTH) satellite, and so many others? Is there another word to describe what is now this vast, complex universe that is the future of television? After all, encompassing so much in the word "television" makes the word meaningless to the listener or reader without there being an understanding between both (or all) parties of what kind of television is being referred to.

As this chapter looks at a future where the television universe is composed of so many parts, it is prescient to consider the futures of the various parts that have been discussed in the different chapters.

First, the broadcast industries. By 2035 at the latest, in the wake of the continuing erosion of their audiences by the ever-growing world of alternative media choices, the networks will have ended all contracts with their local affiliates, preferring to deliver their programming directly to their audiences. Given the inroads being made by the myriad streaming media choices available – including SVOD, AVOD, FAST, and virtual Multichannel Video Programming Distributors (vMVPDs), to remain viable the networks must provide audiences with their programming directly. The networks have begun making the move to direct programming delivery to audiences, as seen in CBS Television/Skydance's Paramount+, Disney's Hulu, and NBC's Peacock. In addition, by delivering their programming directly to the consumer, the networks improve their bottom line by keeping all the advertising time within their programs.

Further, with the advancement of video-on-demand (VOD), IPTV, and fully addressable advertising, as well as enhanced promotional techniques through websites, CTV apps, specialized search engines, and social media, by no later than 2035, the networks will find themselves delivering their entire inventory of programming directly to the consumer through a variety of means. By jettisoning their local stations and moving to direct delivery of programming to the consumer, the networks will find themselves free to explore new avenues of both programming and revenue generation without the need to keep the antiquated system of local television affiliates satisfied.

Local stations, on the other hand, will not fare as well. By 2035, the local television industry will have shrunk dramatically in terms of the number of stations in each market. Whereas the traditional minimum number of stations in a market would be three to six stations – one for each network, plus a public television station and/or an independent television station – by 2035, the number of local stations will be dramatically reduced. With the networks reaching out to the consumer directly, freeing themselves from their local partners, the local stations that were formerly the affiliates of those networks will suddenly find themselves without programming, without advertising slots in those network programs, and without large revenue from retransmission consent fees. The triple-play loss will force the local – now independent – stations to find additional programming to fill their time slots while their revenues shrink to a fraction of what they were previously. Only those few stations who truly understand the future of their industry will make the changes needed ahead of time to remain viable in the television age to come. Most former network affiliate local stations will simply cease to exist, or, more likely, will sell their spectrum allocations back to the Federal Communication Commission (FCC) for reassignment to the mobile phone companies during future rounds of spectrum auctions as those companies continuously transition to ever-more-powerful generations of mobile phones.

Those local stations that do survive will find their niche as hyperlocal television stations, marketing themselves as the station(s) that keeps its finger on the pulse of the local market. While some of their entertainment programming may be syndicated, the prime focus of these stations will be an intense involvement by the station in the daily affairs of the locality in which the station resides. As such, these hyperlocal stations will become the major "go to" locations for all things local. Local sports, local news, and local events will be given prominence on these stations. Local advertisers will continue to reach out to their consumers through these stations as there will be a closer connection between the television station and the community. The local community will feel like the local station is its own, rather than as a network affiliate that also broadcasts a little bit of local news, sports, and weather each day. Those stations that see the writing on the wall have already started to make the changes necessary to prepare for the inevitable and they are the ones that will be in the best position to survive the shakeout.

Likewise, the local public television stations may also struggle to remain viable. While this book has not focused on the public television industry, it is not hard to imagine that the public broadcast system will follow the same route as the networks, finding that their local affiliates are no longer required to deliver programming to their audiences. However, an alternative scenario that is not available to the commercial broadcasters is that delivery of programming directly to consumers could be in addition to traditional local stations. This alternative is due to the differences between the public broadcast system and the commercial broadcast industry. PBS was an early leader in moving toward television in the future but has not continued in that vein in more recent years, so its lead over the broadcasters has slipped away. It is easy to imagine that PBS could have more of a symbiotic relationship with its affiliates than the commercial broadcasters.

Additionally, with the escalation in the amount of work required from production houses to satisfy the abundance of television content providers in the future, along with the continuing development of higher-quality user-generated programming, public television stations will have numerous opportunities to fill their programming days. It is likely that public television will no longer need to depend on the BBC for its programming, although that programming would be available to PBS if the programming was in keeping with the PBS structure. PBS, though, would have many more choices, so the use of BBC (and other international) programming would likely be curtailed significantly.

One other advantage that the local PBS affiliates currently have over their commercial counterparts is that they supply many of the programs run nationally on PBS. As such, local PBS stations are both content providers as well as content distributors. Those stations that are the major producers of programs for PBS will continue to see a positive relationship with the public television system as production facilities for the system's programs. However, production will be their only option in the system, and they will have to compete with the other options mentioned above.

Those independent commercial stations that still exist around the country may have a somewhat easier time responding to the change because they have already had to survive by purchasing syndicated programming to run opposite the network affiliates' programs. The new television reality may place these stations on a more level playing field with their former network affiliate competitors in that all stations will be independent. However, most independent local stations do not have the viewership that local network affiliates currently do, the local brand recognition, or often the resources to compete with those network competitors. As such, their jobs may be made tougher, as they are forced to work harder to build strong brand recognition to compete with the former local network affiliates who already have that strong brand recognition. While there are local independent stations with strong local followings, those stations are the exception to the rule rather than typical. However, given the almost certainty that the number of network affiliate stations will be drastically reduced, independent stations – because of their history of having to survive without a network affiliation – could be better able to survive in the television climate of the future. The other choice for the independent stations would be to sell their spectrum allocations to the FCC during the auctions. It might even be more tempting to those independent stations in smaller markets as they could be sold at significant prices, making it advantageous for the independent stations to sell out. If that is the case, then most independent local stations will not survive.

The cable industry is poised to become one of the major drivers of television of the future and will flourish as a result of new technology and changes. As discussed in previous chapters, cable will become one of the prime deliverers of television, whether it is directly through broadband IPTV or through the various types of home Wi-Fi systems. Capitalizing on their TV Everywhere strategy, cable companies

Final Thoughts and Future Visions 189

will be one of the primary engines of growth for television in the future. However, cable companies will have a number of influences impacting that growth.

Revenue from retransmission fees being demanded by the local network affiliates for the privilege of carrying their stations' programming continues to increase. With the totals reaching $14.3 billion in 2024 and $15.6 billion by 2027, retransmission consent fees will continue to be important to the local television stations as a major supplement to their advertising revenues.[3] However, the broadcast networks are already negotiating directly with the vMVPDs as they are classified separately from the Multichannel Video Programming Distributors (MVPDs), so the vMVPDs are not covered under the 1992 United States Cable Television Consumer Protection and Competition Act.[4] While local station groups such as Hearst, Nexstar, and Sinclair, among others are lobbying for the FCC to reclassify vMVPDs into the same categories as the MVPDs, the FCC is reluctant to do so, deferring instead to Congress, who passed the law.[5] Further, when the networks decide they no longer need the local affiliates, preferring to negotiate directly with the cable companies for the consent fees like they do with the vMVPDs, which will require a change in the law, those costs to the cable companies will likely change dramatically – at least in the short term. Ultimately, retransmission consent fees will cease to be a source of revenue for broadcasters, but it will be too late for most of the cable companies. By 2035, there may only be one or two and certainly no more than four cable megacompanies in the U.S.

Second, as television migrates to IPTV, cable will become less about delivering bundles of channels and more about delivering Internet-connectivity to the home through wired broadband and home Wi-Fi. As such, cable companies will have more in common with Internet service providers. Smaller cable companies have already made the move, becoming broadband companies rather than cable companies. The move away from traditional services is an important one because the television programming seen on today's cable channels will migrate to the various channels'/networks' CTV apps, vMVPDs, and FAST channels. As such, the cable companies will become one of the major providers of the backbone that will deliver television programs to audiences. Additionally, with the government's move to provide everyone in the U.S. with some form of broadband connectivity, cable is currently the most logical way to provide that connectivity, either stand-alone or in conjunction with Wi-Fi broadband.

On the horizon is an even more powerful competitor for the cable industry – the cellular-connected smart TVs, which will likely come on the market in the near future. Today's smart television is connected to the Internet through either a wired broadband connection or through Wi-Fi. The development of cellular-connected smart television sets will allow cellular phone companies to provide IPTV as well as all the apps, video streaming, and web browsing currently available through today's smart TVs. Cellular-connected smart TVs will operate on the same high-speed cellular networks as their mobile phone counterparts, delivering the various options currently available on today's smart TVs, but from a single, integrated source. For many, cellular-connected smart TVs will become the television of choice because they do not require another wire into the home or a wireless router.

In the short term, cable is poised to be the dominant delivery system for television, both through traditional cable services and through IPTV. However, cable must be prepared to meet the challenges of cellular-connected television, ATSC 3.0, and the iWorld, if it is to continue to be a dominant force in the coming television age.

The future is murkier for the DTH satellite industry, and its ability to survive at all in anything like its present form is unlikely at best. It cannot by itself offer telephone, either wired or wireless/cellular. At this time, it cannot offer a high-speed broadband connectivity at reasonable pricing or continuous service because of the distances that signals must travel and the interference of adverse weather conditions that plague the system. As such, both Dish Network and DirecTV have moved to providing streaming options, Dish with its Sling TV and DirecTV with its DirecTV Stream services, both of which are vMVPD alternatives to YouTube TV and others.

Turning to the production companies – although they were not discussed as a separate chapter, what a fabulous time the future will be for them. Because there will be a myriad of content providers clamoring for programming, as has already been shown by the explosion of AVOD and FAST services, the future is likely to be exquisitely bright for the production industry. With the constant demand for new and exciting programming, designed to meet the needs and desires of niche audiences, the production companies will be hard-pressed to keep up with the demand. Further, it may be that some production companies – those desiring to become something more than just content producers – may use their websites and/or develop FAST channels to deliver programming directly to audiences. For both the linear media as well as the streaming media, the idea of the production companies as content providers would be a shift of enormous proportions.

Consider the possibility of an individual production company no longer selling its programs to a network, MVPD, local station, or online provider, preferring instead to deliver programs to the consumer directly through its website or on its own FAST, AVOD, or SVOD channel. A decision of that magnitude turns the production company from a program source for the various content providers to a powerful competitor. Delivering their programming through their websites or online channels would allow the production company to be in charge of their own programming, sell their own advertising, profit from their own subscriptions or pay-per-view programming, and, in general, be in complete control of what they produce.

The decision would be a game-changer and would likely bring about a new wave of mergers and acquisitions as the networks and MVPDs, as well as the streaming television content providers, compete to find programming for their websites. The move would also bring about the development of numerous new production companies providing programming to the content providers starving for their offerings. The move by the production houses to control their programming end-to-end would completely change the television landscape and would bring about wholesale changes in the development of the future television universe.

Internet Protocol television will be the delivery mechanism of the future, with cable, Wi-Fi, possibly ATSC 3.0, and cellular all competing to deliver IPTV to the viewer. IPTV will provide the viewer with the opportunity to enjoy his/her favorite television program anywhere the viewer is, on whatever platform is available, at any time of the day or night, as often as (s)he wishes. With television delivered through IPTV, the viewer will have the ability to enjoy total interactive television if desired, 4K and 8K television, complete VOD, all at the viewer's command. In many respects, IPTV will be the driving force behind the revolution that will be the new television universe of the 21st century and beyond. Appointment viewing and daily television schedules will disappear except for live events such as sporting events, news happenings, and those entertainment programs that are produced and delivered live (*The Voice* and *Dancing With the Stars* are two examples). With IPTV and VOD, viewers will determine their own viewing habits and on-demand viewing will become the dominant way of watching television for the television viewer of the future.

With IPTV, advertising becomes interactive and can be designed for the individual viewer through the development and refinement of Aggregated Targeted Microadvertising (ATMA), Programmatic Advertising (PA), and Dynamic Ad Insertion (DAI). Through the three-step process of ATMA-PA-DAI, viewers will receive commercials designed specifically to meet their needs and interests, making it possible for the viewer to watch only those commercials that appeal to her/him, and advertisers will have the best opportunity to spur the viewer to purchase the products (s)he is viewing. Additionally, advertisers will benefit from ATMA-PA-DAI delivered by IPTV because they will be advertising only to those viewers who are most likely to respond positively to the advertisement. Further, the content provider will benefit from the ability to sell each advertising time slot multiple times, as viewers with different likes and dislikes in terms of advertising will watch the same program, and to sell each slot at a premium because of the high rate of completion.

Additionally, because of the content providers' ability to offer their entire inventory of programs forever, with television in the future a program is never unavailable to the viewer. Because programs are around forever, the opportunity to sell advertising time in any given program never ends. Classic early television programs such as *I Love Lucy*, *Gunsmoke*, and *Perry Mason* will have the chance to experience viewer nostalgia revivals, and along with the program revival will come the possibility to advertise to those viewers.

IPTV also makes it possible for advertisers to make extensive use of product placement. With the ability to turn everything seen in every frame of a television program into an Internet link, viewers will have the ability to learn more about and purchase everything they see on television, while advertisers will have a powerful new tool to draw viewers' attention to their products and services in an immediate fashion, prompting additional impulse buys from the viewers. Content providers will also benefit by being able to sell every opportunity for program placement to advertisers, thus increasing revenues substantially. It will be a "win-win-win" scenario for the viewers, the advertisers, and the content providers.

Further, IPTV will make it possible for viewers to interact with each other and with the television program they are watching in ways that are already being explored, such as social media opportunities, but also in ways not yet seen. By 2035, television viewing will most likely be approaching the type of interactivity imagined by Cisco Systems in its report, and by 2050, the interactivity imagined by Ray Bradbury in *Fahrenheit 451* will likely be fully developed and implemented. Bradbury's television future may even seem quaint and antiquated, as new levels of immersive television become the typical viewing habits of television viewers in the future.[6]

Finally, IPTV makes it possible for content providers to deliver their programs to global audiences immediately and simultaneously. What will be available to one, will be available to all. With the ability to reach global audiences with the entire inventory, the content provider will have the opportunity to deliver advertising to audiences around the world, allowing the content provider the ability to further increase revenues, and advertisers the opportunity to reach new audiences in a more cost-effective manner. IPTV makes it possible for television content providers to have a financial future that is immeasurably bright and exciting.

In the future, all or virtually all of television will be delivered through VOD. The younger generations will demand it. Already there are more and more uses for VOD, whether it is through SVOD and AVOD offerings; niche programming of FAST channels; or through VOD services provided by linear MVPDs. By 2035 at the latest, VOD will deliver all traditionally recorded television programming, and it already provides the possibility of both live and replay viewing of programs that are initially delivered live, such as sporting events.

So, does VOD preclude the scheduling of programs throughout the day? The answer to that is… it depends on the type of program that is being viewed. With all television programming being delivered through IPTV, and with content providers airing their entire inventory of programming through their CTV apps rather than on traditional channel lineups through their local affiliates, there is no reason for daily program schedules. There is no need for seasons (although some would argue that the "season" has disappeared already) when the entire inventory of a network or channel is available all the time. New shows can be added at any time, and there is no reason or need to remove any program, no matter how old or how unpopular it may have been in the past. Further, the concern the networks and cable channels have now for ratings and the popularity of programs will no longer exist, other than as one determining factor for how much to charge for programs. Ratings will not influence whether or not a program is cancelled. Even programs with small but loyal followings will continue to exist because there is no incentive to remove a program from a content provider's inventory.

However, live events will continue to take place at their scheduled times. The opening kickoff, the first pitch, the tip-off of a basketball game will continue to be at a set day and time. The Kentucky Derby will still be run on the first Saturday in May around 6:30 p.m. Eastern Time. Golf will still occupy fans' Sunday afternoons. Those types of events will not change, except that they will also be available for viewers to watch on-demand following the live showing.

The viewer will no longer have to set a digital video recorder (DVR) or wait and hope that one of the sports channels will replay the game, either in full or in an edited form. Missed the Derby because your spouse needed a tree planted in the back yard at exactly the same time? No problem. It will be there for you on VOD three minutes later, four hours later, the next day, or even forty years later if you want to reminisce about "the good old days." (On a personal side note, I would truly enjoy watching Secretariat's triple crown victories in 1973 again and again through VOD rather than the recordings currently available on YouTube. While it is wonderful to have the races available through YouTube, the quality would be much better if the network that broadcast the races made them available through VOD.)

As with so much of television in the future, VOD will be the content provider's response to the viewer's demand to be in complete charge of his or her choices for viewing. Once again, there is no doubt that VOD is the way of the future for watching television and that daily schedules for television programs will disappear. In the future, the position of television programmer will change dramatically from trying to determine the programming strategies that will deliver the largest audience during a daypart to a manager of the current inventory and a purchaser of new programs for her/his company. When it comes to viewing television in the future, VOD will allow the viewer to be in complete control of his/her choices.

The OTT STB industry will not fare well in the future. The STB will become a thing of the past as CTV sets make the OTT box obsolete. As programming, as well as gaming, moves to the cloud, Blu-ray DVD players and videogame consoles such as the Xbox Series S and the Playstation 5 gaming boxes will no longer be necessary because CTV sets will have movement recognition capabilities built into them. However, today's gaming consoles may become gateway boxes to the connected homes of the future in the coming Internet of Things (or, as some like to call it, the "Internet of Everything"), but will have to compete with home systems like Amazon's Echo and Google Home.

The current generations of "smart" CTV sets are on the market, and are produced by virtually every television manufacturer that sells in the U.S., in ultra-high-definition television (UHDTV) and super-high-definition television (SHDTV) models, with screens as large as 115" in diameter by TCL[7] and a TV set by LG that's 325" in diameter and costs only $1.7 million! (This TV set is a true wall-size set, measuring 23.6 feet by 13.3 feet!)[8] The survivors among the current STB industry will be those that create the software that will drive the CTV sets. Apple, Google, and Roku are among the companies at this time that will survive the shakeout in the STB industry and flourish in the new "connected" television universe.

Currently under development is ATSC 3.0. Despite the broadcast industry hyping up how important, exciting, and revolutionary the ATSC 3.0 technology and standard will be, especially in keeping the over-the-air (OTA) broadcasters in the fight, most likely ATSC 3.0 will be short-lived. Should ATSC 3.0 move from its current experimentation phase to delivery, it is still likely to be only marginally successful. While ATSC 3.0 is designed to deliver television to a variety of devices, it is still limited to local stations delivering local television in local markets. While it may remain as an additional method of delivery for those local stations that will still be around, ATSC 3.0 is not the savior it is currently made out to be, nor will it help the OTA broadcasters stave off the coming television universe, no matter how bad they hope or wish that it will. There will be too many less expensive options for both the content provider and the consumer, and more user-friendly alternatives that will supply the same information and entertainment offerings, to make the ATSC 3.0 technology a major player in the long run.

In fact, ATSC 3.0 may never even be fully implemented if it and the hardware needed to receive the signals in a way that is cost-effective are not available to consumers nationwide by 2030 at the latest. Further, the development of streaming services by the broadcast networks suggest that they may have little faith in ATSC 3.0 and are ready to use current app technology to reach their television viewers of the future.

The CTV, with its ability to deliver the full range of IPTV as well as high-, UH-, and SH-definition television, social media sites, Internet surfing, applications, etc., will be the center of the viewer's television universe. Today's televisions that are on the market have grown to 100+ inches in diameter, with sets for commercial application as large as 1,000 inches in diameter.[9] Those dimensions will seem normal to the television viewer of the future.

Internet-connected HDTV and UHDTV sets will continue to grow larger and larger. No surprise there. To reach the imaginings of *Fahrenheit 451* or my ultimate scenario, television sets will need to be the size of a wall – which LG's set approaches. Ultimately, the wall-size CTV will be the hub of the future television consumer's entertainment center. While watching his/her favorite program, the viewer will be able to surf the Web for more information about the actors, producer, director, set designer, or anyone connected with the program, and view statistics or interesting tidbits about the program, characters, scenes, etc. The viewer will be able to select any portion of the television picture to find out more information about the item (s)he is interested in (say, a car used in a scene, a suit or a dress a character might be wearing, etc.) or a nearby location where (s)he might go to purchase the item. The viewer will also be able to chat with other viewers about the program (s)he is watching and post on social media about the program. The viewer will be able to interact with the program in a variety of ways, both in ways that are currently available and through new interactions that have yet to come to market or be envisioned.

3D television sets will be crucial to the future of television, although they will not be the 3D of the recent past. By combining 3D with IPTV-connected sets, along with the development of holographic television imaging and 8K or higher definition TV, the television sets of the future will resemble the holodeck of the Starship U.S.S. Enterprise in *Star Trek: The Next Generation*. For those who choose, that will be the future of television, and it will occur no later than 2070, and likely much sooner, conceivably by mid-century.

It is exciting to attempt to determine the future of the iWorld of mobile phones, tablets, and VR and AR devices, and their places in the television universe of the future. While CTV sets can grow larger and more varied, the potential that smartphones, tablets, and VR/AR devices have to impact television of the future is, in many ways, limitless. Imagining these devices in 2050 – or even 2035 – seems almost beyond the scope of the mind, given where mobile phones were before 2007 and where they are today, to say nothing of the strides that have been made in tablets since the introduction of the iPad in 2010.

Turning first to smartphones and tablets, certainly they are already used to watch television while on the go, including in UHDTV, especially on the latest phones from both Apple and Samsung, the industry leaders in the U.S. In the near future, mobile phones are likely to deliver some form of UHD and SHD television (and whatever might come later) through high-speed 5G, 6G, or 7G (whatever iteration will be available) cellular service or over advanced high-speed Wi-Fi. Television viewers of the future, then, will be able to watch their favorite programs anywhere, anytime, either at home on their television walls or on their numerous mobile devices. As mentioned earlier, mobile phones have already grown to the size of small tablets (for example, the Samsung Galaxy Fold) and their screens continue to increase in size. Additionally, much like today, the phones and tablets of the future will be used for search purposes and will serve as remote control selection devices (no longer channel changers) for their television walls. Those uses, however, will be the most mundane of the mobile phones and tablets of the future.

On the more speculative side, tablets and phones will become integrated parts of the television experience. As television continues to evolve and change, as affordable consumer televisions grow from the current largest of 115 inches in diameter to wall size, and as television moves from passive, lean-back viewing to an immersive, lean-forward experience, the tablet and phone will become just another part of programming that is individually designed and delivered to the viewer/ participant. Television of the future can be described as an "experience" rather than something to be viewed because, in the future television universe, the viewer will have a choice between the traditional lean-back viewing that is today's television, or a totally immersive experience.

When the viewer chooses the immersive experience option, (s)he will be transported into the program and will become a full member of the cast. Cast members who will be 3D hologram figures will ask the new participant questions, expect answers and comments, and will interact with the viewer/participant throughout the length of the program. As the viewer becomes participant, (s)he can expect calls to his/her mobile phone. (S)he may have to look up and read aloud information on a tablet as part of the program, or may compete in videogames. The television experience of the future will be exciting, as everyone can have her/his fifteen minutes of fame – or longer, depending on the length of the program – anytime (s)he wants it. Choose the lean-forward experience and the iWorld delivers.

The iWorld is also preparing to provide future television viewers with the possibility of an immersive television experience outside the home television room. VR and AR systems, initiated by Google's Project Glass first-generation AR glasses and Oculus VR headsets (among numerous others), will set the stage for VR/AR experiences that will provide the television viewer of the future with the chance to enjoy the immersive experience wherever (s)he is. Google's Project Glass glasses did not succeed as a consumer item due to their strange look and the uncomfortable feeling that people had when around a person wearing them. Nevertheless, the project demonstrated what would be possible someday in its corner of the iWorld.

For the future television viewer, later generations of VR/AR glasses have the potential to bring the television universe to the wearer wherever (s)he is without the need for a handheld device. In addition, because glasses can augment reality, the television viewer of the future could also be immersed in the television program's world, providing an exciting lean-forward experience while on the go. Even later generations of VR/AR glasses could take the location of the wearer and build the wearer's travel and actions into a television program, bringing the viewer a fully interactive television experience anywhere and anytime, with the world of the television program revolving around him or her as the viewer moves through the day.

For now, VR systems are (and will be – at least in the near term) used most often in the viewer's home for gaming, but also to create an on-location experience for sporting events and live performances. VR systems place the viewer in the location, providing her/him with the sensation of viewing an event from a 360° perspective. VR systems, then, are the first generation of what will become the immersive holographic experience of the home viewing room and will give the viewer a somewhat similar experience while on the go. By 2030, expect advanced generations of AR and VR glasses and headsets to be commonplace.

This chapter of the book would not be complete without a short discussion of the future of television in the global arena. Television is a global industry. Satellites beam television signals to and from anywhere in the world. Syndicators sell programs across the globe. Comcast, Time Warner, and others, through the development of TV Everywhere, are making their programming available to their subscribers any time, on any platform, and – literally – everywhere a wired broadband, a compatible cellular, or a Wi-Fi signal is available, anywhere in the world.

In the future, television audiences will demand even more – and television will provide. With television's move to the Internet, through the use of IPTV, content providers will no longer be limited by channels, local affiliates, or even national borders. Netflix is today demonstrating what can be accomplished as it is currently in 190 different countries around the world. The television universe of the future will provide the viewer not only the possibility of television anytime, anywhere, and on any platform, but also any program regardless of its country of origin.

With the development of global television as the standard fare for the television viewer of the future comes new opportunities for revenues for content providers. Combining ATMA, PA, and DAI, conducted worldwide, with expanded, Ubiquitous Product Placement (UPP), gives the content provider the opportunity to develop numerous revenue streams by delivering different advertisements during the same commercial insert time and different product placements to viewers around the world. By having the entire inventory of a content provider on its home website, a separate, specialized website, and apps, television content providers of the future will be able to reach their audiences with advertisements and product placements no matter who they are or where they are in the world. The opportunity to provide programming seamlessly to viewers around the world opens up television to an entirely new universe of opportunities for ever-increasing worldwide revenues that makes the future exceedingly bright.

Television In 2070 – A Personal Vision

To finish this chapter and the book, let me take you into my personal television future. While I admit that the following will seem like a science fiction scenario that may, in the mind of some, appear out of place, I prefer to consider the following as speculative science fact. Let me now take you on a journey into the relatively near future.

The year is 2070. Television has come a long way since the turn of the millennium. Once upon a time there were networks broadcasting over the air through their local affiliates or through their local cable companies or DTH satellite services. There were a number of different cable companies all competing for viewers.

In 2070, all that has changed. There are three major companies delivering television to consumers. The first is a combination of Comcast, NBC television network, AT&T/DirecTV, and Google. Second, you have Charter, plus Disney/ABC, Verizon, and Apple. Third is a merger between Cablevision and several other cable companies, plus CBS Television/Skydance, Dish Network, T-Mobile, Facebook, and Amazon/Netflix. These three megacompanies compete against each other for viewers in the U.S. Around the world the major television companies are Eurozone Television Network (which includes the major European channels as well as most of the other European television companies); the BBC/Sky/Star television system, including Fox, the Australian Broadcasting company, and TVNZ; China Television; and a consortium of Korean, NHK, and other Asian television companies. U.S. television still dominates television across the world, but viewers can find more programming to enjoy because of the global competition.

The average viewer watches more television today than at any time in the past, because the television is always with him/her, whether it is on the home entertainment system, or on the go, using her/his various iWorld choices. Besides the traditional computer, mobile phone, and tablet, the viewer also has available an in-car television entertainment system that brings television directly to her/him. For lounging in the car, or out and about, the viewer can watch a favorite program on the latest generation of AR or VR glasses or AR implants if (s)he so chooses – these provide a full 3D, extra-high-definition (16K or higher) television viewing experience. With a touch of a button, a quick motion, or a spoken word – perhaps even a thought – what the viewer is watching is displayed directly onto any surface for sharing. Additionally, when traveling around town or across the country or even in another country around the world in the viewer's autonomous automobile, the automobile can project what (s)he has been watching onto the front, side, or rear window (or any combination of the three) for viewing.

But it is the home television system that has undergone the most remarkable innovation. For the home television system, think of Bradbury's vision of a television room, but one where the interactivity goes even further. Instead of the viewer simply responding to questions à la Ray Bradbury, I prefer to take a page from another science fiction world, the world of *Star Trek: The Next Generation*. The new television room is totally interactive, in which the viewer – if (s)he chooses – is an integral participant in a personalised version of the program – in other words, the television room equivalent of the Enterprise's holodeck. By creating a 3D holographic simulation all around the room, the viewer creates a television program that is experienced, not just viewed – after all, television set manufacturers advertise the idea of a true-to-life television experience. With the hologram television room, that true-to-life television experience really is true to life. Expensive? Absolutely. But television set prices become affordable extremely quickly. As a result of television sets becoming larger; developments in 3D, holographic, and UHD/SHD television, and VR and AR systems; fiber optic cable delivering ever-faster broadband; and cellular telephone systems providing 5G, 6G, and higher capabilities, viewers are able to enjoy the television hologram room.

With television having moved to strictly VOD, viewers have the opportunity to participate in their favorite television programs over and over or to select a new program and be entertained by not knowing what is going to happen. For situation comedies, the missteps simply add to the humor of the program, with the hologram actors and actresses laughing along with the viewer/participant. For action/suspense programs, missteps put the viewer/participant into danger or even life-threatening jeopardy, so the system had to be designed to protect the viewer from harm as (s)he participates in the program. The initial reaction is for the system simply to shut down when it senses the viewer is in danger and it restarts only when the viewer/participant chooses to begin again. As the viewer becomes more accustomed to the program, the viewer is able to correct his/her missteps, and thus the program can safely run from beginning to end. Additionally, video games are enjoyed in the same manner, with the player participating in an immersive manner.

Alternatively, the viewer can choose from a series of levels of interactivity, all the way from the total interactivity that has just been described, to simple passive viewing of the program on a single screen. However, even most passive viewers want to view the program on all the room's screens, which allows them to enjoy the truly immersive aspect of the program without having to worry about interactivity. In this situation, the experience is similar to that of IMAX in the 2020s, except with a more complex immersion opportunity.

Star Trek: The Next Generation has given us another wonderful piece of technology – the tablet computer attached to a cloud storage unit. If you have seen the program, think of the number of times you have watched Captain Picard take a small tablet that provides him with his videophone capabilities, or Doctor Crusher walk around with that same type of tablet sending medical information to the onboard computer. The crew of the Enterprise was working in the iWorld even before Steve Jobs, not to mention using cloud storage before that term was even coined.

Using the cloud, the viewer can take her/his television along no matter where (s)he is going. As mentioned earlier in this section, the viewer has total access to his/her favorite television programming at all times and in all locations. The viewer can begin a program while heading home from work, continue viewing the program when arriving home, and watch the program as (s)he moves around the house. When there is time, the viewer may choose to go from a more passive viewing state to a participatory state by moving into the television room and immersing him/herself in the program.

However, with the continuing development of AR and VR systems from a variety of competitors, the tablet has become a dinosaur in its own right, being relegated to the role that the desktop computer used to play – it is functional, sometimes you want to use it, but it is no longer your computer of choice. With the 2070 generation of AR (and, possibly, VR) implants (no longer glasses or even contact lenses which will come after glasses), television viewers are able to enjoy their favorite programs while on the go, and, with the ability to change from passive enjoyment of television to full holographic, interactive television with just a voice command, the wave of a hand, the tilt of the head, or even the blink of an eye, the viewer can turn any location into his/her own television world.

The television system the viewer chooses provides an opportunity for the viewer to interact with friends, family, and others through chat, social media, and new social experiences. Additionally, the viewer is immersed in advertising (s)he enjoys through the use of an advanced form of fully addressable advertising where the viewer, upon seeing a product of her/his liking, can immediately interact with the product holographically. The viewer can try on that new outfit, sit behind the wheel of that exotic automobile, even test out a set of golf clubs on a range or a few holes at any of the world's favorite courses virtually. Once (s)he decides that a product is the one (s)he wants to buy, the scene shifts to a hologram version of his/her favorite store, where the viewer makes the purchase, and then the (real!) product is delivered to her/him promptly. Further, using extensive product placement, the viewer likewise has the opportunity (in the immersive environment) to try out the product as part of the program itself or select the product if the viewer is watching in some form of traditional, lean-back mode. Purchasing in the immersive role occurs as described above, while the viewer in a lean-back mode first has to move into the immersive mode to try out the product. If the viewer does not need to try out a product in the immersive mode, (s)he can simply select the product on the television and move directly to a website for more information and purchase. Either way, the viewer has the opportunity to interact with the product before purchasing should (s)he choose. Such advertising makes persuading the viewer to buy significantly easier in the long run.

Television in the year 2070 is a fantastic, immersive experience, one that utilizes all the senses and allows the viewer freedom of choice regarding how, when, where, and on what platform to watch television, and whether or not (s)he wants to enjoy a traditional, passive lean-back television viewing or the new, immersive, lean-forward experience that television can provide.

Conclusion

Television in the future is about change – technological changes, programming changes, industry structural changes. It is about innovations. What average consumer would have thought in the year 2000 that his/her mobile phone could be used to watch television, surf the Web, download applications and games, and, generally, do everything a computer could do and even more, and at a price that most can afford? What average consumer would have thought in the year 2000 that tablet computers would be available at reasonable prices, with even greater computing power than their year-2000 desktop computers, and capable of doing much more, including watching television anywhere and everywhere? What average consumer would have thought that television sets would be connected to the Internet and be operated through voice recognition and gesture control? What average consumer would have even understood what "the cloud" is? What average consumer would have thought there would already be VR and AR systems? What average consumer would have thought in the year 2000 that television would have already moved from analog TV, to SDTV, to HDTV, to UHDTV (4K), and SHDTV (8K)?

If these changes and so many more have occurred in the first 25 years of the 21st century, how many more changes will television viewers experience over the next 75 years? For children born in the middle- to late-21st-century, television of today will seem as quaint and antiquated to them, and as far removed from their understanding, as an Underwood or Smith Corona does now compared to the latest iPad. (For those of you who have no idea what an "Underwood" or a "Smith Corona" is, those are two of the more famous makers of manual typewriters. For those of you who have no idea what a manual typewriter is, try Googling "manual typewriters" or go to Wikipedia for an explanation.) They will have no understanding of channels, no concept of schedules, no idea of analog television – the list goes on and on.

In these chapters there have been a number of predictions about the development of the various aspects of television in the future. Some may be idle speculations; most will likely come true. Of those that come true, some may take longer than the time frame offered; others may be on target; still others may occur sooner or even much sooner than the time frame suggested. Regardless, for the future television viewer, television will be an exciting, dynamic, innovative, disruptive, and ultimately, immersive experiential event. So, sit back, relax… no, wait… that is how we watch today's television. Let us try again. So, lean forward, wave your hand or say a few words, and get ready for the most amazing experience you can imagine. Welcome to the television of the future!

Notes

1 "State of the Media 2010. U.S. Audiences and Devices." The Nielsen Company. [Note taken directly from article footnotes.]
2 "Netflix Earnings Call," October 2010. [Note taken directly from article footnotes.]
3 Adgate, Brad, "TV Stations & Broadcast Networks at Odds Over Streaming Content Fees," *Forbes,* (May 3, 2024), https://www.forbes.com/sites/bradadgate/2024/05/03/tv-stations–broadcast-networks-at-odds-over-streaming-content-fees/.
4 Adgate, Brad, "TV Stations & Broadcast Networks at Odds Over Streaming Content Fees."
5 Adgate, Brad, "TV Stations & Broadcast Networks at Odds Over Streaming Content Fees."

6 Katzmaier, David, "TCL's Huge 115-inch TV Is Among the Biggest, Brightest Screens I've Seen," *CNET,* (January 8, 2024), https://www.cnet.com/tech/home-entertainment/tcls-huge-115-inch-tv-is-among-the-biggest-brightest-screens-ive-seen/.
7 Hood, Bryan, "LG's New 325-Inch 8K TV Takes Up the Whole Wall and Costs $1.7 Million," *Robb Report,* (September 15, 2021), https://robbreport.com/gear/tvs/lg-dvled-325-inch-8k-tv-1234636088/.
8 One example of this size set is Samsung's "The Wall," which can be configured to any size because it uses small panels that connect seamlessly together. A 146" set from Samsung is available for consumers and costs approximately $22,000. It can be purchased directly through the Samsung website (samsung.com).

Index

Note: Page references with "n" denote endnotes.

3D holographic television sets 86, 109, 198; *see also* holographic television
4K television 8, 45, 47, 51–53, 58, 60–62, 83–84, 187
8K television 8, 45, 48, 51–52, 83–84, 86, 99n16, 113n14, 191, 195
2024 BrandZ Top 100 Most Valuable Global Brands 169

ABC 3–4, 14, 22, 54, 61, 75
ABC's World News Now 48
addressable advertising 77, 119, 121–122, 131–132, 134, 150–151, 163, 187, 200
adult television programs 144
Advanced Television Systems Committee (ATSC) 51; *see also* ATSC 3.0
advertisements: addressable 77, 119, 121–122, 131–132, 134, 150–151, 163, 187, 200; delivered to targeted audiences worldwide 135; different, delivered to different audiences 135; higher success rate of attention/engagement 133; interactive 134–135; placed in content provider's library of programs 135–136; in streams cannot be skipped by viewer 134; used throughout all viewers' choices 134
advertising-driven video-on-demand (AVOD) 19, 31, 71–72, 81, 108, 118–119, 173, 187, 191
agenda-setting 148
Aggregated Targeted Microadvertising (ATMA) 8, 121–123, 126–129, 149, 166; reaching the future television viewer 124–127; working of 122–124
All-Channel Receiver Bill 21–22

Amazon 2, 5, 62, 83, 108, 118, 167, 169, 172; Alexa 120; cloud 104
Amazon Fire TV 108
Amazon Instant Video 16, 20, 94, 145
Amazon Prime Instant Video 59, 71, 82, 143
Amazon Prime Video 30–31, 33, 72–73, 76, 112, 167
American Film Market 167
American Idol 9, 76, 144, 145, 149–150
Anderson, Chris 47
Android phones 91–92
Android TV 60–61
Anypoint Media 137–140, 142n32
Apple Corporation 91–93, 145, 169
Apple Powerbook 2
Apple's iCloud 104
Apple TV 3, 31, 46, 49, 61–62, 65, 83, 167
appointment viewing 7, 31, 69, 75, 77, 191
apps: future of 95–96; and television 94–96
artificial intelligence (AI) 8, 110–113; benefits and challenges 130; future, in television 113; future of 103–113; and Programmatic Advertising 129–130
Ashton, Emma 148–149
ATSC 3.0 7, 22–23, 24, 51–54, 64, 109, 165, 191, 194–195; challenges 53; digital rights management (DRM) 53
AT&T 30, 38
audiences: American 14, 20, 33; global 157, 170, 173, 192–193; going global and 167–169; niche 110, 120; "pay-TV service" 55; primary/secondary 160; rural 14; specialized 153; targeted 135, 137; younger demographic 84
augmented reality (AR) 98, 112, 187; defined 89; and television 89–90

Barnes and Noble 5
barter opportunity 146
Batchelor 145
Batchelorette 145
The Big Bang Theory 154–155
Big Brother 111
big data 129, 130
The Biggest Loser 9, 144, 150
Blackberry 90
Blattburg, Eric 128
Bloom, David 52–53
Bob Hearts Abishola 18
Bove, Michael 85
Bradbury, Ray 17, 192
branded entertainment 146
British Broadcasting Corporation (BBC) 49, 70, 164, 188–189
broadcast industry 187; future of 13–25; local network affiliates 21–25; networks 14–21
Bulova Watch Company 117
Burrell, Gordon 23
business agility 104

cable television 2, 14, 28–34, 187; cable future 31–34; cable today 30–31; history 28–30; summary 34
Cambridge Digital Interactive Television Trial 70
C-Band satellite systems 35–36
C-Band television receive-only (TVRO) dish and system 35–36
CBS 3–4, 13, 17–19, 22, 54, 61, 94
CBS Television/Skydance 14, 17, 167, 187
Charter 33
Chat GPT 111
China Central Television 164
Cisco Corporation 9, 179, 192
Clarke, Arthur C. 35
client-side ad insertion (CSAI) 132
cloud: future of 103–113; private 104–105, 108
cloud computing 103–110; cloud advantages 105–108; cloud television 108–109; cost of 107; flexibility (mobility) 106; green computing 108; portability 107; safety 106; scalability 107–108; summary 109–110; types of clouds 104–105
"cloud television" 108–109
CNBC 29, 164
CNN 163–164
Cole, Jeffrey I. 18, 126
Coleman, Elaine B. 126

Comcast 17, 32, 33, 197
community antenna television (CATV) 28, 29
connected television (CTV) 187; search function 153; sets 108, 164
connected television (CTV) industry 7–8, 31–32, 81–84; future of 83–84; ultra-high definition (UHD or 4K) 83–84
Consumer Electronics Show (CES) 78, 83
content providers and advertisement 133–134
Cooper, William 49–50
Corden, James 18
cord-nevers 82
cord-shavers 82
cost savings 104
Crackle 72, 118
CU-SeeMe video conferencing software 48
CW TV 17

Dancing With the Stars 75, 192
DBSD 37
Deal or No Deal 111
Defense Advanced Research Projects Agency (DARPA) 2
DeFranco, James 36
Deloitte Corporation 20, 126, 155
digital rights management (DRM) 53
digital video recorder (DVR) 2–3, 31–32, 56, 58–59, 69, 75–76, 147, 193
direct-to-consumer delivery of programming 20
direct-to-home (DTH) satellite signal television 3, 6, 13, 18, 30, 119, 187; current/today 37–38; future of 38–39; history 35–37
DirecTV 30, 34, 36–37, 39, 163, 167, 191
DIRECTV STREAM 37
The Discovery Channel 153, 163, 164, 173
Dish Network 30, 34, 37–39, 163, 167, 191
Disney 17, 173, 187
Disney+ 118
Dude Perfect 72
Dukes of Hazzard 144
Dynamic Ad Insertion (DAI) 122, 131–132, 149, 166; defined 131; history of 131; today 131–132

Early Bird I 35
Echostar Communications Corporation 36–37
The Ed Sullivan Show 161
Ellison, David 4
Ellison, Larry 4

Ergen, Charlie 32, 36–37
ESPN 120, 163, 173
EuroNews 173n2
EuroSports 173n2
external hard drives 105–106

Fable Studio 111
Facebook 108, 124–125, 129, 157, 159
Fahrenheit 451 (Bradbury) 9, 17, 192, 195
Fatty Arbuckle, 143
Feder, Bart 24–25
Federal Communications Commission (FCC) 21, 22, 37, 53
Financial Times 89
Fire TV 62
flash drives 106
flexibility (mobility), cloud computing 106
Flower program 137–140
Fox 15, 163
Fox Sports 164
free ad-supported streaming television (FAST) 21, 31, 53–54, 77, 81, 108, 173, 187, 191
FREE: The Future of a Radical Price (Anderson) 47
FreeVee 118
The Future of Television: Sweeping Changes at Breakneck Speed report 179–186
future television viewer 124–127

Game of Thrones 111
The Garage 143
General Motors 36
Generation Y 126
Gen Z 155
globalization 163–164, 171
global television market: future of U.S. television in 163–173; going global and audiences 167–169; going global and revenues 169–172; potential impediments to 172; TV Everywhere 165–172
going global: and audiences 167–169; and revenues 169–172
Google 3, 91, 94, 129, 167, 169; Google Home 120; Project Glass glasses 196
Google Chromecast 60–61
Google Drive 104
Google TV *see* Android TV
Grease 146
green computing 108
Greenfield, Howard 46, 47
Gunsmoke 192

Hatsune Miku 86
HBO Now 94
Hearst 95, 190
Hill Street Blues 14
The History Channel 120, 153
holographic television 85–86
Home Box Office (HBO) 16, 29, 35
Houston, Julie 148
Hubbard, Stanley S. 36
Hughes Electronics 36
Hulu/Hulu+ 16, 20, 21, 108, 145, 187
Hulu+Live TV 94
hybrid cloud 104
hyperlocal stations 24, 25

IBM Simon 3
IBM Thinkpad 2
I Love Lucy 161, 192
individual advertisement 132–133
Instagram 108, 125, 157, 159
Intelsat I satellite 35
Interactive Advertising Bureau 122
Interactive Television Institute's *itv dictionary* 122
Internet Business Solutions Group (IBSG) 179
Internet of Things (IoT) ecosystem 96
Internet Protocol (IP) 77
Internet protocol television (IPTV) 6–7, 9, 45–51, 71, 81, 108, 117, 120, 165, 187, 189, 192–193; defined 45; development and future 48–51; reasons for growth of 46–48
iPad 93
iPad2 93
iPad mini 93
iPhone 8, 22, 81, 90–91, 93
IPTV and Internet Video (Simpson and Greenfield) 46
IPTV Guidex 49–50

The Jeffersons 161
Jenna Marbles 72
Jessell, Harry 54

Kantar 169
Kindle Fire 5
Kurtz, Phil 52, 54

Lanzano, Steve 23
The Late, Late Show 18
Lazarsfeld, Paul F. 147
Let's Make a Deal 144
linear (formerly legacy) television 6, 187

Linkedin 45, 157
Lippman, Walter 147
live sporting events 144
local network affiliates 21–25; local television future 23–25; local television history 21–22; local television today 22–23
local television: future 23–25; history 21–22; today 22–23
Lovelace, Graham 49–50

Magnum P.I.'s 144
Marché International des Programmes de Communication (MIPCOM) 167
Marché International des Programmes de Télévision (MIP-TV) 167
Masayoshi Son 38
Mashable 89
McCombs, Maxwell 147
Miami Vice 144
Microsoft 62, 92, 169
Microsoft OneDrive 104
Millennials 126, 155
Moffett, Craig 82
Moonves, Les 19
Moore's Law 47
MrBeast 72
multicast backbone (MBONE) 48
Multichannel Video Programming Distributors (MVPDs) 15, 189–190; cable television industry 28–34

NASCAR 149
National Association of Broadcasters (NAB) 1, 34, 51, 142n32, 165
National Association of Television Program Executives (NATPE) 167
National Institute for Standards and Technology (NIST) of DoC 104
National Institute of Information and Communications Technology (NICT) 85
National Television System Committee (NTSC) 51
Natz, Jacques 95
NBC 14, 17, 163, 187
NBC SuperChannel 164
NBC Universal 173
near video-on-demand (NVOD) 73
Netflix 3, 16, 20, 72, 94, 95, 108, 118, 143, 145, 165, 167, 172, 197
network television 14–21; current 15–16; future of 17–21; history 14–15
Nexstar 190
NextGen TV *see* ATSC 3.0

NextTV 52–53
Nook Tablet 5

over-the-air (OTA) broadcast television 1, 3, 13, 16, 145, 189, 190
Over-the-Top (OTT) Set-Top Box (STB) conference, San Jose, California 179
over-the-top (OTT) set-top boxes (STBs) 1, 3, 7, 13, 31, 54–65, 82, 167; future of 63–64; history of 54–59; stand-alone STBs 59–62; videogame consoles 62–63

Palm Pilot 2, 90
Paramount+ 17, 20–21, 60, 72, 94, 167, 187
Paramount Global 4, 17
PBS 188–189
Peacock 17, 20–21, 72, 94, 119, 187
Peaky Blinders 111
peer groups 147–148
Perry Mason 192
PewDiePie 72
Philo TV 13, 59, 74, 78, 118
Pinterest 157
Playstation 4 62
Playstation 5 62
Pluto TV 77, 118
portability, and cloud computing 107
premium video-on-demand (PVOD) 73, 187
The Price Is Right 144
Primestar 36
The Prisoner 144
private cloud 104–105, 108
product placement: as barter opportunity 146; branded entertainment 146; defined 143; future of 149–150; history of product placement 143–145; and promotional fee 146; works 145–149
Programmatic Advertising (PA) 121, 127–130, 166; artificial intelligence and 129–130; audience-based advertising transactions 129; automation 129; data-driven 128–129; industry standard 129
Programmatic Media Buying 121, 149
Project Echo 85–86
promotional fee 146
public cloud 104
Public Opinion (Lippman) 147
Puopolo, Scott 179

Rakuten TV 77
Research in Motion (RIM) 90
revenues, and going global 169–172
Richie, Lionel 150

Robertson, Pat 35
Roku 31, 59–60, 77, 83, 108, 118, 167
Rowan and Martin's Laugh-In 161

safety, and cloud computing 106
Samsung 4, 54, 62, 77, 83–84, 92–93, 97, 143; "The Wall" 201n8
scalability, and cloud computing 107–108
screens 96–98
second-screen devices (The iWorld) 90–94; development of tablets 92–93; smartphones 90–92; tablet computers 92; tablets and TV 93–94
server-side ad insertion (SSAI) 132
set-top boxes (STBs) 108; OTT STBs (*see* over-the-top (OTT) set-top boxes (STBs)); stand-alone STBs 59–62, 65
Shaw, Donald 147
Shook, Perry 19
Showrunner 111
Simpson, Wes 46, 47
Sinclair 190
Sirius 39
Skydance Media 4
Sky News 33
Sky Sports 33
Sky Television 33, 173n2
Sling TV service 37, 39
smartphones 97–98
"smart" TV 31, 81, 84
The Smithsonian Channel 153
SnapChat 125, 157
social networking 124
Softbank 38
Sony 3, 62
The Sound of Music 146
Spencer, Jaime 24
Sprint Nextel 38
stand-alone STBs 59–62, 65
Star Television 173n2
Star Trek: The Next Generation 86, 195, 198–199
subscription video-on-demand (SVOD) 19, 31, 71–72, 172, 187, 191
Suddenlink Communications 33
super-high definition (SHD) 109

tablets 92, 97–98; development of 92–93; and television 93–94
television 108–109; in 2070 197–200; and apps 94–96; and augmented reality 89–90; changes in future 1, 5; content search and promotion 153–162; evolution of 2; future of artificial intelligence in 113; programming 69–78; and tablets 93–94; and virtual reality 88–89
television advertising: Aggregated Targeted Microadvertising 122–127; Anypoint Media 137–140; case study 137–140; Dynamic Ad Insertion 131–132; future of 117–140; Programmatic Advertising 127–130; three-step process 132–136
television delivery systems: ATSC 3.0 51–54; future of 45–65; Internet protocol television (IPTV) 45–51; OTT STBs 54–65
Terrestar 37
Thrilla in Manila 29
TikTok 108
Time Warner 32, 197
TiVo 147
T-Mobile 38
TPG 39
traditional advertisements 132–133
transactional video-on-demand (TVOD) 71, 73, 187
Tubi 108, 118
Turner, Ted 15, 29, 35
Turner channels 173
TV Everywhere strategy 32–33, 109, 165, 189
TV NewsCheck 52, 54
"two-step flow" theory of communication 147–148

Ubiquitous Product Placement (UPP) 149–151, 163, 166
ultra-high definition (UHD or 4K) CTV 83–84, 109
ultra high frequency (UHF) stations 21–22, 28, 63
United States Cable Television Consumer Protection and Competition Act 189–190
United States Satellite Broadcasting (USSB) 36
Univision 15
user-generated sites 160–161
U.S. Federal Communications Commission (FCC) 131, 144, 188–190

van Der Velden, Eline 111
Verizon 30, 38
very high frequency (VHF) stations 21–22
videocassette recorder (VCR) 2, 3
video-on-demand (VOD) 7, 16, 25, 31, 69–70, 74–76, 117, 153, 187; future of

Index 207

73–76; overview 70–71; pay-per-view services 70; types of 71–73
virtual Multichannel Video Programming Distributors (vMVPDs) 4, 7, 15, 30–31, 34, 78, 167, 187
virtual private network (VPN) 76
virtual reality (VR) 8, 19, 86–88, 98, 112, 153, 187; defined 87; and television 88–89
Virtual Reality Site 87
The Voice 75, 192
Voice over Internet Protocol (VoIP) 95

Wanamaker, John 125–126
WebTV 83
WhatIs.com 89
WhatsApp 157
Wheel of Fortune 144, 145

Wireless World Magazine 35
WNBT (later WNBC) 117
Woodford, Chris 87
World War II 118, 163
World Wide Web 1–2, 131

X 125, 157, 159
Xbox One 62
Xbox Series X 62
XM 39
Xumo 118

YouTube 3–4, 16, 72, 94, 108, 145, 159, 161, 167, 172
YouTube TV 4, 16, 31, 78, 94

Zucker, Jeff 8